St. Andrews

St. Andrews

Cradle of Golf

Dawson Taylor

South Brunswick and New York: A. S. Barnes and Company
London: Thomas Yoseloff Ltd

A. S. Barnes and Co., Inc.
Cranbury, New Jersey 08512

Thomas Yoseloff Ltd
108 New Bond Street
London W1Y OQX, England

Library of Congress Cataloging in Publication Data

Taylor, Dawson.
    St. Andrews, cradle of golf.

    Bibliography: p.
    Includes index.
    1.   Golf—St. Andrews, Scot.—History.   I. Title.
GV984.T39   796.352'068'0941292   74-16
ISBN 0-498-01442-8

Also by Dawson Taylor:
The Secret of Bowling Strikes
The Making of the Pope
The Secret of Holing Putts (with Horton Smith)
Your Future in the Automotive Industry
Aim for a Job in Automotive Service (with James Bradley)
The Masters: Profile of a Tournament

Unless otherwise indicated, all photographs are presented through the courtesy of Mr. George M. Cowie, St. Andrews, Fife.

PRINTED IN THE UNITED STATES OF AMERICA

To
Laurie and Bea Auchterlonie
for their friendship and help,
To
the Royal and Ancient Golf Club
for its cordiality and counsel in making this book possible,
especially its Secretary, Mr. Keith MacKenzie.
And to all the kindly citizens of the Auld Grey Toon.

Respectfully,
Dawson Taylor

Contents

Foreword

*by Laurie Auchterlonie**

Just after Tony Lema's victory in the Open Championship of 1965 at St. Andrews I first met Dawson Taylor. He came into my little golf shop "around the corner from Granny Clark's Wynd" and gave me a copy of a book on putting, told me that he was the co-author of the book with Horton Smith. He also said that he was considering writing a book about the Old Course.

I told him that I had known Horton well and admired him as a great gentleman of golf. During the next nine years, Dawson and I became good friends. We both could sense, in a rather instinctive way, our mutual respect and love for golf and what it represents. Although he came from thousands of miles from St. Andrews, I had never met a "Yankee" who had greater knowledge of the most obscure facts about the Old Course.

As his book on St. Andrews progressed toward completion (Dawson came back to St. Andrews three more times, incidentally) I was pleased and honored to be able to help him obtain even more information on the history of the famous links and their great champions. I feel that golf has been so good to me and to my beloved wife, Bea, that anything I could do in my power to return my thanks to golf I would do gladly in the hope that I, too, was adding my "wee bit" to the history of golf.

That Dawson Taylor happened along at this late moment in my life was fortuitous for me because my memory remains still clear and undimmed about the old days on my home links. True, I may forget the name of an old acquaintance now and

then but surprisingly enough I still remember whether it was a mashie or a mashie-niblick some ancient champion used in a match fifty or more years ago.

When Dawson Taylor requested that I write a foreword for this book I was very pleased but I told him that I was no writer. His answer was, "Do your best. Just try to tell us what it was like to grow up in the shadow of the Old Course and to be a part of its history all your life." I accepted the challenge and hope, most humbly, that if you find this foreword of interest, it is primarily because it comes from the heart. I am no writer, a good club-maker perhaps, but the words come with difficulty. Be that as it may, this that follows is the foreword I have composed for Dawson Taylor's book, St. Andrews, Cradle of Golf. I sincerely hope that it conveys to you an idea of what I feel has been a most happy life in love with two great ladies, the Old Course and also the former Miss (Beatrice Lyle), my faithful and long-time beloved companion down the fairways and roughs of life.

Dear Dawson,

My father, Willie Auchterlonie, won the Open Championship in 1893, a number of years before I was born. It was both a blessing and a curse to grow up in St. Andrews as the son and only child of a famous champion. I was well-known to all my schoolboy chums as the offspring of a man who was very famous in their eyes. But, on the other hand, I was always in his shadow. He became the Honorary Professional to the Royal and Ancient Golf Club after the death of Andrew Kirkaldy in 1934.

*Honorary Professional, The Royal and Ancient Golf Club

9

My father was also a well-known clubmaker in St. Andrews so it was most natural that I would follow in his footsteps, as I did, and became a clubmaker, too. Our house was not very far down South Street, about a 4-par distance from the first tee of the Old Course, and that was not very far for a young Scot to walk in those days.

My first recollection of the Old Course is of one Saturday afternoon with my Father walking across the Old Course toward the New Course. I was probably four or five years old at the time but I distinctly remember the old stone bridge which, of course, is and always has been a great landmark of the Old Course at St. Andrews' links.

We go from there to the first time I remember hitting a golf ball. I would say that I was no more than seven years of age then. I remember banging a golf ball up against the sea-wall behind the Royal and Ancient golf club, hitting the ball in the sand and the ball coming off the stones of the wall so I would have to duck quickly in order to avoid being hit.

Then, as a boy, they tell me, I spent all my summer holidays on the golf course. Each evening they would have to come and collect me. Eating never came into my picture once I had found golf.

Now, a word about how I got wrapped up in club-making. That was something I inherited from my father. He was exactly the same as I am, incidentally, in his love for the trade, the title "master club-maker." When he won the Open Championship he was back at the bench two days after. He never looked on the championship as anything of great importance. He was almost embarrassed about it. He was such a humble man, so unassuming.

He gave me a lot of encouragement in my efforts to make good golf clubs. He never spoke to me in front of the other workers to tell me I had done something wrong. Later on in the evening after we had finished our work and were having our evening meal he would say something like, "I don't think you did that particular job very well. You must take more time. You were in too big a hurry." That was quite an ordinary remark for him to pass at me.

And while he was looking at a club I had just finished, I might say, "What do you think of that?" He would look it over very carefully, turn it over and over in his very large hands, hands that I inherited from him, by the way, and then he would say, "Oh, it's no' bad"!" That was the best that I could ever get out of him. However, he was a wonderful man, a delightful man, and even when he was confined to bed in his later years, when he lost

part of his leg, he would tell me stories about all the great golfers of the past, about old Tom Morris and young Tom, Allan Robertson, Bob Martin, Willie Park, Braid and Herd, Alex and David Strath. These were all men he knew personally except for young Tom, who died when my father was a boy.

My father was the sort of man who would never tell you any sort of fable. Anything he told you, you knew was the truth, and if he wasn't sure he'd say, "I've heard them say, but I'm not sure. I wouldn't vouch for it."

So you can see I got a wonderful grounding in the game of golf, especially golf as it was and is played on the links at St. Andrews. I got into collecting old clubs, photographs and mementos of the old golfers, mainly through knowing so much about them and being so interested in them.

Now, a little about my memories of some of the great championships and champions. The first big championship I remember distinctly was the Centenary Open of 1910. Since I was born in 1904, you can see I was only a little boy at that time. I remember a terrible thunderstorm coming down during one of the early rounds and being in the shelter down near the first tee of the New Course. All the good players had gone in there, too. I remember looking up at those big men and marveling that I would be so fortunate as to be in their company. Strangely enough, the Centenary Open of 1960 suffered another similar thunderstorm. The Royal and Ancient steps became a regular waterfall. It was almost exactly fifty years before that the 1910 Open had been washed out. I remember both of them as clearly as if they happened yesterday.

Jock Hutchison's victory in 1921 was the next Open Championship that was really an exciting one, as far as I am concerned. I was seventeen at the time and considerably more knowledgeable about golf. The course was quite hard, a true seaside links, and every shot had to be exacting. The ball had to be pitched onto the precise spot to get it to break straight in to the flag. If you missed that spot anything could happen. Jock won the cup and although he was then an entrant from the States, everybody thought it was a great victory because he was truly a home-town boy making good. Roger Wethered actually played one stroke less than Jock did, but, as you know, he suffered an unfortunate penalty in an early round when he stepped on his own ball by mistake. However, even though he lost in the replay with Jock, it was a great breakthrough for Roger, who went on to a most distinguished career in golf, including the

Amateur Championship of 1923 and that marvelous showing against Bobby Jones in the 1930 finals.

I remember the great excitement that occurred in 1924 when Ernest Holderness beat E.F. Storey in the finals of the Amateur championship. That was an interesting championship in many ways. There were many new amateurs coming to the fore at that time. There was only one American, a Mr. Francis Brown, who actually was from the island of Honolulu. He had them all scared. He was a tremendous golfer, a great striker of the ball. He hit his tee-shots very low but a long, long way. He was beaten by an unknown amateur on an absolute fluke. I had played with him once or twice in practice so I was very interested in his progress. On the day of his match I walked out to meet him. I think it was in about the third round of the championship. He was coming down the 16th and his opponent, Birnie of Inverness, hit the Principal's nose. His ball hit the bridge between the two bunkers and bounced over, and believe it or not, he hit his second shot right on the head. This shot bounced and scooted up onto the green and he was almost stone dead. To top it all, he holed the putt for his 3. Francis Brown, of course, was so mad that he cut an awful chunk off the shed coming down the seventeenth, took too big a bite, you know, and his ball landed in the coal sheds. So he was beaten 2 and 1. It was most disappointing because this Francis Brown was a terrific golfer and it's a shame that he didn't get to play Holderness. But, on the other hand, Holderness was a beautiful golfer, too, a consistent striker of the ball, a beautiful iron player and a very steady putter. He just went steady on through that championship without any trouble at all.

But, as far as I am concerned, the story of Bobby Jones at St. Andrews is the true "history of St. Andrews." He was such a fine golfer, and such a great gentleman that the course and Jones make a story in themselves. I will tell you my own favorite recollection of Jones. It was another very exciting championship tournament. The year was 1927, the year Jones won his second championship. He had won the previous year at Lythann-St. Anne's and he won again with a very fine total of 285. His scores were 68, 72, 73 and 72, which was great golf.

I followed him all the way around in his final game. The coolness of Jones was the thing that struck me most. He played a poor pitch at the third hole and the ball bunkered at the left of the green. He walked quietly into the bunker and flippd the ball out of the bunker stone dead and got his 4. He got into another bunker later on and just as he was about to make his swing, a camera clicked. He stopped his swing and just looked in the direction of the sound. It was just as if he were saying, "Now, please don't do that. It is very upsetting." Then, most calmly, he went about making his stroke and put the ball up and out of the bunker close enough to make his par after all. It was his calmness and composure that were most striking.

So he went in steady par figures until he hooked his tee-shot badly on the fifteenth hole. It went so far that it ended up on the other side of the fourth fairway. Then he hit a magnificent shot. He very wisely did not play over the bunker guarding the flag. He played into the corner of the green and rolled up his putt without any trouble at all.

On the sixteenth he whipped it around his neck again. Once more he played a great golf shot, well thought out, and placed the ball on the face of the green. He wasn't going to be too fancy with it because there was a bunker in the corner on the left. The ground gathers the ball there and swings it into the bunker if you get anywhere near it. So he flipped his ball off the face of the green, rolled it up close and holed his putt again, and got his par. At seventeenth he got his par again and then he came to the last hole.

It was a tremendous climax to a wonderful championship. He hit the ball right up between the road and the Valley of Sin and as he was playing his shot something must have taken his eye. He had barely enough room to swing his club back. The crowd was right up against him in a horseshoe. Well, his shot went up the face of the green and then came back down into the Valley of Sin. He calmly walked up, took his putter and stroked that ball up about six inches from the hole. It was a most magnificent finish to a great championship.

Jones was quite something and I don't think there'll ever be anyone who could ever stroke a long putt with the control that Bobby Jones had, especially on those greens. He always putted so well at St. Andrews. He must have had great confidence in himself because those greens could be very tricky. It was like putting on ice, you know.

And so the years went on, championship after great championship. You will tell the story better than I, I am sure, but it has been a wonderful life. The final touch was being named Honorary Professional to the Royal and Ancient Golf Club. I was so pleased to be following in my father's footsteps so many years later. You cannot imagine how proud I was that morning when I walked down to tee the ball for the Captain of the Royal and Ancient in September, 1964. The Captain at that time

was Sir Alec Hill. I was a very nervous person. I don't know whether the Captain was shaking more with nerves than I was. It is hard to say.

It always gives me a great thrill to walk down to that tee in mid-September, about the 19th or 20th on a Wednesday or Thursday morning to tee the ball for the new Captain. That's a wonderful tradition. The little cannon is shot off, sometimes on the downstroke of his swing, I swear, though it's probably right before, and the caddies, all strung out down the fairway, scramble to retrieve the ball and get the gold sovereign they always give as the reward.

I do hope this has given you the material you wanted from me. It has been a pleasure to reminisce with you. In the meantime, Bea joins me in sending you and your good lady our tenderest regards. We wish you every success with your book!

The beloved honorary professional of St. Andrews, Willie Auchterlonie, in the painting which hangs in the Royal and Ancient clubhouse. Auchterlonie was Open Champion in 1893 in the tournament played at Prestwick

How This Book Came to Be Written

I am a true golf fanatic. I love the game of golf and I love great golf courses. I have been playing "the gentleman's game" for more than forty-five years, usually with success. My early instruction in golf came from a delightful Scottish professional, Fred Lamb, who taught golf to the sons of members of the Detroit Athletic Club in the wintertime in a small damp room in the club basement. He had a driving net and a canvas backstop. I can still hear Fred's Scotch "burr" when I turned to him after a particularly satisfying "thwack" of a drive against the bull's-eye on the canvas, as I said to him, "Wasn't that a good one, Mr. Lamb?" and heard him reply, "Aye, the results were fine but the method was incorrect!"

And so he would start once more, patiently working on my grip or the position of my hands at the top of my swing. My game developed rapidly. Once I had found golf—at the age of eleven—there was no other sport that interested me. True, I played baseball and football, but even now I can remember clasping and unclasping the "Fred Lamb grip" in surreptitious fashion while studying in high school years. By the age of fifteen I was playing on the University of Detroit High School golf team in matches of the City League, and scoring in the low 80s. At seventeen, I was occasionally in the low seventies, went on to play college golf at the University of Detroit and was team Captain in my senior year. The fact of the matter was that all other members of the team had graduated and so the captaincy devolved on me of necessity.

College golf brought with it the opportunity to play famous Oakland Hills Country Club in Birmingham, Michigan, renowned as one of the finest golf courses in the world, designed by Donald Ross and later redesigned, amid some controversy, by Robert Trent Jones. As early as 1936 I first viewed the great Oakmont course outside Pittsburgh where "Bobby" Jones had lost an Amateur Championship in 1919 and where he came back six years later to win the same crown for the second time, having won at Merion the year before.

The footsteps of Bobby Jones seemed to be in front of me all through my early years in golf. Although I was too young at the time to realize it, the great Jones had accomplished an unbelievable feat on the Oakland Hills course during his play in the United States Open Championship of 1924. Jones eventually lost there by three strokes to a virtual unknown, a diminutive Englishman named Cyril Walker. But in the playing of one of his rounds Jones made a golf-shot that my Father saw and often recounted to me later. In an early round of that tournament, Jones sliced the ball first up and then out of a bunker with a spoon, put it out over Lahser Road, which was out-of-bounds of course, and then let the wind bring the ball back safely onto the green some two hundred and thirty yards away, where he "saved his par."

In 1927, *Down the Fairway* was published by Minton, Balch and Company. This was the story of Bobby Jones's career told by Jones himself and his "Boswell," the Atlanta reporter, O.B. Keeler, who followed Bobby's career all his life and told the world about it in the pages of the *Atlanta Journal* and the golf magazines of the day. For a birthday present, I was given this wonderful book.

The thrill of a lifetime. Dawson Taylor, the author,
on the first tee at St. Andrews in September, 1964.

Remember that the height of Jones's career was yet to come, in 1927, 1928, 1929 and 1930 when he would win eight of his eventual thirteen major tournaments. I hope that the reader will understand how and why, at such an early age, I happened to become such an admirer of Bobby Jones, the golfer and, later on after I had met him, Bobby Jones, the gentleman.

Time passed into the '50s. I had become an autobile dealer in Detroit, Michigan, after serving in the U.S. Navy as a Radar Officer on the destroyer U.S.S. *Brown* in World War II. Now a member of the nearby Detroit Golf Club, I had even had the pleasure of meeting Robert T. Jones, Jr. when he came to Detroit Golf Club to participate in the unofficial Ryder Cup "Challenge" matches held there in 1941 when Britain, then at war, could not send a representative team. For the first time in my

life, I saw with my own eyes his beautiful rhythmic swing. Watching him perform on my own "home course" added even greater pleasure to the occasion.

The next part of my story deals with how I happened to fall in love with the Old Course at St. Andrews. Like all golfers of the world, I was certainly aware that somewhere in Scotland there lay an historic and undoubtedly great golf course. I knew that Bobby Jones had had several personal triumphs there, knowledge derived from *Down the Fairway* and subsequent Jones-authored books.

At some time in the late '40s I happened to see a beautiful color reproduction of a photograph which showed a view of the eighteenth green at St. Andrews with Robert T. Jones, Jr. putting in his match against Roger Wethered in 1930. The print was marked "H.O. Quinn, Ltd., Fleet Street, London E.C. 4" and soon afterward I managed to

14

obtain a copy of it for my own office. I remember, too, that the price of the print was just seven dollars. Similar prints today cost fifty dollars.

The print was framed and hung across from my desk. "How could anyone possibly two-putt on such a huge green?" "That must be the famous 'Valley of Sin,' that dip in the front of the green." These were my thoughts as I gazed on this great photograph and began to wish that some day I might putt on that immense green, play that obviously difficult and historic golf course.

The next step in what I call my "love affair" with "The Old Course" (as if I were discussing a dignified and great Old Lady) happened when a friend of mine, a wealthy man, was fortunate enough to be able to make a pilgrimage to Scotland to play the St. Andrews links. True, he had business connections in London, but I could not get over the luxury of a golfer traveling those thousands of miles from Detroit, Michigan all the way to Scotland to see and play the wonderful golf course that Jones, among many others, had made famous. I envied my friend and wished, down in my heart, that I could drop my business then and there and accompany him on his trip. I did nothing of the sort, of course, but continued to work and dream of the day that I might go over to Scotland myself. Before my friend left, I commissioned him to get for me, if he could, a scorecard of the Old Course. When he returned a month or so later, he not only had a scorecard but he also had bought me a beautiful color-chart of the Old Course printed by the *Dundee Courier and Inquirer*. There before my eyes was the complete aerial view, a plan lay-out, most artistically done, of every hole and bunker, including the names of all the famous caverns and " 'umps and 'ollows." For the first time I could see how "the Loop" went from the seventh through the twelfth holes, how huge "Hell Bunker" really was, the treachery of "the Road Hole" with Auchterlonie's drying sheds on its right and the stone fence which marked out-of-bounds for drives at the seventeenth hole.

My friend also brought a small booklet called *How to Play the Old Course, St. Andrews,* published by J. and G. Innes, Ltd., of St. Andrews, which, in about forty small pages, gives hole-by-hole line drawings of the various holes of the links along with suggestions on how to avoid "the often unseen troubles" of the course. My knowledge of the Old Course was increasing by leaps and bounds. Now I could actually play the course in my imagination. I could entertain myself no end with my tremendous make-believe drive down the left side

John Whyte Melville, famous and beloved Captain of the Royal and Ancient Golf Club. Captain in 1823. When he died, the Club left his post open in respect to his memory.

of the first fairway at the Old Course, my 6-iron into the imaginary east wind, carrying the Swilken Burn (of course!) and my comfortable two putts for a par. Oh, I'd let myself get into trouble occasionally and I'd take a three-putt or two but I was always able to play "the Road Hole" to perfection, drive over the corner of the sheds, put my long brassie second shot onto the green and get my coveted 4 to "save the round."

So for years I continued to dream of the day I would make my pilgrimage to St. Andrews. The opportunity finally came in 1964 when a fine group of golfers, gentlemen all, invited me to join them on a jaunt to Scotland and Ireland. With much trepidation I approached my charming wife, Mary Ellen, with the proposal that I leave her alone for three weeks in mid-September. Most surprisingly, her answer was "Yes, I think you should go now before you have your first coronary!" I was delighted at her response.

So I went to Scotland in the fall of 1964. We played many of the famous courses, Portmarnock, Royal Dublin, Turnberry, Troon, Carnoustie and Gleneagles. But the height of my pleasure there was the first drive down the fairway of "the Burn hole" at St. Andrews, on my way, of course, to a splashed second shot into Swilken Burn. One of our players, Mr. Herbert Trapp, had had the thrill of a hole-in-one at "Dollymount," or Royal Dublin, so when we reached Dundee the next day we celebrated the occasion with a grand party, complete with skirling bag-pipes and decorated with some pretty Scottish lassies in tartans.

I arranged for a photograph of the group with Herb holding up the "hole-in-one" ball in triumph. The photographer was Mr. George Cowie of the *Dundee Courier and Inquirer*. I asked Mr. Cowie if he would follow my round of golf the next day at St. Andrews and photograph my shots from some of the "hallowed places." He came the next day and the result was an unusual album of sequential photographs of myself and of some of the rest of our party playing the Old Course at St. Andrews. There were some very interesting sequences of searches in the gorse and heather, of striking the newly-found ball and then searching for it again a few feet ahead where it had once more disappeared from view. There was an interesting photograph of my own explosion from "Shell" bunker over "Strath" bunker at the famous eleventh hole, where the great Bobby Jones "picked up," certain that he had put himself out of contention in the Open Championship of 1921 with a bad 6 or 7 on that hole after a first nine score of 41 strokes.

These photographs proved to be a great consolation and pleasure to me later, especially when they could be reviewed and the game replayed mentally. I began to call this pastime "imaginary golf." By this time, Mr. Thomas Yoseloff of A.S. Barnes and Company, fine publisher of all categories of books but especially of sports books, had published my first two books, *The Secret of Bowling Strikes* and *The Secret of Holing Putts* (with Horton Smith as co-author). Upon my return to America after the impressive trip to St. Andrews I submitted to Mr. Yoseloff the suggestion that I write a golf book, aimed at the "arm-chair" golfers of the world, which would use top-grade photographs to enable them to play "imaginary golf" at St. Andrews, to understand the tactical situation and difficult terrain through the medium of good drawings and good photographs of the renowned golf course.

In his wisdom, Mr. Yoseloff suggested that while the idea was a good one, he thought that the first effort along that line should be directed toward a famous American golf course in order to gauge the public reaction to such an approach. Then, if the idea worked, the St. Andrews story might be the next effort. He recommended, too, for even more universal appeal, that a history of the golf tournaments held on that site be included so as to achieve a comprehensive coverage of the famous golf-course, one which might be brought up-to-date yearly with subsequent issues.

The outstanding and famous Augusta National Golf Club, which holds the annual "Masters Tournament," was then selected for the book project of "imaginary golf," plus the history of the various tournaments held there. The book would also report assorted records and highlights of the championships over the years 1934 to the present.

So, in March, 1973 *The Masters, Profile of a Tournament* was published by A.S. Barnes in exactly that format. The book had an immediately favorable reception from the press and golf-readers. It was clear that *The Masters* would be a success. The way was now open for the follow-up effort, the even bigger project of a book concerning St. Andrews Old Course.

After receiving permission from the Royal and Ancient Golf Club to visit and research their records and archives, I had the great pleasure of spending a week in marvelous sunny weather at St. Andrews, Fife, Scotland this fall (1973). Again, Mr. George Cowie took the desired black and white photographs and "colour" transparencies of the Old Course. Since he had already spent the greater part of his life photographing the course and its players, his files yielded many interesting old pictures which, in this volume, we hope will add to the reader's interest and enjoyment as he peruses its pages. The Royal and Ancient Golf Club graciously granted permission for Mr. Cowie to make copies of many of its historic photographs, oil paintings and records. For this cooperation, the author and publisher are most grateful, especially to its Secretary, Mr. K.R.T. MacKenzie, M.C., whose help has been invaluable. The United States Golf Association, too, kindly supplied photographs and various records from its library. The U.S.G.A. was most helpful in locating former Walker Cup players whose comments added greatly to the author's ability to tell the story of the Walker Cup matches at St. Andrews. Mr. Desmond Muirhead, famous golf course designer, was most obliging and supplied a recent topographical survey of the Old Course which Mr. Kenneth Seaquist used in making the beautiful and accurate drawings of the individual holes at St. Andrews.

The story of the Old Course and the city of St. Andrews, the history of the tournaments and the players over nearly a century of golf is truly a monumental one. If this author has failed to complete the task, it is respectfully requested that forgiveness be granted. If the golfer-reader has already made the pilgrimage to St. Andrews I hope that this book will cause him to fall even more in love with the Old Course than before. If the reader has never been there, then may this book cause him to fall in love with that "Grand Old Lady," the Old Course in the Auld Grey Toon, and may he some day walk those hallowed fairways accompanied by the ghosts of those great golfers of the past and present, may his golf-ball successfully carry Swilken Burn, and may all the putts "run truly in" in the "splendour, the splendour of it all!"

Dawson Taylor

Acknowledgments

I would like to express my deep and sincere appreciation to the following persons without whose help and encouragement this book could not have come to completion:

First and foremost, to Laurie and Bea Auchterlonie for their friendship, for their locating those obscure books on St. Andrews, for the delightful tape-recordings of reminiscences of the Old Course, and for the foreword of the book which sets the mood so well.

To the Royal and Ancient Golf Club for its cordiality and cooperation in making available the remarkable archives of the Royal and Ancient and especially to its Secretary, Mr. Keith MacKenzie for suggesting and finding additional sources of information that proved most productive.

To the United States Golf Association for its similar kindness and cooperation. Many of the photographs which proved elusive in Scotland were found in U.S.G.A.'s library under the custodianship of Miss Janet Seagle, its curator. My thanks to Janet for her friendship and to the U.S.G.A. for permission to reprint the Walker Cup material from the U.S.G.A. *Record Book*.

To the Ladies' Golf Union of Great Britain and its Secretary, Miss K. Hannay, for locating the rare material concerning the Ladies' Golf Championship of 1908 and other valuable photographs.

For personal interviews in connection with their participation in the championships of St. Andrews I would like to thank Jack Nicklaus, always charming and accommodating, Bruce Devlin, delightful and friendly "Aussie," Bill Campbell, John Farquhar, Allen Miller, Bill Hyndman, as well as many other American Walker Cup stars. In Scotland, Sandy Saddler was most helpful concerning Great Britain's Walker Cup teams.

My thanks also go to Roger Wethered and his sister, Joyce, both great British golf champions many times over, especially to Roger for his kindness in supplying the text of his address at the commemoration ceremony held in honor of Robert T. Jones, Jr.

To Cyril J.H. Tolley for his reminiscences of his famous match with Bobby Jones,

To Enid Wilson for her friendship and the story of the Wethered-Collett match,

To Glenna Collett Vare for her friendship and her remarkable memory of the 1929 Ladies' championship

To Cecil Leitch for her recollection of the 1908 championship

To Jack Tower in appreciation of his friendship and for allowing access to his extensive golf library materials and books,

To Joe Murdoch, for his kindness in locating some difficult-to-find materials,

To Gary Wiren, for finding in his library the ancient *History of the Royal and Ancient Golf Club*.

To Cassell and Company, Ltd., London for permission to reprint material from *A History of Golf in Britain*.

To Doubleday and Company for permission to reprint material from *Golf is My Game* by Robert Tyre Jones, Jr., (c) 1960.

To John Murray Ltd. and Houghton Mifflin Company for permission to reprint Mr. John Betjeman's poem "Seaside Golf" from *Collected Poems* (1959).

To The Hamlyn Publishing Group Limited for permission to reprint material from *Bobby Locke on Golf.*

St. Andrews

PART I

The Old Course

1

The Birth of a Course

Nature was her architect, and beast and man her builders. In the formation and stabilization of the Scottish coastline, the sea at varying intervals of time gradually receded from the higher ground of cliff, bluff and escarpment to and from which the tides ebbed and flowed. And, during the ages, as the sea withdrew it left a series of sandy wastelands in bold ridges and significant furrows, broken and divided by numerous channels up and down which the tides advanced and retired, and down certain of which the burns, streams and rivers found their way to the sea.

As time went on these channels or furrows dried out. Then, by the action of the winds, they formed into dunes, ridges, knolls, denes, gullies, and hollows of varying height, width, and depth.

Then nature took over and sent the birds there to nest and breed. The burns, streams and rivers brought silt down to the water's edge. The bird droppings provided the manure to help in the germination of the seeds blown there from the inland areas and carried there by the birds. Soon vegetation began to appear. Eventually all of these areas became grass-covered, from coarse marram on the exposed dunes, ridges and hillocks and the finer bent grasses and fescues in the sheltered dunes, gullies and hollows, to the meadow grasses which surrounded the river estuaries and the mouths of the streams and burns. From the spreading and intermingling of all these grasses there came to be established the thick, close-growing, hard-wearing greensward that is the feature of true "links" turf.

In due course of time, where the soil was suitable, heather, whins, broom and trees took root and flourished in drifts, clumps and coverts, the sort of terrain which would attract and sustain animal life.

The rabbits came first, then the beasts of prey and finally man. The sequence of these events had a definite effect on these sandy wastes which were waiting to be turned into links by the golfers who would come along later and recognize them as useful for sporting pursuits. The rabbits linked up their burrows by runs in the dunes and ridges and they frolicked in the sheltered oases flanked by whins and broom. The runs were gradually worn into tracks by foxes, and when man the hunter came, he widened them into paths or rides.

Then, when man adopted golf as one of his favorite pastimes and went in search of suitable ground for its pursuit, he found it lying right before him in these warrens, paths and tracks, in the whins, the gorse, the brush, the broom.

The tracks and paths leading from one assembly place to another provided the basis for each fairway, the wild and broken country over which the rides threaded their way provided the rough and hazards; and the sheltered areas the rabbits used for their "dancing floors" became the obvious sites for greens. The area known as St. Andrews's links is an outstanding example of the alliance between nature, beast and man.

This information excerpted from an article by Sir Guy Campbell in *A History of Golf,* London: Cassell and Company, Ltd. 1952.

The Queen Victoria Jubilee Vase, in constant play since 1887.

A Grand Match at Golf, *a picture from 1850.*

2

A Sunday Morning at St. Andrews

The burns shimmer in the sunlight and the traitorous whins stir in the breeze of St. Andrews Bay. It is early Sunday morning and already there can be seen a lone golfer, heavily sweatered, plodding along toward the north on the New Course at St. Andrews. Why not on the Old Course? No. The Old Lady rests on Sunday as she has for years and years. Old Tom Morris once said, "Even if the golfers do not need a rest on Sunday, she does!"

The gulls are feasting on the empty fairways of the seventeenth and eighteenth holes. They march like soldiers in flank formation. There are exactly fourteen of them and one in particular seems to be the leader. Suddenly something frightens them, a golf ball perhaps, and they all take flight at once. But soon they land again and continue their breakfast on the deserted fairway.

The view from the top of the Old Course Hotel is a breath-taking one. To the right and south is the Royal and Ancient Golf Clubhouse, mists sweeping around it as it stands guard over its entrusted golf courses. The sun is rising in the east now and the mists are being eaten up by the warmth of its rays. Several more pairs of golfers are now coming down the first fairway of the New Course, one of them attended by a large collie dog on a leash. As the golfer makes his stroke the dog patiently lies on the ground nearby awaiting the execution of the shot. Then, with the swing completed, both proceed in leisurely fashion on to the next one, where the ceremony is once more repeated.

One can see traps everywhere; the burns, (streams), the whins, (clusters of soft-looking green shrubs with skin-tearing thorns on them). When the wind whips off the bay, the ball that started out as a slice turns into a hook. When the mist rolls in in the late afternoon, it is sometimes impossible to see the end of a club held in one's hand. It would seem that it has always been like this at St. Andrews, for hundreds and hundreds of years. The stories of great golf rounds of a hundred years ago are told as if they happened yesterday and as you look down upon the scene, the mounds, the dips, the rolls, the dark yellow spots that mark the bunkers, the forbidding clumps of whins and gorse, you understand why—because this place is timeless and will continue to be timeless long after you and I have finished our rounds of golf at St. Andrews.

Where else could they still tell of Maitland Dougall? While Dougall was awaiting the starter's traditional "Play away, please" in the club championship 105 years ago, a violent tempest sprang up in the bay and a ship was seen to be foundering.

"I'll take the stroke oar," roared Dougall, leaping into the lifeboat, and for five hours he and his mates battled the sea as they rescued the beleaguered crew. Naturally, Dougall returned to win the championship.

This is the home of golf. There is no discussion here about the various theories that attribute the origin of the game to the Romans or to the Belgians. Long before the swells came up from England to drink at the Black Bull Inn (and be carried back to their hotels in sedan chairs) the details of the game's birth had been pinpointed with precise vagueness.

A Scottish shepherd was swinging at round stones with his crook one day and hit one into a rabbit hole.

"I wonder if I can do that again," he murmured to his flock, completely unmindful of the summer madness he was about to unleash upon the world.

Although this is the oldest golf course with recorded games back as far as the 14th and 15th centuries, the Royal and Ancient is only the second oldest club. It was begun in 1754, one year after the Honourable Company of Edinburgh Golfers, and its annals include the fining of one gentleman two bottles of port for failing to wear his scarlet coat to a club function.

The Royal and Ancient, as it is called, does not own the famous Old Course, nor does it own the three other 18-hole courses that twist and turn between the town and the bay. After hundreds of years of squabbling, including the case of one Mr. Dempster who inflicted his rabbits upon the links, the course was declared to be common land by an Act of Parliament and its future official custody was taken over by the Town Council of the City of St. Andrews.

The four courses are open to the public except during tournaments and a few special days set aside for the Royal and Ancient. Bookings should be made in advance of play, especially for the Old Course. Customarily the names of prospective players are placed in the "ballot" and drawn in late afternoon for the next day's play. You may choose morning or afternoon starting times, but Lady Luck must be with you to get the choice time to play. The cost of play is very low. As of this writing, the fee for the Old Course is one pound Sterling, a little over two American dollars.

Old Tom Morris died in the last century. He was, of course, one of the elder statesmen of golf and particularly St. Andrews, its first Honorary Professional to the Royal and Ancient Golf Club. In the private museum his benign bearded face still watches over such Royal and Ancient relics as the "Track club," which was specifically made in 1760 to scrape golf balls out of carriage ruts, the featherie ball (covered with leather like a small indoor baseball and stuffed tightly with exactly one silk-topped hat filled with feathers.) and grape-like clusters of gold and silver golf balls attached to silver golf clubs.

The silver balls commemorate each Captain of the Royal and Ancient, the gold balls each Royal Captain (including the Duke of Windsor when he was the Prince of Wales in 1922) One American Captain was Francis Ouimet, who was given this great honor in 1951.

There are now about 1,700 members, most of them from the British Isles, about 250 from the United States. The Royal and Ancient Golf Club is undoubtedly the most important club in the world. Despite its lack of ownership, The Royal and Ancient regards the Old Course as its sacred trust. The Old Course is in wonderful hands.

*Tom Morris, four-time winner of the Open Champion-
ship between the years 1861 and 1867, when the tournament was played at Prestwick.*

*Francis De Sales Ouimet "plays himself into office" as
Captain of the Royal and Ancient Golf Club in 1951.
It was in 1913 that Ouimet won the U.S. National
Open Championship in a famous play-off with the
"foreign invaders," Harry Vardon and Ted Ray.*

Harold H. Hilton, the second amateur to win the Open Championship, in 1892. Hilton won the Amateur Championship in 1900, 1901, and 1911. He was runner-up in 1891 and 1892.

Created in honor of the 50th anniversary of the championship, this certificate was used as a prize for other golf club champions of that time. "The Golfers' Diploma" is a special panorama of Open Champions from 1810 to 1860.

The bridge at Swilken Burn: golf at St. Andrews in the 1890s.

"Old Tom" Morris, the first professional of St. Andrews.

Bing Crosby, a fine amateur golfer, drew tremendous crowds when he played in the Amateur championship of 1950. He played well but lost in an early round.

Alan Darlington Cave plays himself into office as Captain of the Royal and Ancient Golf Club in 1971. Laurie Auchterlonie is at the left.

Sir John Simon plays himself into office as captain of the Royal and Ancient Golf Club in 1936. Courtesy U.S.G.A.

Family recreation on a Sunday afternoon at St. Andrews in 1896.

3

The Old Course at St. Andrews

by Robert Trent Jones

As you can see, the Old Course at St. Andrews is very much with us when we build our courses today. And it is also very much alive in its own right, remaining one of the world's greatest tests of golf. There it is as it has always been, winding out and back along the narrow thumb of linksland between the Firth of Forth and the Firth of Tay. There is only one Old Course, and nature built it. It would be outright folly for any architect to attempt a duplication. The Old Course is only right at St. Andrews.

If you are an ardent golf fan and have dreamed for years of visiting St. Andrews, your first look at the Old Course will result either in exhilaration or let-down. The let-down is the more common reaction, at least for Americans who are used to courses which divulge all their secrets and present all their beauty at first sight. The aspect from its first tee is not impressive, nor is there any other visible hint of its right to its honored position. Perhaps one should never play the Old Course at St. Andrews without first getting the spirit of the town. It is like no other town in the world. The very backbone of the town is golf, and it is supported by its four golf courses, its beaches, and its University. What delightful sources of revenue! The spiritual feeling for golf is matched only by the spiritual feeling for religion. Sunday is the one

day on which you cannot play the Old Course. The Royal and Ancient clubhouse lies but a block from the main street. Bordered by the sea, it sits there monumentally, a thing apart, which is as it should be, for the Royal and Ancient is the oldest and most respected club in the world, celebrating its two-hundredth season in 1954.

The first few rounds a golfer plays on the Old Course are not likely to alter his first estimate that it is vastly overrated. He will be puzzled to understand the rhapsodies that have been composed about the perfect strategic position of its trapping, the subtle undulations of its huge, double greens, the endless tumbling of its fairways, which seldom give him a chance to play a shot from a level stance. Then, as he plays on, he begins to realize that whenever he plays a fine shot he is rewarded; whenever he doesn't play the right shot, he is penalized in proportion; and whenever he thinks out his round hole by hole he scores well. This is the essence of strategic architecture: to encourage initiative, reward a well-played, daring stroke more than a cautious stroke, and yet to insist that there must be planning and honest self-appraisal behind the daring.

Of all the splendid holes at St. Andrews, the most renowned are the eleventh, or the Eden; the fourteenth, or the Long Hole; and the seventeenth, or

An aerial view of the Old Course taken in the 1930s. Swilken Burn can be seen winding across the first fairway at lower right. The black area in the left center of the photo is the coalyard, the "drying sheds" which were such an interesting and dangerous out-of-bounds hazard along the right-hand side of the 17th hole. Courtesy Aerofilms Limited.

Road Hole. The strategy of the eleventh, which measures 164 yards, is developed by its key hazard, the Strath bunker, a deep heavy-lipped bulldog that patrols the access to the right-hand side of the green. The Strath sets up perfectly the function of Hill bunker to the left of the green and of the green itself, which slopes back-to-front at a very severe angle. When the wind is out in full force and blowing down the slope, it is next to impossible to keep a downhill putt from running off the green, no matter how gently you tap it. (I feel that at no other place but St. Andrews would such a slope be countenanced.)

The Seventeenth, the famous Road Hole, is a par five, as we would rate it here, which measures 467 yards. It is a very possible 4 and a very possible 7. To be in a position to reach the green in two, the golfer must take his courage in his hands on the tee and drive over Auchterlonie's drying sheds, which are situated in an out-of-bounds area that noses into the direct line between the tee and the choice of the fairway. The long second shot must be played with true precision. A deep trap at the left of the green forces the player to hew to the right; there, running diagonally behind the green, is the road, and behind the road a stone wall. They

36

A view of the town of St. Andrews, the Royal and Ancient clubhouse, and the Old Course from the southeast looking northwest. Picture taken in the 1930s. Courtesy Aerofilms Limited.

play as part of the course, and any guess at how often they have proved to be the difference between a match that was won and a match that was lost would be an almost astronomical figure. (Here again I feel that at no place but St. Andrews would such hazards be acceptable; on the Old Course, they are as natural as the gray stone of the houses which line the closing hole.)

As for the fourteenth, the Long Hole, the longest on the course, a brute of 527 yards, we have here the apotheosis of one cardinal tenet of golf architecture: a great hole always offers the golfer an alternate route to the green. The fourteenth, in fact, offers the golfer a choice of three alleys: left, center, and right. The intelligent golfer will wait until he arrives at the tee and take into account how the wind is blowing at that moment, as well as other immediate conditions, before he chooses his route for that particular round. By any of the routes, he must tack his way skillfully to the green, avoiding the bunker-groups that lie in wait to change his peaceful sail into a hapless Odyssey.

The links of St. Andrews can never be known by the casual visitor. One ought to have known and loved and played over the links for a long while; and I can lay no claims to such knowledge as that. I can speak only as an occasional pilgrim, whose pilgrimages, though always reverent, have been far too few. I do not know by instinct whether or not my ball is trapped in "Sutherland"; I only know the difference between "Strath" and the "Shelly" bunker; I could not keep up my end in an argument as to the proper line to take at the second hole—I am, in short, a very ignorant person who means thoroughly well.

This article first appeared in *The Complete Golfer*, edited by Herbert Warren Wind.

4

The Charm of St. Andrews

by Bernard Darwin

There are those who do not like the golf at St. Andrews, and they will no doubt deny any charm to the links themselves, but there are surely none who will deny a charm to the place as a whole. It may be immoral, but it is delightful to see a whole town given up to golf; to see the butcher and the baker and the candlestick maker shouldering clubs as soon as the day's work is done and making a dash for the links. There they and their fellows will very possibly get in our way, or we shall get in theirs; we shall often curse the crowd, and wish whole-heartedly that golf was less popular in St. Andrews. Nevertheless, it is that utter self-abandonment to golf that gives the place its attractiveness. What a pleasant spectacle is that home green, fenced in on two sides by a railing, upon which lean various critical observers; and there is the club-house on one side, and the club-maker's shop and the hotels on the other, all full of people who are looking at the putting, and all talking of putts that they themselves holed or missed on that or on some other green. I once met, staying in a hotel in St. Andrews, a gentleman who did not play golf. That is in itself remarkable, but more wonderful still, he joined so unobtrusively in the perpetual golfing conversation that his black secret was never discovered. I do not know if he enjoyed himself, but his achievement was at least a notable one.

I am writing this chapter (I am but newly returned from St. Andrews), after having watched all the champions of the earth play round the course for three strenuous days. The weather was perfect; there was scarcely a breath of wind, and violent storms of rain had reduced the glassy greens to a nice easy pace. Scores of under eighty were absurdly plentiful, and, indeed, if someone had come in with a score of under seventy I think the news would have been received without any vast degree of astonishment. Yet with all this brilliant, record-breaking golf being played over it, the course never looked really easy. The champions certainly got their fours in abundance, but they had to work reasonably hard for most of them. Nor did one suffer from the delusion, as one does when playing the part of a spectator upon simple courses, that one could have done just as many fours oneself. St. Andrews never looks really easy, and never is really easy, for the reason that the bunkers are for the most part so close to the greens. It is possible, of course, to play an approach shot straight on the beeline to the flag, and if we play it to absolute perfection all may go well; but let it only be crooked by so much as a yard, or let the ball, as it will often do, get an unkind kick, and the bunker will inevitably be our portion. Consequently, the prudent man will agree with Willy Smith of Mexico, who declared that it was unwise to "tease the bunkers"; he will not attempt to avoid these greedy, lurking enemies by inches or even feet, but he will give them a good wide berth and avoid them by yards. The results of this policy is that the man who is getting his string of fours has to be continually lay-ing the ball dead with his putter from a reasonably long way off, and so St. Andrews is a fine course for one who can do good work at long range with a wooden putter.

This article first appeared in *The Golf Courses of the British Isles* by Bernard Darwin.

Andrew Kirkaldy, Honorary Professional of St. Andrews from 1910 to 1934.

The "Long Room" of the Royal and Ancient club-house. The windows look out over the first tee and the 18th green on the Old Course.

The unique traffic light for pedestrians who wish to cross Granny Clark's Wynd.

The Treasury at St. Andrews. A Royal and Ancient Captain adds a silver ball after his captaincy, a Royal Captain adds a gold ball.

The Duke of Windsor (then Prince of Wales) with Lord Castlerosse in 1922.

5

How to Play the Old Course

by Laurie Auchterlonie

Laurie Auchterlonie in his "museum of golf."

View from the Old Course hotel rooftop overlooking the Old Course to the southeast.

Dawson Taylor playing the Shell bunker over Strath bunker at the 11th hole.

HOLE NO. 1 368 YARDS, PAR 4
BURN HOLE

This is a nice sunny morning at St. Andrews. It could be a day in June, July, August or September and there is a little wind from the west. Today you can fly the ball in to the greens from any angle. The greens are all watered and soft. They will hold a shot well, but in the old days when the wind had blown for a few weeks and there hadn't been any rain it would take a lot of skill to carry the Swilken Burn and stop the ball before it went through the green. In fact, it was considered quite a feat to do so. We'll play the course as Bobby Jones would be playing it in the late 20s and 30s. The line for your tee-shot is just left of center. This gives a fine shot into the green, a 6-iron or a 7-iron. There is nothing in the way except the Swilken Burn which you must be sure to carry. With the excellent equipment of today you should be able to stop the ball on the green and get your two putts for your par 4. And you are off to a good start.

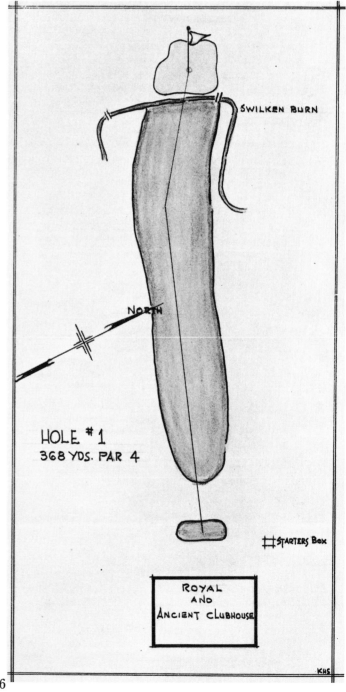

SWILKEN BURN

NORTH

HOLE #1
368 YDS. PAR 4

STARTERS BOX

ROYAL
AND
ANCIENT CLUBHOUSE

46

HOLE NO. 2 401 YARDS, PAR 4
DYKE HOLE

The line to the hole doesn't matter as much as it did in the time of Bobby Jones. You should take the line to the hole which will take you as close to the bunker on the left as possible. This gives you the face of the green square on for your second shot. A 5-iron or 6-iron will probably do. The green breaks a bit from left to right but the ground in front of the green breaks from right to left so it's a case of your hitting the ball straight into the face of the green and holding it against the break of the green. In championship play they usually have the flagstick on the left. It is not good policy to play for the flag as the bunker is just waiting for you there. With two putts, you have your par 4.

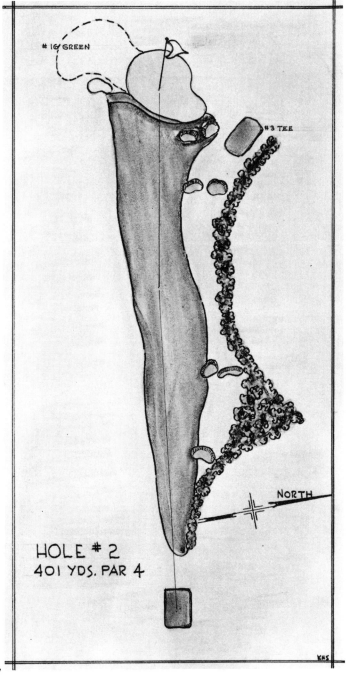

#16 GREEN

#3 TEE

NORTH

HOLE #2
401 YDS. PAR 4

HOLE NO. 3 356 YARDS, PAR 4
CARTGATE HOLE

Hit the drive down the right-hand edge of the fairway. There are three pot bunkers down the center which you want to keep clear of, if you can. The shot in to the green is an 8-iron or a 9-iron. If you want to fly the ball in you will probably use the 8 or 9. Or you might want to play a pitch-and-run shot as it should be played in true St. Andrews style, that is, play a half-shot and let the ball bump in to the green. If you put your tee-shot left you have a difficult second shot to play. The prevailing wind blows from left to right and will affect your shot more when you are on the left. You will find it hard to get your ball near the flagstick from that side. In general, remember that it never pays to get on the left side of the flag at St. Andrews going out.

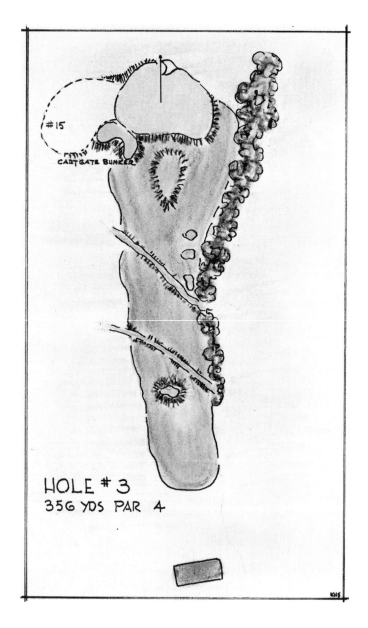

HOLE NO. 4 427 YARDS, PAR 4
GINGER-BEER HOLE

This hole is fairly straightaway with no trouble for you if you take the line directly to the hole. However, there are two troublesome bunkers on right-hand side of the rough waiting to catch your drive and you must be careful of the Students' bunkers on the left side of the green. There is a little hump in front of the green and you must be aware of it so that you can decide which way you can expect your ball to break as it comes off the hump. You should reach this green easily in two strokes, probably with a 4-iron second. It is better to stay to the right of the flagstick. More birdies are made from that approach to the hole. A comfortable par 4 for you here.

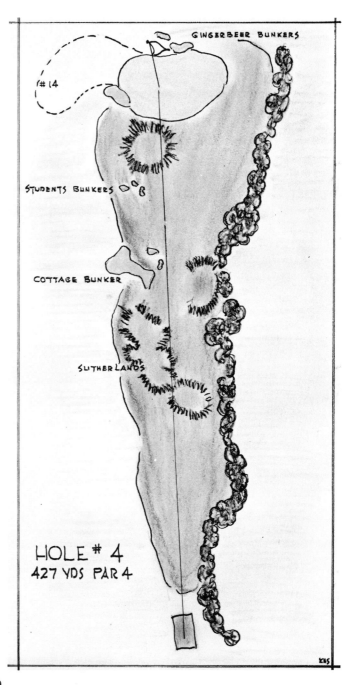

HOLE # 4
427 YDS PAR 4

HOLE NO. 5 530 YARDS, PAR 5
HOLE O'CROSS (OUT)

The fifth hole is one of the fine long holes of the course. You should hit your drive on the left "spectacle," the left bunker of the two you see about 450 yards from the tee. If you hit your drive on the line toward the left one you are left with a full wood shot in between those bunkers to the green. And, if you hit a very fine second shot you can get home in two shots provided that the wind is not too strong in your face. It is difficult to get your ball dead to the hole and you may easily face a 100-foot approach putt because the green is so large. Get your two putts and you have a great par 5.

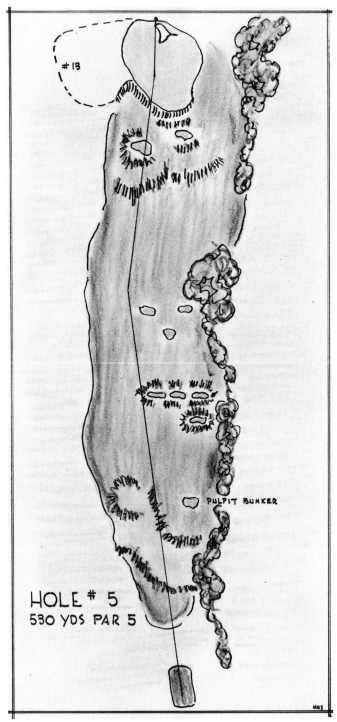

HOLE NO. 6 367 YARDS, PAR 4
HEATHERY HOLE

You must skirt the edge of the whins very accurately. There are six bunkers along the right-hand side and you must guide your ball by them. If you hook your ball there are three bunkers in a row waiting for you on the left. So this is one of the most demanding tee-shots on the course. From there it is about a 6-iron in to the green but because there is a dip in front of the green your second shot must be hit boldly to make sure you are going to get up. Two more putts and you have another pleasant par 4.

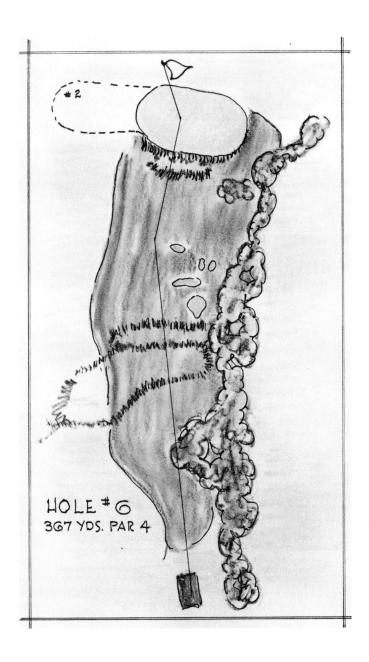

HOLE #6
367 YDS. PAR 4

HOLE NO. 7 353 YARDS, PAR 4
HIGH HOLE

The seventh hole is the only real dog-leg on the course. Play your tee-shot on the right shoulder of the hummock. If it is a good shot you will get clear of the hollow, leaving you approximately a 7-iron to the green. Again there is a big bunker guarding the green. Also, there is Strath bunker to the left of the big one. So you have to be very accurate with your second shot. It must be thrown up to the left of the flag because the ball breaks very quickly to the right once it hits on the green. There's a big slope that takes the ball to the right. A par 4 here is a reward for excellent golf.

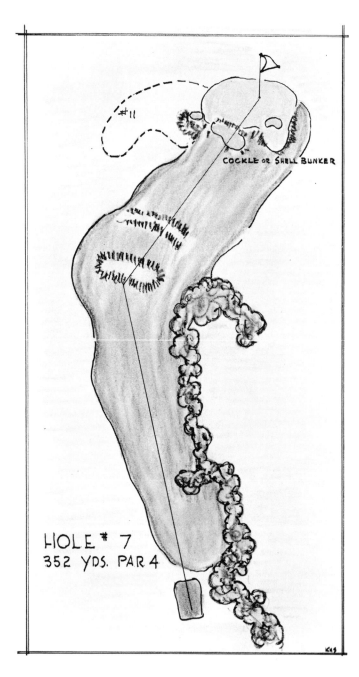

#11

COCKLE or SHELL BUNKER

HOLE # 7
352 YDS. PAR 4

HOLE NO. 8 150 YARDS, PAR 3
SHORT HOLE

The eighth is a very simple-looking hole but if your tee shot is the least bit short your ball will pitch into the bunker off the face of the green. While the bunker is small it gathers from a long way out. So be careful with this tee shot. Be sure you take enough club to get you up onto the green. Two putts here and you have a great 3.

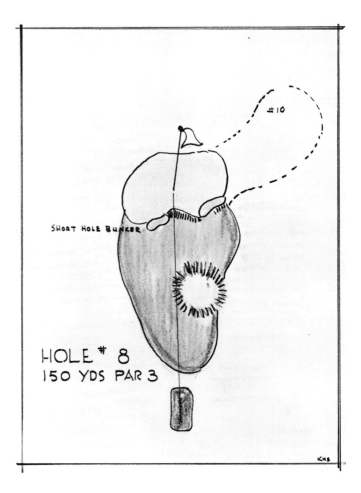

HOLE NO. 9 314 YARDS, PAR 4
END HOLE

The drive on the ninth hole is normally up to "Boase's Folly," the bunker on the right. From there it is just a pitch-and-run in to the flagstick, but, strangely enough, while this is a very simple looking hole there are more 5s on it than 3s. Two putts will give you your par 3.

You have now finished your "Outward Half" in 36 strokes. You've got four 4s, a 5, then two 4s, a 3 to the 8th and a 4 on the 9th and that is golf without any mistakes!

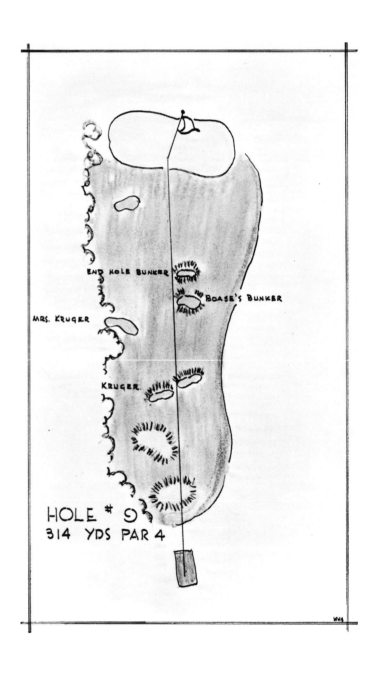

END HOLE BUNKER

BOASE'S BUNKER

MRS. KRUGER

KRUGER

HOLE # 9
314 YDS PAR 4

HOLE NO. 10 312 YARDS, PAR 4
ROBERT T. JONES, JR. HOLE

We start to turn toward home now. The tenth hole is one that is very often driven with the tee-shot but it must be a long, accurate tee-shot, one that carries the hummock that bars the way. If you do carry the hummock the ball will fall in a slight downshoot and it's possible to get home. But pushing the ball slightly will put you into a bunker ready to clap you on the right and there's one on the left, too, ready to get you into trouble. Remember that a little bit of draw will put you into the heather and that can be an unpleasant experience. It's one of the simpler holes on the course, like the ninth, an easy 4 if you just play it reasonably.

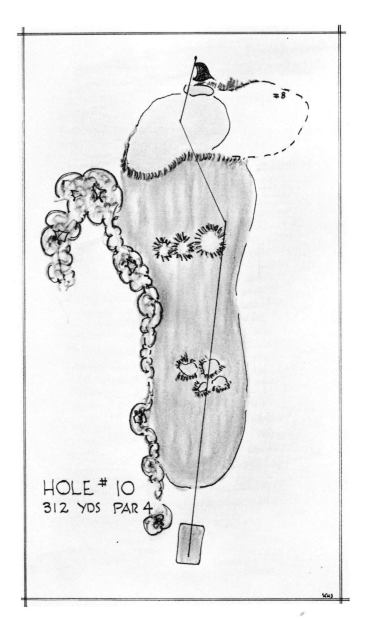

HOLE NO. 11 164 YARDS, PAR 3
HIGH HOLE

This is one of the most famous one-shot holes in golf. The wind is usually blowing in your face here and the green is on a very steep slope. The ball must be hit very boldly in to the flag. The correct way to play this hole is to "kill the ball" by hitting it into the face of the green so that it will hit the front slope and bounce in to the flagstick. If at all possible, stay on the low side of the hole as the putt from above the cup is a most difficult one. There's a lot of trouble here. The club is usually a 4-iron or a 5-iron depending upon the wind. If you cut your tee shot a bit you're in Strath bunker, the same bunker you had to contend with in playing the seventh hole. It's a little bunker but it's very deep and can be quite treacherous. The bunker on the left is Hill Bunker, the one that Sarazen put his ball into in the 1933 Championship. He took three strokes to get it out. Strath, of course, is the bunker that gave Jones his trouble in the Championship of 1921. The great Ted Ray, a big strong fellow, took four or five shots in Strath bunker and lost an important tournament right there in 1921. It is terribly deep, about eight feet when you are in the bottom, and it has a very straight face so it is not easy to get out of it. My best advice to you is, "Don't get into it!" but if you do and waste a few shots don't be ashamed. You will be in the company of a lot of fine golfers of the past. A great par 3 for you.

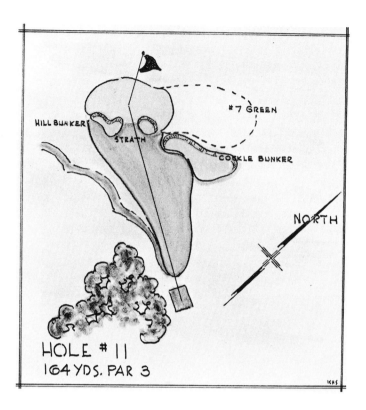

A bunker on the 11th hole at St. Andrews, the famous "Strath Bunker." Note the impossibility of lofting the ball forward. This shot would have to be played out sideways.

HOLE NO. 12 314 YARDS, PAR 4
HEATHERY HOLE (IN)

We are on the edge of the Eden now and we are turning for home. The wind will be blowing off our right side. Where the flag is placed will make a big difference in determining where to hit your tee-shot on the twelfth hole. If the flag is on the right side of the green then you want to put your tee-shot on the left in order to get your second shot into the corner of the green. If the flag is on the left, try to put your tee-shot down the right. That will help you get your tee-shot into the other corner of the green. There are two corners to this green and it has a very narrow ledge. You simply cannot pitch the ball onto the green and stop it there because the green is so narrow. You must pitch your ball over the hummock and let it run into the green. This is a shot that requires a lot of "local knowledge" which I am trying to give you in advance. Take my advice, it's good, and try to pitch your second shot over the hummock and up the face of the twelfth green. If you succeed you will have a most satisfying result, a ball nestling close to the hole for a birdie putt.

If you hit your tee-shot down the middle of the twelfth fairway you run the chance of being bunkered because there's a big, long bunker at about 160 yards carry and two smaller ones on the next ridge about 30 yards farther on. So you have a carry of nearly two hundred yards in the air if you hope to miss them all and if you don't make it, the chances are strong that one of these bunkers will catch you. With two putts you have another par 4.

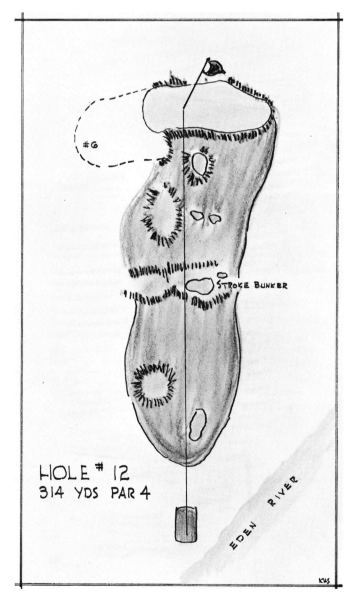

#6

STROKE BUNKER

HOLE # 12
314 YDS PAR 4

EDEN RIVER

KHS

HOLE NO. 13 410 YARDS, PAR 4
HOLE O'CROSS (IN)

The thirteenth is one of the fine holes of the course. There are three bunkers about 20 yards apart running down the left-hand side of the course. You try to miss those bunkers (the right-hand side is best) but miss them if you can even if you go left. You are left with a 5-iron or 6-iron to the green. This second shot must be hit right into the green because there's a nasty bunker on the left shoulder of the green. A ball can hit 20 yards short of the green and the pitch of the land will take it right into that bunker.

Notice what is called a grass bunker cut right into the middle of the face of the green here. You must fly your ball right over that grass bunker onto the green. Your best line is to play between the two flags and take your two putts, if you can, because it is a very fine and difficult four. You should be proud to make a 4 here.

The view of the drive at the 13th hole, "Hole O'Cross."

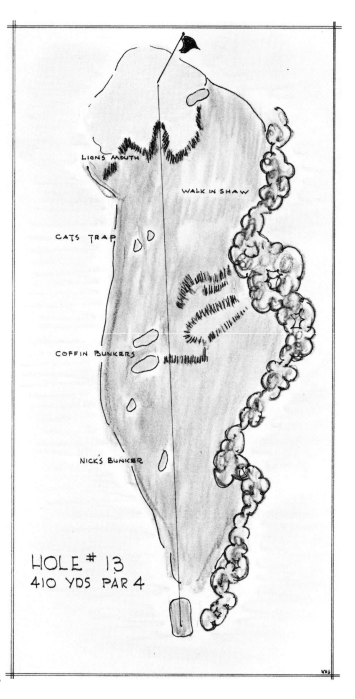

LIONS MOUTH

WALK IN SHAW

CATS TRAP

COFFIN BUNKERS

NICK'S BUNKER

HOLE # 13
410 YDS PAR 4

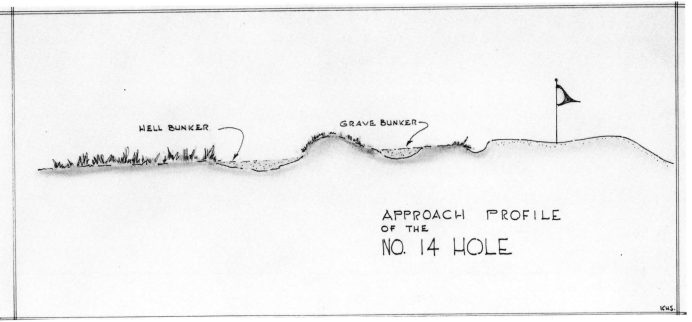

APPROACH PROFILE
OF THE
NO. 14 HOLE

HELL BUNKER

GRAVE BUNKER

HOLE NO. 14 527 YARDS, PAR 5
LONG HOLE (IN)

This is an exceptionally fine driving hole. The tee has been put back farther than it used to be in the early days. The hole is much improved thereby. Your tee-shot comes over the corner of the out-of-bounds wall on your right. The Beardies are those small bunkers on your left. They are very dangerous. Stay away from them if you can possibly do so. There is not a great deal of room to place your tee-shot. You need a fairly long carry, too, so you will soon realize why I say it is a fine driving hole.

If the wind is helping you from the right side, as it often is, and if the ground is running exceptionally, you can get down far enough with your tee-shot to have a "go" at the green in two. But it takes two mighty fine shots to reach that green. The usual way is to hit your second shot over the left-hand corner of Hell Bunker which will land your ball short of the green, of course. Then you play your pitch and run up into the green from there. That would be the way the average golfer plays the hole. Only the long hitters can get home in two. With two good shots the second dodging Hell, your pitch-and-run up over the face of the green and two good putts and you have your 5, a good one.

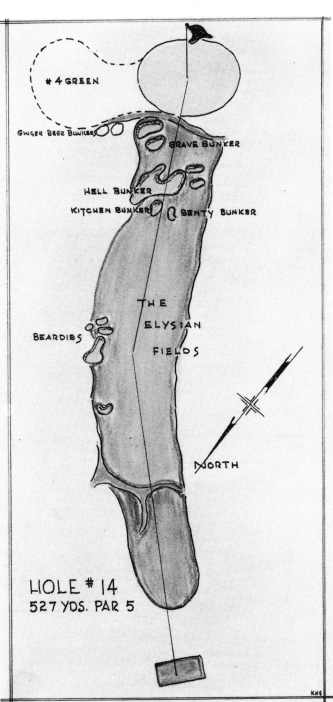

#4 GREEN

GINGER BEER BUNKERS

GRAVE BUNKER

HELL BUNKER

KITCHEN BUNKER

BENTY BUNKER

THE ELYSIAN FIELDS

BEARDIES

NORTH

HOLE #14
527 YDS. PAR 5

A close-up view of the awesome "Hell Bunker" on the 14th or "Long Hole In."

HOLE NO. 15 409 YARDS, PAR 4
CARTGATE HOLE

Your drive should carry over the right-hand corner of the Cottage Bunker. That's the long bunker that stretches almost across both fairways. This is where Jones holed his approach in his match against Sid Roper in 1930. Then you will be playing straight into the saucer of the green from that angle which is slightly left of center. Two putts here and you have your par 4.

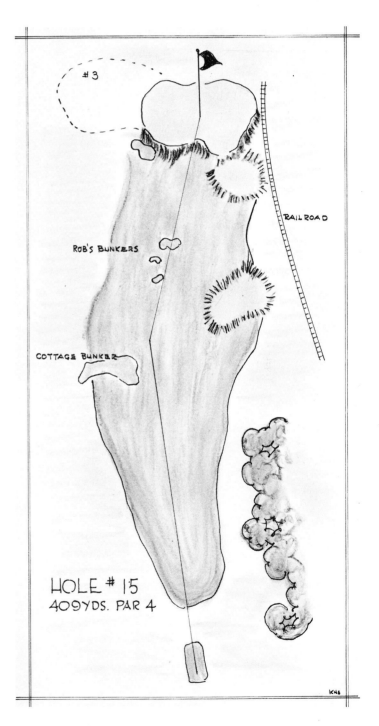

HOLE NO. 16 348 YARDS, PAR 4
CORNER OF THE DYKE HOLE

The sixteenth hole is one that must be played in from the left side. You hit your ball down past the Principal's nose on the left and then you have the face of the green square on to you. Your second shot can be a 7-iron or even an 8-iron into the green. Once you have played safely there is not a great deal of trouble afterward. There is a bunker on the left side of the green which will catch a shot that is slightly hooked but ordinarily it is a straight-forward 4. You should get your par here if you are the least bit careful.

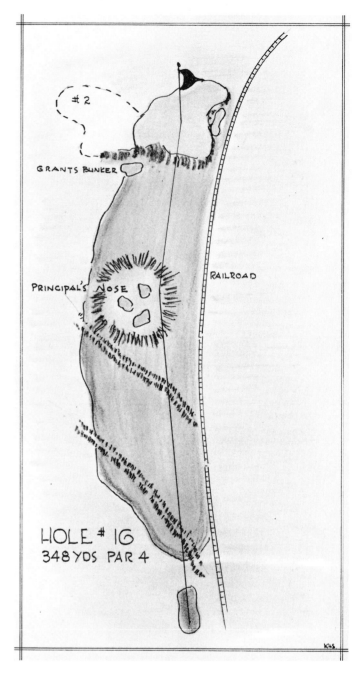

Putting on the 16th green. A view taken before the demolition of the so-called "black sheds" on the seventeenth hole.

HOLE NO. 17 467 YARDS, PAR 5
ROAD HOLE

Your tee-shot comes over the wall missing the out-of-bounds on the right. This is where the coal-yards used to be, the "drying sheds," as they were called. Now the Hotel is there but the screen in front of it still captures the danger and excitement of daring to drive the ball out-of-bounds for a few moments of flight so as to land it on the fairway beyond the stone fence. The safe shot is to play your second down near the front of the green. You have more of a chance of getting your 4 from there than from any other place. You can putt a run-up putt the way the old-timers used to do and you have your four. Many fours are gotten that way at the seventeenth. There's a bunker on the left, of course, the famous Road bunker where so many champions have foundered. That bunker can catch your second shot easily and that's why you don't go so boldly for the green with your second. The ground breaks toward that bunker. That's one of the strange features of St. Andrews. You can have a ball that lands twenty yards away from a bunker but it might have a slight "cut" on it or a slight "draw" so the ground takes the ball and shoots it straight into a nearby bunker. There's a "long cut" into many of those bunkers out there. They gather a ball from a long way out. Especially in the old days when the course was running you couldn't afford to pitch the ball into the greens. You had to pitch it short, into an exact spot, and let it bounce up into the green. One foot left or right sometimes and you find that bounce taking you right into trouble.

So play the Road Hole very carefully. Stay to the left on your tee-shot and come in on the right-hand front of the green for your third shot into the plateau green. A good chip-shot, or a "St. Andrews run-up shot" up the green front slope and you have a moderate putt for your birdie. Take the two putts and be thankful for your par 5 here.

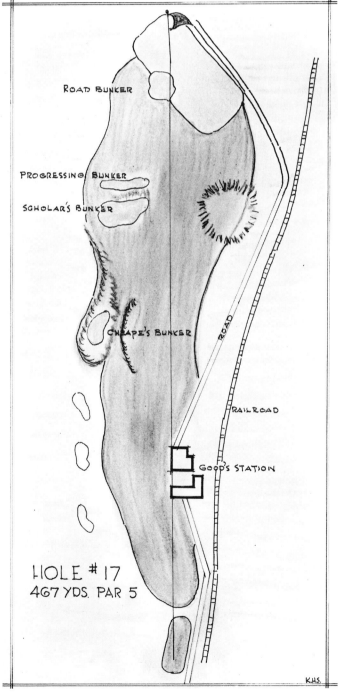

HOLE # 17
467 YDS. PAR 5

The "Road Hole," the 17th. Note the wicked whins at right. A ball caught in the whins is usually unplayable.

A contemporary view of the drive from the seventeenth hole now that the "black sheds" have been replaced by the Old Course Hotel. Notice how the screens are placed at the corner of the hole so as to give the golfer who dares to be brave with his tee-shot the same opportunity to "cut the corner" in a short-cut toward the green.

"The Golfers."

Mr. William Innes, Captain of Blackheath Golf Club.
Courtesy Blackheath Golf Club.

Mr. John Taylor, Captain of the Honorable Company at Edinburgh Golfers, 1807.

Mr. Francis Benoch.

Spectators following a match at the 17th hole in the 1950s.

An aerial view of the 17th, the "Road Hole," before the black sheds were torn down and during the construction of the Old Course Hotel. Courtesy Aerofilms Ltd.

HOLE NO. 18 364 YARDS, PAR 4
TOM MORRIS HOLE

This hole is also straightforward. You should hit your tee-shot on the clock which is in the face of the Royal and Ancient Golf Club. Then the Valley of Sin is straight on for you. That is the big dip in front of the green which has caused disaster to so many good players over the years. There is a slight rise from right to left coming down the green and so you usually are able to check your shot fairly quickly when it alights on the surface of the large green. The important thing on this last hole is to be "up" onto the plateau where the flagstick is usually placed. Two careful putts now and you have your par 4, a very satisfying one, on another one of the great holes of golf. On your way back in you have had a 4 and then a 3 and a 4. Then a 4 at the thirteenth and a good 5 at the 14th. The Fifteenth and Sixteenth fell in par 4s for you and the Road Hole was conquered in that fine par 5. When you downed your second putt on the eighteenth hole, you scored a great 37 on that nine, which added to your first nine would give you 73 strokes, a par round. Once more, golf without any mistakes! Congratulations on your fine round! The "Old Lady" will get back at you tomorrow, just wait and see!

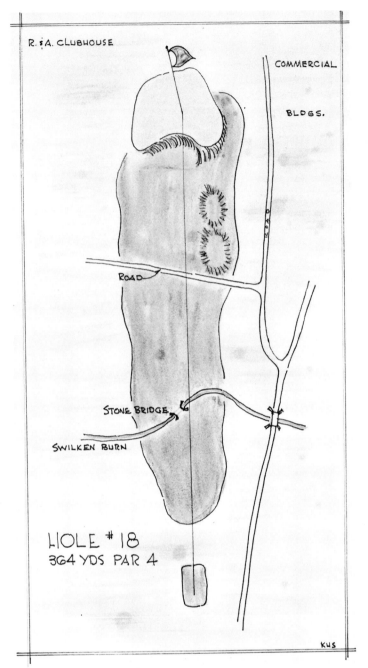

HOLE #18
364 YDS PAR 4

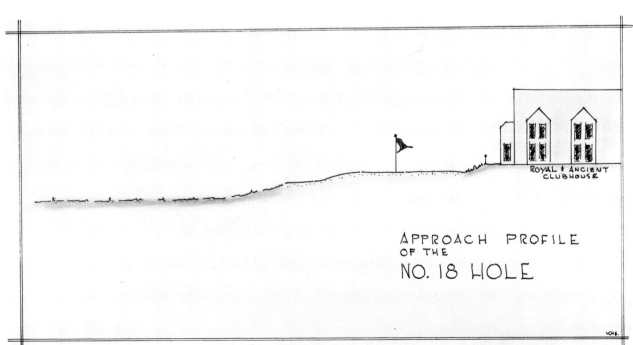

APPROACH PROFILE
OF THE
NO. 18 HOLE

PART II

Golf at St. Andrews

6

The Old Timers

ABE MITCHELL AND GEORGE DUNCAN

At the end of the First World War George Duncan was 36 and Abe Mitchell 32. These two players became to Britain in the years after the Great War what the great triumvirate of Vardon, Taylor and Braid had been as a trio before the war.

Mitchell and Duncan travelled together, played countless exhibitions together and strove mightily against each other in the championships. Mitchell, it seems, was never destined to win "the big one." He was a unique swinger, "stood with his feet rooted to the ground, grasped the club in a pair of massive hands, and quietly and with little outward effort gave the ball a tremendous two-fisted clout with his arms, hands and wrists."

In the first tournament after the war, on the Old Course at St. Andrews, Mitchell and Duncan tied.

In the first post-war Open in 1920 at Deal, Mitchell's first two rounds put him six strokes ahead of the field and thirteen strokes in front of Duncan, who had turned in a pair of 80s. Duncan, with nothing to lose, played in relaxed fashion and turned in a final 71. Mitchell had not yet started his last round. Abe three-putted the first hole, continued to fritter away stroke after stroke on the round, finished in 84, and lost every one of the strokes in his huge lead. Duncan won with 303. Mitchell never did win "The Big One."

George Duncan, having won at Deal in 1920 in the dramatic thirteen stroke comeback to displace Abe Mitchell from his leading position, defended his title the next year at St. Andrews. The winner was a Scotsman-turned-American, Jock Hutchison, and when Jock won it was the beginning of many successive victories by American "invaders."

HARRY VARDON

Here is contemporary reporter Horace Hutchinson's story of Vardon's first victory in the Open Championship:

J. H. Taylor had won the title two years before at Sandwich in 1894 and again at St. Andrews in 1895. When Taylor tried for his third win in succession, Vardon and he tied at the end of seventy-two holes. They played a thirty-six hole play-off and Vardon won. Taylor played well but Vardon played better. Most notably, Vardon putted better. Even after Taylor had gotten back the considerable lead which Vardon had gained early in the match, Vardon did not allow himself to become flustered. He kept on the even tenor of his ways and won the match. The manner in which he won the match, his perfect coolness, the absence of swagger, and yet the perfect possession of confidence, these are very typical of Vardon and his style.

Vardon played with golf clubs considerably shorter and quite a bit lighter than those that are used by the great majority of golfers and he drove half of the body have taken a great part of the swing. Seldom will you see anyone rising so freely on the toe of the right foot, bending the left knee so much or even allowing the left shoulder to come so far under. It is in these particulars that Vardon's swing is big.

In Vardon's downswing it is evident that he has made every movement with ease. There has been no pressing, no forcing, no wild hitting with the arms. The body has been allowed to follow the turn of the swing with wonderful freedom. Vardon ends his swing facing quite straight in the direction in which the ball is going, and that without an effort, with the left foot planted just as it was when the stroke was delivered. The right heel has come away off the ground with all the freedom of action that we see in his left foot at the top of his swing, the turn at the hips has been very free and com-

The great Harry Vardon. Note, the "Vardon grip" with the little finger of the right hand overlapping the forefinger of the left hand. Although Vardon made this grip famous, it was actually originated by J. H. Taylor.

very long distances. He drove farther than Taylor who is certainly not a short driver and who has all the appearance of being the stronger man. Vardon drove without appearing to force the stroke at all, appearing rather as if he could hit the ball a good deal harder if he so pleased, as if he were always playing within himself with a good measure of reserve strength to be called upon occasion. Vardon hit every ball perfectly cleanly with his club-head always traveling in the right direction.

Vardon's swing is not a long swing. The club does not come even so far around behind him as to reach a horizontal line. The turn of his body is great. The legs, the hips, the feet, all the lower

Harry Vardon at top of swing.

70

plete. His right shoulder has come around, following it. The two parts of Vardon's swing, the upward and the downward, match each other perfectly.

Hutchinson ended his commentary on Vardon, the man, and Vardon, the golfer by saying: "His temperament as a golfer seems to have all the qualities of his style, qualities that seem to have very few defects attached to them. The quietness and control of his swing are reflected in the modest confidence of his manner. He is universally liked as a man and universally feared as a golfer."

The Book of Golf and Golfers
by Horace G. Hutchinson
Longmans, Green & Co., London 1899

At Muirfield last May, when the great body of onlookers went surging after the victorious Hagen, there were a few, liking art for art's sake, apart from victory, and disliking a crowd, who went elsewhere. This little band of connoisseurs, at once so modest and so select, was to be seen following Macdonald Smith and Harry Vardon. The one might well have won, but had had a bad time and was out of the hunt; the other, born in 1870, could not hope to win at this time of day. So they were to be watched purely because they were two of the most graceful and beautiful of all golfers.

Till they got to the greens there was nothing in it between them; the older man was fully holding his own in the power of his long game, in the crispness and accuracy of his iron shots. Only when it came to the putting did Vardon's old enemy beset him; he moved his body, he stabbed at the short ones, he went off "at half cock." Otherwise the years might have rolled away. Here was still a great master; we might almost have been looking at the invincible player who had dominated golf at the beginning of the century.

I am not going to argue as to whether or not Vardon is the greatest golfer that ever lived. Such comparisons are futile. It is enough that he was the golfer of his time. He won the British Open Championship in 1896, 1898, 1899, 1903, 1911 and 1914; he won the American Championship in 1900. He was probably at his very best in 1898 and 1899, before his visit to America. In point of health and strength he was not quite the same man afterwards and he himself has said that he thinks he left a little of his game there. It was not till some little time later that his actual and very serious illness developed. He won two more championships after he was well again, but never again did he show the same utterly crushing superiority, which caused Andrew Kirkaldy to say that he would break the heart of an iron ox.

Harry Vardon and Arthur Havers in 1921. Vardon was Open champion six times. Havers once, in 1923.

Of the "triumvirate"—Vardon, Braid and Taylor —Taylor is actually the youngest by a few months, but he was the first to make his name. He leaped into fame in 1893 when he began knocking down the big men like ninepins. In both 1894 and 1895 he was champion. Very few people had heard of Harry Vardon then, nobody perhaps save a few golfers in the north of England who had backed him in a home-to-home match against Sandy Herd and seen him badly beaten. In the winter of 1895-96 half a dozen leading professionals were asked to go out to play at Pau, France; someone of discerning judgment made Vardon one of the party and the rest of the world asked "who is this fellow Vardon?"

Then, in the spring of 1896, Taylor, twice the champion, played Vardon on his home course at Ganton in Yorkshire and came away beaten by a pocketful of holes and declared that here was the man that he feared most in the coming championship. It was a sound piece of prophecy, for the two tied at Muirfield and Vardon won the playoff. In the next year the new star waned a little and then in 1898 blazed out in full glory.

For the next two years, if Vardon was in the field,

no one looked any further for the winner; he crushed everyone. He once beat Taylor at Newcastle in Ireland by twelve and eleven and Taylor was playing his game. In 1900 he went to America and after that he was, right up till the war, one of the two or three unquestioned best, but he was never again as he had been, in a completely different class from all the other golfers.

Well now, what were the characteristics, both of his method and its results, that made him so devastating a conqueror? Results are easier to tackle and I will take them first. Vardon was first of all a magnificent driver. He could shoot a guttie ball an uncommonly long distance, especially down the wind, and he was very straight. Taylor had been regarded as inhumanly accurate and so he was. Now here came Vardon, who rivaled his accuracy and added to it a little something more of freedom and power. He had a gift of hitting long carrying shots and, because of his upright swing, the ball would sit down where it pitched with but little run. This gift was of enormous value through the green. The brassie was not atrophied then, there were lots of wooden club shots to be played up to the pin, and Vardon, who often played them with his driver, could and did put the ball nearer the hole than other men could with their mashies. It was his most overpowering stroke and, even if he had been a bad putter then (which he was not), it left him little putting to do.

But then, he was superb with all iron clubs. He could command great length, if he needed it, and had at one time a driving mashie which was as a driver in his hand. He was beautifully accurate in all pitching shots. Taylor had got there first and acquired the reputation of the greatest mashie player in the world, but I think Vardon was just as good. He was a good approach putter and at any rate an adequate holer-out, though without the touch and delicacy of the really outstanding putter.

As to his style, photographs of him are probably familiar to the reader and give at any rate some impression. One thing noticeable in those pictures is that by comparison with the modern school, Vardon certainly made no fetish of the stiff left arm. Another thing is the uniform beauty of the follow-through. Time after time he would come right through, drawn to his full height, the club right round over his left shoulder, the hands well up, the left elbow tolerably high. It was the ideal copybook follow-through and he did it every time with an almost monotonous perfection.

Neither photograph, however—the top of the swing nor the finish of it—gives any real notion of how he took the club up. His method is very un-like anybody else's. First of all, he was a conspicuous example of the doctrine of "hands leading." In his day the books used to tell us that the head of the club should go back first and the wrists begin at once to turn away. In fact, I do not believe that any of the good players did anything of that kind, but they thought and taught that they did and the human eye was not quick enough to detect the fallacy. In Vardon's case, however, it was clear that he did none of these things; one could actually see the hands leading and the club-head going back for some distance in a straight line before he slung it to the top of the swing. Neither does any photograph convey the small but still perceptible touch of lift in the upswing nor the little touch of sway. His was essentially an upright swing in the days when orthodox swings were flat. He took the club up very straight, "too straight" as any self-respecting caddie would have said in instructing his master. Then, by way of natural compensation, he flung the clubhead well out behind him and brought it down onto the ball with a big sweep. It was a beautifully free movement of one having a natural gift for opening his shoulders and hitting clean. And, of course, like the movements of all really great golfers, it was an instinct combined with that mysterious thing called rhythm. No golfer in the world, not even Bobby himself, was ever more perfectly rhythmic than Harry Vardon.

In re-reading what I have written I find I have said nothing about the Vardon grip. Well, Vardon certainly discovered it for himself and made it popular; but Taylor at Westward Ho! had also discovered it for himself while Vardon was doing the same in Jersey and Mr. Johnny Laidlay had discovered it long before either of them, at North Berwick, while those two were tiny boys. Still, it is a convenient name and I hope the day will never come when some young golfer who has just learned it asks "Who was Vardon?"

This article first appeared in *The Complete Golfer*, edited by Herbert Warren Wind.

JOHN BALL

"The supreme match player," was the name given to John Ball by his writer contemporary, golf expert Bernard Darwin. His record was magnificent. Eight times British Amateur Champion starting in 1888 and ending in 1912, an unbelievable twenty-three year span. Besides that, he picked up the Open Championship in 1890, at medal play of course, was one of the few amateurs ever to beat the professionals on their own terms. Ball's first

Ball customarily played in the Scottish tweed jacket which all golfers of that time wore. He always had a boutonniere in his lapel and walked with his head down, eyes straight forward as he concentrated on his "business," to get a par. Ball may have been the originator of the strategy of the great match players such as Jones and Joyce Wethered, in which the golfer tries to block from his mind all knowledge or even care about what his opponent is doing and merely concentrates on playing Old Man Par. It seemed that the more intense the crisis Ball encountered, the more he was able to pull within himself and play his own game.

Ball was said to be "lethally accurate" with his shots, and had what was described as "a beautiful swing." Darwin said he preferred to watch Ball rather than Jones or Vardon, that Ball's swing defied analysis, that he, Darwin, could not put the rhythm of Ball's swing into words.

John Ball, the first amateur player to win the Open Championship (1890, at Prestwick). Ball had won the British Amateur Championship already in 1888 and went on to win a total of eight times through 1912, a remarkable span of excellence.

John Ball, Jr., Open Champion in 1890, when the tournament was contested over thirty-six holes. His score was 164.

five Amateurs were played with the "Guttie" ball, the last three with the rubber-cored ball.

Ball was truly the subject of golf hero worship of the kind that later was seen concerning Robert T. Jones, Ben Hogan and Arnold Palmer. He was a silent, retiring, resolutely dour fighter. He was almost "obstinately modest." On one occasion, it is related that when Ball had won the Open at Hoylake his fellow golfers at Royal Liverpool Golf Club, Ball's home club, made extensive preparations to meet him and greet him at the train station. The crowd waited and waited for him but he never arrived. He either knew about the planned welcome or sensed one so he had left the train at an earlier station and walked home alone across the countryside.

Ball's style was unorthodox as far as today's swings go. His feet were noticeably far apart and his legs were stiff. His early swing had the ball very far back toward his right foot, his shots amazing to the spectators in the way they started on a low trajectory, rose gradually in flight and then fell dead on touching the ground. The "Guttie" ball was especially suited for this action and later on, with the rubber-cored ball, Ball narrowed his stance somewhat and played the ball farther forward but with no decrease in accuracy or distance. Ball also had the ability to stop his backswing wherever he wanted and thus had great control over the "half-shot" or "three-quarter" shot to the green. An extraordinary fact about Ball was that he played with clubs no more lofted than a mashie, even out of the deepest bunker. He would lay the face of his club open and loft it as high as he wished and stop the ball the way anyone else might do with a niblick. He claimed in his later life not to understand the whole battery of numbered clubs that came into vogue when golf equipment manufacturers began to cater to every whim of the golf devotee. John Ball was truly a golf marvel of the 1890s and early 1900s. He should be ranked alongside the first "Big Three of Golf."

WALTER TRAVIS

At the United States National Open Championship at Myopia Country Club in 1908 all the great golfers of that day were having terrible trouble with the twelfth green, a very tricky and difficult green. One by one they pitched mechanically to the green, stepped nonchalantly up with their putters, casually glanced at the lie, gave the ball a tap—and missed by a mile. One after the other, they took their second, then their third putts, ruefully shook their heads and walked away.

Then down the fairway came Walter Travis, greatest golfer, beyond all doubt, of the day. His approach shot to the green was a trifle too strong and it came to rest several feet behind the cup. From that angle the green's bad features, its speed and its downward, irregular slope were accentuated.

Slowly, Travis walked out on the green and carefully picked out the spot where the ball, if propelled at just the proper speed, would almost come to a dead stop before, yielding to gravity, it would turn down the next slope toward the cup. Then he called to his caddie to stand on the special spot he had picked out so carefully. He eyed the caddie's feet intently, then motioned the boy away and played. The ball, perfectly judged, wended its way down the slope, turned at the exact spot—and rimmed the cup. Technique, plus thought, had enabled Travis to pick up a valuable stroke where his more careless opponents had been willing to leave too much to chance.

In many respects Walter J. Travis will stand as the most remarkable golfer that ever lived. Just consider, as a starter, these two facts. He won the first tournament he ever entered at the age of thirty-five, a month or so after he had hit his first golf ball. He won the last tournament he ever entered, the Metropolitan Championship, at the age of fifty-four, in 1915, and on his way through he beat Jerry Travers, the United States Open Champion of the same year.

Here was a man who started golf at middle age, or well beyond the competitive prime of life. He began a difficult game, a game demanding the imitative power of youth, at the age where most men leave off as champions. He was of slight physique, with rather small hands and slender wrists. He weighed no more than one hundred and forty pounds. Yet against all these handicaps he wrested four national championships from the best golfers of America and Great Britain.

Few learn golf in a lifetime. Championship golf is usually a matter of many years of struggle from a young start. Travis picked up his first golf club in October, 1896, when he was nearly thirty-five years old. Two years later he had reached the semifinal round of the Amateur Championship. Within four years of his golfing debut he was the amateur champion of his country, and for four years—1900, 1901, 1903 and 1904—he was champion of either American or Great Britain.

He was forty-four years old when he invaded Great Britain and brought back the famous cup from Sandwich. After that invasion such American stars as Chick Evans, Jerry Travers, Francis Ouimet, Fred Herreshoff, Bob Gardner, Bobby Jones, Bill Fownes and many others were to try in vain for twenty-two years to match him. It was not until 1926 that Jess Sweetser duplicated the Travis achievement, and Sweetser at the time was twenty years younger than his famous predecessor had been.

Many years ago, when Walter J. was in his prime, the late George W. Adair, who played with him often, made this comment on his golf game: "Travis can beat any golfer that ever lived on a golf course only ten yards wide with a keen wind blowing."

Some of his forgotten achievements are remarkable. In one match at the old Westchester course he hit the flagstick three times and missed it only by inches on other occasions.

In a thirty-six-hole match with "Snake" Ames at Garden City he had 36-36-72 in the morning and 36-36-72 in the afternoon. He had exactly par on thirty-four of the thirty-six holes played. On one of the most testing of all golf courses this must stand as a record for deadly consistency.

On another occasion at Garden City he had six consecutive 2s in one week on the difficult and elusive second hole. At the age sixty he had 66 and a 68 in one of the Florida championships and at the age of sixty-four he played Garden City in 73, even par, and just two strokes above the record of the course.

It must be remembered that such great golfers as Bobby Jones, Jess Sweetser, Walter Hagen, Johnny Farrell, Tommy Armour and Gene Sarazen started golf when they were seven, eight or ten years old, under good instruction, from which it was possible to develop a fine swing instinctively. They also had superlative physical powers.

But consider the case of a rather slight, slender middle-age man who started at thirty-five to build up his own game without any outside help, and who, within a short while, stood as the amateur champion of the two greatest golfing nations in the world.

Walter J. Travis could do more with a putter than any golfer in history. He was probably no better than Jerry Travers upon the green itself. But he could also use the putter effectively off the green and from bunkers where the ball was lying well.

He devised the scheme of smaller holes on the practice course at Garden City, holes only a trifle larger than the ball. He practiced here for hours. When you can drop them steadily in a two-inch cup, one double the size looks like a keg.

One of his main angles in regard to putting was to imagine he was driving a tack into the back of the ball and let the putting blade go on through. He considered putting largely a right-handed affair and the right hand predominated in his grip. The left was merely a steadying aid.

But he was something more than a magnificent putter. He was straight down the course from the tee and almost every type of iron usually left the ball fairly close to the cup. He had a peculiar grip, no overlapping or interlocking, with the right hand well under, but he understood the value of flexible wrists that were firm but never tight or tense.

One of Travis' greatest contributions to American golf was a detail which frequently made him enemies. This was an insistence on playing the game to the letter and spirit of the rules. He would tolerate no deviation from the correct path, even in a friendly round. In the early days of the game,

when there was an even greater laxity in playing by the rules than anyone can know today, he set a standard which gradually took effect.

There was still another feature to his play—he never played a careless, indifferent shot. No matter how unimportant the match, he played every stroke as if he were in a championship test. He made careful, accurate golf a habit. He thought too much of the game to desecrate it with any indifferent effort. Every shot was a problem to be worked out and worked out in the right way. His rank as a course architect was high, for he knew the value of holes and how they should be arranged to call for skill and to keep up sustained interest.

He was fifty-four years old when he faced Jerry Travers, his leading rival for many years, for the last time, at Apawamis in 1915. Travers had been his hardest barricade. He had checked Travis out of many championships. In this last meeting they came to the final hole all square with the Metropolitan Championship at stake, and, for old time's sake, Travis sank a thirty-foot putt to win, one up. He knew this was his last chance to beat a victorious opponent from many years gone by and yet no one ever swung the blade of a putter with a smoother, steadier stroke as he sent the ball spinning across the green into the cup.

It was always a treat to play with the Old Man. Even though his conversation was scarce, one could learn more from him in a few words than from almost anyone else in a long day's talk. He had the courage of an unbroken will and an unbreakable determination. There was no faltering in any crisis, where he was usually at his best.

There has been only one Bobby Jones in golf. And there, also, has been only one Walter J. Travis.

JAMES BRAID

James Braid first came to the official notice of Vardon and Taylor when he displaced both of them in the Open Championship of 1897 and finished runnerup to amateur Harold Hilton, who beat all three of these players to the finish line and the title at Hoylake, England. Taylor had played against Braid in an exhibition match several years before and when Braid tied him, Taylor knew Braid would be a future threat in professional golf.

Although Braid did not break through to win his first Open Championship until four years later at Muirfield in 1901, where he won out over Harry Vardon, his strong driving was gaining him quite a reputation among his fellow professionals. Horace Hutchinson, Amateur Champion himself and, later

*Six great Open Champions. Top row: Jim Braid,
Horace Hutchinson, Harry Vardon. Bottom row: J.H.
Taylor, Tom Morris, Willie Park.*

on, golf writer, had these comments on Braid's swing: "His style is not attractive to watch. Sound it certainly must be or it could not obtain the results it does; but one would not call it orthodox. Notice the comparative shortness of his swing, computed by the position of the club at its highest. It is scarcely allowed to make more than an angle of 45° behind the back. In Braid's swing, it is evident that the club has been held firmly in the right hand throughout the upward swing and is held no less firmly throughout the downward swing. Braid looks a little 'tied' in his backswing as if certain bits of his anatomy were saying to him, 'You cannot get back any further.' Braid's answer is, 'I do not want to go back any further,' and he points to his next drive to clinch any argument."

From 1902 until the beginning of the First World War there were twelve Open Championships. The "Big Three" of early golf, Jim Braid, Harry Vardon and John Henry "J.H." Taylor dominated the field of golf in those early years, particularly the Open Championships, by accounting for nine of them, Braid four, Vardon three and

Taylor two. These three great golfers had different styles of golf swing because they were of distinctly different physical builds. Jim Braid was tall and wiry and when he was playing his best was very flexible. He was six feet, one and a half inches tall and weighed 174 pounds. Harry Vardon was five feet, nine inches tall and weighed 154 pounds. He, too, like Braid was very wiry in build. "J.H." Taylor was only five feet, eight inches tall, was on the short stocky side and outweighed Vardon at 161 pounds. The new rubber-cored ball probably helped "J.H." more than the other two because he never had the length of the others and was losing distance on his drives as a result of age. All three of these great players swung with their left wrists under the shaft at the top of their swings. This is known in golf instruction parlance as "shut-faced" as contrasted to the so-called "American" method of "open-faced" position at the top of the swing, which results from keeping the back of the left-hand in a "flat-plane," in line with the left forearm during the wrist-cock at the top of the swing.

Braid had his left hand more on top of the shaft

than either Vardon or Taylor and as a result was at times a big hooker.

Braid positioned the ball unusually far forward toward his left foot. After he had hit the ball, and it was always with terrific power, it seemed to observers that he was still straining to put more power into the shot even though it had already flown from the face of his club. Braid faced toward the line of flight after hitting the ball and let his body follow freely with the stroke. His body weight came far forward into his left leg in what was said to be not a "graceful stroke but one of undeniably terrific power." Braid was reported to "press hard" with every drive. The great feature of his style was his power of concentration along with perfectly trained eyes and muscles which allowed him to keep his tremendous power under perfect control.

Hutchinson also said of Jim Braid: "In spite of his lack of grace, and partly by reason of its lack of grace, it is a peculiarly fascinating style to watch. There is a special delight in seeing the kind of divine fury with which he 'laces into' the ball and yet the wonderful accuracy with which he hits it. He is a fine player to watch. Nor should Braid be viewed only as a tremendous driver. He is also a finished approacher with his irons. While he is very powerful with them at long range, his manner of using them is less forcing than in his driving. It was said that now and again Braid's putting was weak, but that 'only proved him to be mortal.'"

EDWARD "TED" RAY

Edward "Ted" Ray was a huge lumbering figure of a man who "lurched" into the ball with all the power he possessed. While he had great overall rhythm in his swing, he had a distinctly timed sway as he moved into his hitting position. His philosophy of golf was well expressed in his answer to a question about how to drive the ball farther when he said, "Hit it a bloody sight harder!"

Ray used a whole battery of deep and deeper faced mashies, mashie-niblicks and niblicks. He would explode up and over towering trees and out of impossibly deep lies in the heavy rough, and more frequently than not the ball would be observed soaring to great heights like a projectile, only to come to rest finally on the putting surface. For a large man and for one with so explosively violent a swing, Ray had a delicate touch with his putter. In 1913, Ted Ray was one of the players in the three-way tie for the United States Open Championship at Brookline, Massachusetts, along with Harry Vardon and the young Francis Ouimet.

Although Ray and Vardon both lost to Ouimet, Ray returned in 1920 to long and difficult Inverness at Toledo and, at last, put his name on the U. S. Open trophy. There is no question that Ray was a remarkably good golfer with a style all his own and should be ranked high among the best golfers of all time.

FREDDIE TAIT

The spring and autumn meetings at St. Andrews are held at a time of year when the greens are impossible to pitch on, and frustrating to putt on. Freddie Tait realized that if he was to be successful on his home green he would have to cultivate a style of approaching which would stand him in good stead not only when the green was easy but also when the green was hard. He found that the only shot which answered his problem was the

Freddie Tait, one of the greatest of the old-time golfers. Tait kept a daily golf diary for years.

The Freddie Tait painting in the Royal and Ancient clubhouse. Tait's dog, "Nails," is at his side. The caddie is a blind boy.

*Freddie Tait holing out on the 18th green. Tom
Morris is holding the flagstick. Notice the relationship
of the 18th green to the clubhouse in comparison with
its present position.*

*short pitch and long run. This shot he played so
well that his biographer, John L. Low said, "I cannot help thinking it the most perfect achievement
of golfing skill that his genius and science have
ever produced. No turf could be taken, so hard
was the lie from which the ball had to be played.
This cleanness of hitting the ball or rather of nip-
ping it up off the hard ground was the lesson which
St. Andrews taught him."*

*Two incredible shots of Freddie Tait deserve
mention in this book. Here are Low's words describing them:*

Going to the sixth or "Heathery" hole at St.
Andrews, a mound with an almost trench-like
grassy hollow beyond it guards the green. The
green itself is a tableland, and on that day, the
hole was situated on its nearer side. Tait's ball lay
some 120 yards from the hole. The wind was a

following one and blew also somewhat from the
left. The hollow was partly full of casual water, so
that a purely running shot was out of the question.
It was equally impossible to pitch on to the green
and not run 30 or 40 yards past the hole, as the
green was keen, the hole just over the hollow, and
the wind strong. To play the push shot against the
bank, which is only about two feet high, it would
have been necessary to have allowed a good deal
for the cross wind from the left, and the ball would
during the latter part of its course, both before and
after it pitched, have been at the mercy of the
golfers' greatest enemy. Tait played the shot quite
straight, counteracting the force of the wind by
the upward turn of the right hand, and at the same
time by hitting the ball in the centre; just as the
club was beginning to rise, he put the forward spin
on it which gave it no chance of refusing to take

79

the hill. This was his "leg-break" shot, most useful in counteracting wind or slope of ground.

The other shot I have spoken of was played at the fourteenth hole at St. Andrews; it was Tait's third shot. It was played in the course of the Spring Medal Competition of 1899. Tait at the time was leading Mr. Laidlay, his keenest rival, by one stroke. There was a north-westerly wind blowing down and across the course, and Tait had played his second shot well out to the left into one of the grassy hollows which lie to the left of "Hell." He had got so far to the left that the pot bunkers at the foot of the plateau-like green were directly between him and the hole; the green was very keen, and Tait's ball lay on the downward slope of a rather steep hill. The obvious shot to play was the one we have just described. With this shot he could have *pulled* the ball on to the right-hand corner of the green without crossing the bunkers at all. Two things were in Tait's mind against doing this; the first was that the hole was not on right-hand corner but in the middle of the green, and the second was that he knew he could get but little pull on his ball, even with the help of the wind, owing to the hanging lie. To play the ball straight for the hole from such a lie it was necessary for him to cut it, but no amount of cut would have enabled him to pitch the ball on to the narrow tableland and yet stop it from going down the slope beyond. The hole was about 120 yards off, and Tait, taking all risks, picked the ball up almost clean, with but sufficient slice on it to counteract the wind, and drove it hard and low over the bunkers against the face of the green; the ball struck the face and gave one bound into the air, the life was taken out of it, and it lay dead at the side of the hole. One foot lower or higher and the shot must have been a complete failure. The shot was so clearly meant, and the execution so wonderfully carried out, that I shall always regard it as the most skillful stroke I ever saw Freddie play.

This article first appeared in John L. Low, *F. G. Tait: A Record*

Course Record Score of Freddie Tait in 1894

Here is the account of Freddie Tait's record round of 72, which was made on February 5, 1894, one under par, breaking the former records of 73 by Hugh and Andrew Kirkaldy, which had stood since 1889. It is taken from the magazine Golf *of February 16, 1894:*

In view of Mr. Tait's marvelous feat, it may be that golfers, especially those abroad, will not find it wearisome if we describe the round somewhat minutely. First, as to the position of the holes: The first was on the medal green to the right, the tee some 70 to 80 yards from the railings; the second, on a newly made green to the right (the putting here being rough), rather farther on than the medal hole; the tee to the third hole was 30 yards farther forward than on medal days, and a good deal to the right, among the rough grass. From that point every hole and tee was much about the same as on medal days, as far as distance is concerned, until the end hole, which was only some ten yards past the small bunker, and just to the right of it. Turning homewards, though the tee was a little more forward, the balance was about restored by the hole being placed about the same distance further back—the eleventh hole was far to the left, close to the Eden, on a small table with steep sides, and immediately behind the bunker; it could not have been reached from the tee save by a driver of exceptional power, such as Mr. Tait himself. Thus it will be seen that the next hole was considerably shorter; in fact, Mr. Tait, with a terrifically long ball, could, and actually did, reach the green. From this point the only alterations were from the "Hole O'Cross" to the Ginger-Beer"; a much longer hole than on medal days, by reason of the tee being put very far back; and at the eighteenth hole where the same remark applies. While he did not play the "medal course," had he played the same game on the exact medal round as he did on this occasion, his score would probably have been as good. If the ninth and twelfth holes were easier, the distance was quite made up by the extra length of the long hole home and of the last.

Here then, is the actual score

OUT	5 4 4	3 5 4	5 3 3	= 36
IN	3 3 3	5 5 4	4 5 4	= 36
			Total	72

Details as thus:

1. Two long drives over the Burn to left; short loft; two putts.
2. Two, rather to right; short pitch; putt (two yards).
3. Drive; pitch; two putts (almost a three).
4. Very long shot; driving mashie; putt (10 to 12 yards).
5. Two drives onto a narrow table fronting green; approach; two putts (nearly a four).
6. Very long drive; approach a little past; two putts.
7. Drive drawn into second bunker; niblick; approach; two putts.
8. First very wide to right; approach putt two yards past, third in (good recovery).
9. Very long drive; nearly home; two putts.
10. Drive to foot of green; approach 10 or 12 yards past; third holed out.

80

11. Long shot to left of teeing ground; putted up; holed out from 10 yards.
12. Very long drive which just reached green on left; two putts.
13. Carried all the bunkers; indifferent iron shot, heeled; three putts.
14. Two very long drives; an iron shot quite straight; two putts, (almost a four).
15. Long drive; cleek shot to foot of green (too heavily taken); approach dead; one putt.
16. Drive; wrist approach; two putts (almost a three).
17. Drive somewhat drawn to left; second to right of bunker; running loft onto green; two putts.
18. Long drive; cleek shot past hole; two putts, the first of which hit the cup for 71 and ran about a yard past. The crucial putt was well holed by Mr. Tait amidst loud plaudits.

This article first appeared in John L. Low, *F. G. Tait: A Record*

Note: This score, of course, was made with the gutta percha ball.

7

Some Champions and Championships

The Open Championship of 1895.

*Frank Stranahan, British Amateur champion of 1948
at Sandwich and 1950 at St. Andrews.*

Bob Martin, Open Champion of 1885.

John H. Taylor, known as "J.H.," five-time winner of the Open Championship from 1894 through 1913.

Hugh Kirkaldy, Open Champion of 1891.

BRITISH OPEN CHAMPIONSHIPS
AT
ST. ANDREWS

Year	Winner
1873	Tom Kidd
1876	Robert Martin
1879	Jamie Anderson
1882	Robert Ferguson
1885	Robert Martin
1888	Jack Burns
1891	Hugh Kirkaldy
1895	John H. Taylor
1900	John H. Taylor
1905	James Braid
1910	James Braid
1921	Jock Hutchinson
1927	Robert T. Jones, Jr.
1933	Denny Shute
1939	Richard Burton
1946	Sam Snead
1955	Peter W. Thomson
1957	Arthur D. Locke
1960	Kelvin D. G. Nagle
1964	Tony Lema
1970	Jack Nicklaus

BRITISH AMATEUR
CHAMPIONSHIPS
AT
ST. ANDREWS

Year	Winner
1886	Horace Hutchinson
1889	John Ernest Laidlay
1891	John Ernest Laidlay
1895	L. M. Balfour-Melville
1901	Harold Hilton
1907	John Ball
1913	Harold Hilton
1924	Ernest W. E. Holderness
1930	Robert T. Jones, Jr.
1936	Hector Thomson
1950	Frank Stranahan
1958	Joseph Carr
1963	Michael Lunt

WALKER CUP MATCHES
AT
ST. ANDREWS

1923	United States 6, Great Britain 5, one match halved
1926	United States 6, Great Britain 5, one match halved
1934	United States 9, Great Britain 2, one match halved
1938	Great Britain 7, United States 4. one match halved
1947	United States 8, Great Britain 4
1955	United States 10, Great Britain 2
1971	Great Britain 13, United States 11, two matches halved
1975	United States 15½, Great Britain 8½

Leslie Balfour-Melville, at finish of drive.

THE OPEN CHAMPIONSHIP OF 1876

In the Open Championship of 1876 at St. Andrews, Bob Martin and David Strath tied with a total of 176 strokes. A protest was lodged against Strath, alleging that his approach at the seventeenth hole had struck a spectator. The Royal and Ancient Golf Club ordered a play-off of the tie but Strath refused to play off the tie until a decision had been given on the protest. No decision was given and thus Bob Martin was declared the champion.

Horace G. Hutchinson, Amateur Champion of 1886 at St. Andrews.

HORACE HUTCHINSON

BRITISH AMATEUR CHAMPION OF 1886

The first British Amateur Championship to be held at St. Andrews was played on the Old Course in 1886. It was the second championship in point of time, the first having been held the year before at Hoylake, where there were 44 entries and A. F. McFie, won while Horace Hutchinson was runner-up. The winner by a resounding margin of 7 and 6 was Horace H. Hutchinson, who defeated Henry Lamb in the eighteen-hole final round.

Hutchinson was a would-be "stylist" of the early days of reported golf and even allowed himself to be the golfer model for the gold medal presented to the Amateur Championship winner. By our standards, Mr. Hutchinson would be considered unorthodox but, in view of the fact that no true "style of play" had yet developed in golf, it must be admitted that the unorthodox portions of his golf swing, as well as those of other prominent winners were widely imitated among many of the leading golfers of his day.

Hutchinson showed a loose, double-palm grip at the top of his backswing. His back would be turned on the hole by reason of the fact that his left foot was up on its toes with the sole of his shoe partially opened toward the hole as well. His left arm was moderately bent at the top of his swing and his club had reached a position about 15 degrees below the horizontal line. Hutchinson, himself writer of *The Book of Golf and Golfers* in 1899 "yielded to the extremely injudicious advice" of his publishers and gave two illustrations of his own swing. He pointed out, however, rather embarrassedly, that "two points seem worthy of attention; the bend of the right knee at the top of the swing. This is quite worth any beginner's study as it must give an instability and inaccuracy to the whole swing. And secondly, the swing has an inadequate follow-on, the turn of the body is checked and freedom lost by the fact that though the heel of the right foot has come away from the ground, there has been no turning of the foot."

Mr. Hutchinson also exhibited a high right elbow at the top of his back-swing. He was the model not only for the "gold medal golfer" but also for a silver statuette figure of a golfer in action. His comment about his "flying right elbow" was that if he were making the model now (1899, that is) he would have had the elbow even higher than it was when made four years previously. At the top of his swing, Hutchinson's head moved to a point almost directly over his right foot, while in his "follow-on," or "follow-through," as we call it today, his head reached a position directly over his left foot, denoting a monstrous slide of the head and entire body from left to right and then from right to left again as he accomplished what was, no doubt, a well-timed stroke.

Mr. Hutchinson had a full-flowing bushy mustache, wore a warm cloth jacket and woolen knickers as well. His hat was the usual short-visored Scottish cap so necessary in the wind.

Horace Hutchinson in discussing the merits of the putting cleek as contrasted with a straight-faced putter said that "the merit of the slightly lofted club for putting becomes apparent when the first few yards of the putting line are broken and rough. The loft on the club enables the player to continue to use his ordinary putting weapon, and yet put enough carry on the ball to pitch it over the broken ground and allow it to run on over the smooth."

However he pointed out that "the difficulty of putting with these lofted clubs is that to most players it is harder to guage the strength accurately when the ball is lofted at all than when it is run along the ground all the way."

Horace Hutchinson was an excellent writer on badminton as well as golf. His book *Golf* went through six editions while his *Hints on the Game of Golf* enjoyed nine editions. His style of writing was a forerunner of that of Bernard Darwin and since he himself was a golfer and champion, although unorthodox in method by our standards of today, Horace Hutchinson made a great contribution to the game of golf not only in his play of the game but also in analyzing for the first time the various styles of golf of such great players as Vardon, Braid and Taylor. The golfers of today owe a debt of gratitude to Horace H. Hutchinson, British Amateur Champion of 1886, one of the first golf analysts of the world and a champion golfer, as well.

JOHN ERNEST LAIDLAY

BRITISH AMATEUR CHAMPION OF 1889 AND 1891

The fifth British Amateur Championship was held in 1889. For the second time the venue was the Old Course at St. Andrews. The winner was J. E. Laidlay, who was considered "by a large majority of the golfing world" to be the best amateur player in Scotland. In 1888, when the Championship was held at Prestwick, Laidlay had gone to the final round with the great player, John Ball, only to lose the match to Ball, 5 and 4, and settle for the runnerup position for the first time.

Laidlay had a "peculiar swing," it was said. He struck all his shots off his left leg. His left elbow was slightly bent, pointed out on the line to the hole. He exhibited a tremendous, even exaggerated follow-through and must have had a great sense of timing in order to keep striking the ball repeatedly with the success he achieved.

In his younger days, Laidlay was renowned as one of the best slow bowlers in cricket and was also an excellent photographer.

One of Laidlay's "foibles" or extravagances was that he thought he could play better with a new brassie than he could with an old, familiar one. Before an important match he would go into Tom Morris's shop and come out with a brand new club that he had never seen before and play all his second shots with it, in the words of writer Andrew Lang, golf observer, "as if he had been teethed on it." However, it is possible that Mr. Laidlay's brassie trick caught up with him one day in 1893 because Bernard Darwin reported that "a topped brassie shot into the cavernous recesses of the bunker (at the seventeenth hole of Prestwick) was generally thought to have cost Mr. Laidlay the championship when he played Mr. Peter Anderson and lost by a score of one down in 1893." Or perhaps Mr. Laidlay played the ball a little too far forward off his left foot that day and it wasn't the brassie after all that did him in. (Note: Incidentally, the Peter Anderson who defeated Laidlay at Prestwick was the twenty-one-year-old son of the Reverend Mark Anderson of the Town Church in St. Andrews. Peter and another student named J. Proudfoot were equally low in funds and being equally good, if not the best, amateur players in the University Club flipped a coin to see which player would go to Prestwick. Peter won the toss and the title, too.)

Laidlay was a remarkably good putter. He went far down on the shaft of a lofted cleek and had the habit of passing the club over the ball in mid-air on the line he intended to use. In fact, he had this mannerism, it was said, on all his shots, particularly his pitches to the green. Laidlay had learned his game on the short course at North Berwick where "all the holes were on greens so small and so beset by hazards that it was essential to pitch the ball right up to them and make it stop there, as if a string were tied to it." Laidlay had that stroke down to perfection. He believed in gripping all of his clubs lightly. In this matter he was diametrically opposite to the style of J. H. Taylor, who advocated gripping the club very tightly. Laidlay said "The more lightly I grip my clubs the better I play." Laidlay's handles were unusually thin to the golfers of his day.

Here is a contemporary report of Laidlay's grip by his friend and golfing rival Horace Hutchinson, himself Champion in 1886 and 1887:

"Laidlay's delicacy of touch on the club is illustrated by the way in which he 'fingers' the club. He does not hold it in any coarse, brutal grasp of the palm of the hands; the thumb and the fingers are sensitively gripping it, ready to feel every subtle suggestion of difference in the manner of striking the ball."

While Laidlay's backswing on his full shots was considered "short" by the analysts of the golf swing of the 90s, his "follow-through" was so striking that it was said he appeared to have come forward as if he had been "shot out." Laidlay's power, and it was considerable, was obtained by perfect timing. Since pictures of Laidlay swinging show considerable movement of his head in his "follow-through," it is evident to us today, with present emphasis on the "steady head" or "fixed axis" of the modern swing, that Laidlay takes to the hold.

J. E. Laidlay was renowned as a great "finisher," a golfer most likely to "lay up a long second close up on the green of the last hole when the match was all even with one hole to play." His nerves were very good and that, of course, made him "hard to beat" when the chips were down."

Laidlay's favorite golf-balls were the "Clan" and the "Agrippa." He played a great deal of his golf at Muirfield where he was, of course, a member of the Honourable Company of Edinburgh Golfers. As early as 1883, Laidlay's name started to appear in the various lists of champions. He won the first of many silver and gold medals in 1883 with two rounds of nine holes each at nearby Musselburgh totalling 85 strokes. Laidlay continued to win these prestigious competitions during all the years between 1893 and 1919 for a total display of no less than twenty-five medals against such formidable opponents as L. M. Balfour-Melville, Amateur Champion of 1895, and other leading golfers of his era. All in all, J. E. Laidlay was a remarkable, if unorthodox golfer, and a worthy British Amateur Champion.

Leslie Balfour-Melville, Amateur Champion of 1895. Melville was also runner-up to Laidlay in the Amateur Championship of 1889.

THE BRITISH AMATEUR OF 1895

The records show that Leslie Balfour-Melville defeated John Ball at the 19th hole in the final match at St. Andrews to win the 1895 Amateur Championship. There were 68 entries this year, the most in the eleven year history of the event. John Ball had been the champion of the previous year and by that time had amassed a total of four championships, including those of 1888, 1890, and 1892.

Leslie Balfour was considered the most capable representative of amateur Scotch golf in his early years and in his later days, because of a tendency to weak putting, he was ranked among the top five. He was not only a terrifically long driver but he was also a very straight driver, as unusual a combination then as it is now. His drives started off with a low trajectory, continued in flight longer than might be expected and then, after touching the ground, had considerable run. Balfour-Melville

(he took the Melville name later in his life after the death of an ancestor) was a "painstaking golfer" who consciously and deliberately set himself into the address position with much precision. He had a smooth and even swing. He followed on "straight and far after the ball."

Horace Hutchinson, who played with Melville frequently, said that: "Mr. Balfour-Melville's swing possesses all the orthodox elements. The weight is thrown completely on the right leg, the turn of the body on the hips is sufficiently free, and is aided by the bend of the left knee and lift of the left heel. The left shoulder comes well around. The hands are brought well away from the shoulder, high above it at the top of the swing. The club comes just a little below the horizontal line behind his head. At the finish of his swing we can see that his arms have been greatly extended throughout the whole swing. This may be the secret of his exceptionally fine driving. His body is facing in the direction of the ball's flight, the right shoulder working under, the body turning on the hips, the right knee and foot aiding the action."

There are no contemporary accounts of the 1895 matches and thus we are unable to tell the drama of the final round with Mr. John Ball. However, by a fortunate coincidence, this author had the pleasure of meeting a distinguished gentleman, Mr. R.L. Balfour-Melville, the present Secretary of Gullane Golf Club at nearby Gullane, Scotland. Upon being introduced to Mr. Balfour-Melville in summer, 1973, I remarked upon his unusual combination name and, having just completed some research into the British Amateur Championship of 1895 which was won, of course, by Leslie Balfour-Melville, I asked him whether he might possibly be related to the former Amateur champion.

He answered that, indeed, he was, that the champion had been his own grandfather, that his grandfather had had a long and happy life in golf, in cricket, and in billiards, that he had excelled in all three sports. He told me that Leslie Balfour-Melville played eight holes of golf each day in his last year of life, (he died at eighty-two) that upon his death he left an estate which included more than one hundred various types of putters. He also remarked, and I thought that this came a little nostalgically, "Do you know that the last words he uttered on his death-bed were, 'You know, I never could putt!' "

Leslie Balfour-Melville possessed probably the finest record of all the golfers listed in the record book of the Royal and Ancient Golf Club of St. Andrews. His name first appears in the records as winner in 1874 and 1875 of the Gold Medal of King William the Fourth and the St. Andrews Club Gold Medal with scores of 97 strokes and 93 strokes. The last appearance for his name was in 1908, when he won the George Glennie Medal for the seventh time with a thirty-six-hole score of 162. In other words, he was able to play championship golf for more than thirty-four years of competition. His lowest record score was a 79 in taking the George Glennie Medal in 1903. But, we must remember that the Old Course was played with much more difficulty in those days than it does in our times. And there have been great improvements in golf club and ball manufacture. Here is Leslie Balfour-Melville's record at St. Andrews club events:

Winner of the Gold Medal of King William the Fourth: 1875, 1876, 1877, 1883, 1896 1902.
Winner: The Silver Club and Queen Adelaide medal: 1906.
Winner: St. Andrews Club Gold Medal: 1874, 1880, 1881, 1885, 1903, 1908.
Winner: The Silver Cross of St. Andrews: 1890, 1898.

Winner: The Silver Medal: 1879, 1880, 1883, 1885, 1894, 1896, 1897.
Winner: The George Glennie Medal: 1885, 1886, 1889, 1890, 1896, 1898, 1908.
Winner: The Queen Victoria Jubilee Vase: 1892.
Winner: The Amateur Championship: 1895.
Note: Mr. Balfour-Melville's winning scores were in the 90s in the 1870s with 97 in 1874 and 93 in 1875 and slowly came down to lower figures. His winning score in 1908 was a thirty-six-hole total of 162, and in 1903 he won the Club medal with a 79.

THE BRITISH AMATEUR OF 1913

Harold H. Hilton came into this Amateur Cham-

Harold H. Hilton, the first amateur to win the Open Championship. His first victory was in 1892, his second in 1897. He also won the Amateur Championship four times from 1900 through 1913.

pionship riding on the crest of a remarkable career in golf. At the age of twenty-three in 1892, he had first startled the world of golf by winning the first of his eventual two Open Championships. This year he would add his fourth Amateur Championship to those he had taken in 1900, 1901 and 1911.

His great rival, John Ball, was the defending champion this year having won at Westward Ho! in 1912. Furthermore, these two golfers had had a long and bitter rivalry for golf honors. Ball had won the Amateur title no less than eight times between 1888 and 1912. He was truly a "boy wonder" golfer, as Locke would be called later on, in that at the tender age of fifteen years he was able to finish sixth in the Open Championship of 1876.

Another confrontation between these two great golfers was certainly in the making this year. The galleries were already anticipating the match.

Then a most unfortunate accident happened to Ball on his way from Hoylake, England to St. Andrews. While riding a motorcycle he had taken a nasty spill on a slippery road and, lucky to be alive, reported to St. Andrews tournament headquarters the next day well-battered up and with both a sprained wrist and sprained ankle. Ball consulted with the doctors in St. Andrews to see if some quick relief could be given him, but his own aching body told him he must withdraw from this tournament, and regretfully, he left the field. Hilton had a wide-open chance now and he was determined to make the best of it.

The American entrants were only six and of them, there was not one known in America as a strong capable contender for the title. Strangely enough, as we shall see, one American player, Heinrich Schmidt, was an "artisan golfer" in the language of Scotland. In our language perhaps the expression a "blue collar-worker golfer" might be the equivalent. Schmidt, twenty-three years old, had a "beautiful smooth swing. His driving was excellent, a long straight ball down the middle of the course." His approaching was "deadly in accuracy." He had worked his way through college, Worcester Polytechnic Institute in Massachusetts.

Schmidt's father was a tailor. Heinrich had been a caddie and saved his money for college and for the trip to Scotland. He had come over in second-class on a "cattle boat" to save money. His only win at golf thus far had been the Massachusetts Amateur Championship of 1912. His friends said that Schmidt had "indomitable spirit and great desire to win.

In the words of Henry Leach, the English "golfing writer," a victory by Schmidt would be "most popular among the Scottish artisan golfers, who say they are tired of seeing the amateur championship won by rich men who devote their whole time to golf."

It is interesting to read the New York Times report of this amateur championship. Henry Leach, was filing his stories about the tournament at St. Andrews from London, England. The heading on the reports read "Transmitted by Marconi Wireless Telegraph to the New York Times." The stories were one day late, which was not unusual considering the transmission difficulties and time differential. Leach was probably sending his copy down to London from St. Andrews by rail. The reportage of Leach is interesting in itself. For example, when the pairings of two American players, Findlay Douglas of Long Island and C. W. Inslee of Oneida, New York, were announced, Leach said, "Douglas and Inslee are fairly well drawn but British golfers hardly believe they will get very far, thinking their golf not scientific enough for a severe testing over a course like St. Andrews." By "well drawn" of course Leach meant that they had tough opponents in their first matches.

Schmidt was drawn in the most difficult bracket of the pairings and Leach said, "Schmidt cannot get very far unless he is in great form." The Americans had come over early and were practicing on the course assiduously and were "very much impressed with the difficulties of the course."

The difficulties were rather abnormal at the moment since all the bunkers were flooded as a result of recent heavy rains. The City of St. Andrews had loaned its beautiful new fire engine to help the tournament officials to pump out many of the flooded bunkers. The weather had cleared by tournament time, fortunately, and the matches began as Andrew Kirkaldy, the celebrated Honorary Professional of St. Andrews, made the prediction that "no American would get past the third round."

Edward Blackwell and "Abe" Mitchell, along with Hilton, were the favorites to win. Mitchell, another "artisan golfer," a chauffeur in everyday life, was the galleries' sentimental hope to win.

Schmidt played well and surprised a lot of canny Scots watching him. He made one particularly fine "watershot" from the bunker at the second hole on his way to beating Captain Prideaux Brune by a score of 6 and 5. Schmidt's putting was "exceeding good" and "he had not a severe task in winning that match." In the third round Schmidt came up against E. A. Lassen, the Amateur Champion of 1908 and runnerup to Harold Hilton in the tournament of 1911. Lassen got off to a great start against Schmidt and was three up after the fifth hole. Schmidt's putting stroke had deserted him temporarily, it seemed. However, Schmidt played "a great game coming in" after being two down at the turn and eventually eliminated Lassen, 3 and 2.

A great deal of interest centered upon the match between Blackwell and Mitchell. Both were great hitters and "much speculation was manifested regarding which would drive the longer ball." Blackwell eked out a 1-up victory. The "better ball of the pair" was a 68 so it can readily be seen that the golf was of high calibre. Then Mitchell lost on the 19th hole in his next match against Gillies.

In the meanwhile, Harold Hilton had been playing spotty golf, good and bad, but fortunately good enough to win. Hilton took on Gillies after Gillies had beaten Mitchell and Hilton "just scraped through" in his match with Gillies, winning at the nineteenth hole.

Schmidt had "fairly smothered" Willie Grieg, of the New Club, St. Andrews, and won by an 8 and 6 margin. The match of Schmidt against Hilton, the youth versus the veteran, now became a reality in the quarter-finals. Reporter Leach said, "The form he (Schmidt) showed against Grieg was in such striking contrast to that displayed by Hilton, who just barely won from Gillies, that the Massachusetts youngster has been made an even money choice against the renowned English player."

But, it was not to be, apparently. Once more they went to the nineteenth hole and there the experienced Hilton holed a 25-foot putt for a 3 to win the match. For eighteen holes, Schmidt made the Englishman fight every inch of the way. In rimming four putts, not one of them dropped or he would have been away to a comfortable lead. Both players played well though not spectacularly.

The first nine scores were 39 for Schmidt and 38 for Hilton, their final scores approximate 75s.

A gallery of 2000 watched the match. Young Heinrich remained "as cool and collected as the most seasoned veteran." He lost in sportsmanlike manner, saying later, "I did my best to carry the championship to America. But I have only had two weeks' practice this year. You see, I work for a living. Hilton is a fine sportsman and a good fellow. He is well entitled to his victory."

Hilton won from Aylmer of West Surrey one up while Robert Harris of Acton, Scotland entered the final round from the other bracket. The final thirty-six hole match saw Hilton regain his basic great form. He won 6 and 5 over Harris. It was his fourth championship, the last one of his illustrious career.

THE OPEN CHAMPIONSHIP OF 1921

The Championship of 1921 had some remarkable golf and golf incidents in it. Jock Hutchison led the field on his first round with a 72 but included in the score-card were a 1 and a 2 at the 8th and 9th holes. Jock aced the 8th and it was said that if a spectator had not rushed up to remove the flagstick at No. 9 the ball might have holed rather than switched away from the cup as it did.

Roger Wethered had the misfortune of stepping on his own ball during the third round. Since Roger and Jock later tied it has often been said that Roger would have been the winner but for the penalty stroke assessed him for moving his own ball. However, it might also be pointed out that on his last round, needing a 4 to tie Jock, Roger pitched his ball short into the Valley of Sin and then took three more strokes before he finished the hole. His 71 was nevertheless a great final score and Jock, aware of it and playing behind Wethered, knew what he had to do, a 70 to tie and accomplish the same score as Roger.

On the last day Wethered, who was seven strokes off the pace (Sandy Herd was leading with 222) got permission to play his last rounds early so that he could catch a train and play elsewhere in, of all things, a cricket match. Apparently the starting times of those days were not as rigidly enforced as they are now, for Wethered was granted an earlier start than he might have expected and was off to the two great final rounds which earned him the eventual tie for the cup.

Roger's 72 in the morning round brought him up to within three strokes of Herd and one stroke ahead of Jock Hutchison.

The play-off between Wethered and Hutchison was what you might expect when a great amateur golfer meets an even greater professional golfer. Roger's morning round of 77 left him only three strokes behind Jock's 74 but in the afternoon Roger's game, probably from physical tiredness and mental strain, left him completely and he struggled in with an 82 nine big strokes behind the "invader" from America, Jock Hutchison.

Roger Wethered has been kind enough to search his memory these many years later and in a recent letter had these comments about the unfortunate penalty incident in the third round:

"At that time I was an undergraduate at Oxford University, twenty-three years of age and just be-

Jock Hutchison and Laurie Auchterlonie.

Jock Hutchison, Open Champion of 1921, winner after a play-off with amateur Roger Wethered.

ginning my career in golf. I had played without any success in the first International Match between Great Britain and the United States at Hoylake and so when I asked my father if I might go and play in the Open, he naturally lifted his eyebrows and only reluctantly, I thought, agreed to my proposal. As the records show, I went from strength to strength and eventually tied Jock Hutchison and lost to him in a play-off. I was an early starter, expected by none to have a chance of winning, and so was under no real pressure at any stage of the game. It is clear that the Fates did not intend me to win. Since I was a more or less inexperienced young amateur, it was probably as well in the long run that I did not. But the field had their work cut out to stop me in the long run. As the record books relate, Jock Hutchison enjoyed two remarkable strokes of good fortune: an ace at the eighth which was followed by a deuce at the ninth, almost a second ace in a row. Besides that, he had a magnificent three in one of his rounds, almost a two at the "Long Hole In," the 14th. In contrast to Jock's good luck, I remember taking four putts on the 11th, treading on my ball and incurring a penalty stroke at the 14th and finally I took four strokes to get down at the very last hole of all from a drive which was not more than forty yards from the pin. Of course, on the last hole I visited the Valley of Sin, from which the inevitable three putts were taken.

"I would like to relate the true story about my treading on my ball on the 14th hole. It has never been told before. It happened because of a straightforward lapse of memory on my part. There was a large gallery on the adjoining fairway and until it had passed it was impossible for me to play to the 14th green until the way was clear. My tee-shot lay on the Elysian Fields, in a perfect position in front of Hell bunker. While I was waiting for the field to clear I stood on the small rise in front of my ball and I must have forgotten exactly where it lay so that in stepping backwards, contact between the heel of my shoe and the ball occurred. Other stories had it that I was on the upslope of the green. That was not true. I have always felt that if the play had continued at its normal tempo the event would never have happened, but no one will ever know that or not. The important part, as far as I was concerned, was that the penalty did not have an adverse psychological effect on my game. I was still able to make my par on that difficult hole and did not lose my equanimity. I am very pleased to be able to tell the true story of this "famous accident of golf" these many years later.

THE BRITISH AMATEUR OF 1924

Ernest W. E. Holderness, a winner of the British Amateur Championship two years earlier when the event was held at Prestwick, Scotland, won his second amateur crown this year at St. Andrews, defeating E. F. Storey in the thirty-six hole final round by a score of 3 and 2.

The "American Invasion" this year was constituted of one single golfer and he, although an American citizen, was in fact a resident of Hawaii. Francis I. Brown, small of stature, but strong of body and thirty-four years of age had traveled 10,000 miles to see whether he couldn't wrest the coveted cup from a field which included many past British Amateur Champions: Harry Hilton (1913), J. L. C. Jenkins (1914), C. J. H. Tolley (1920), W. I. Hunter (1921), E. W. E. Holderness (1922), and defending champion Roger Wethered, who had won at Deal, England, in 1923.

That Francis Brown's challenge was taken seriously is borne out by a newspaper report which said that: "The chances of Francis Brown of the Omaha Country Club of Hawaii, the only American entrant for the British Amateur were discussed by the experts. Andrew Kirkaldy, the famous local professional said: 'He is a very possible winner.' " Brown had a brilliant 34 "coming home" in a four-ball practice match with three birdies "obtained mainly by perfectly judged iron shots and putts of three and four yards." Brown was said to have been "out-driving the prodigious Mr. Tolley," whose long driving ability was renowned. Tolley had won the championship in 1920 at Muirfield, beating the American star, Bob Gardner, at the 37th hole, and although he would lose out this year he would win again in 1929 at Sandwich, England.

In the qualifying rounds, Brown started off with a rush by breaking the course record of the New Course with a 67, to which he added a 70 on the Old Course. He added this record score to four other course records he already held, one especially notable, a 68 at Del Monte in California.

Roger Wethered was the favorite to win again, for it was said "He is always at his best at St. Andrews."

Both Wethered and Tolley won their early matches, Wethered by 8 and 7 over former champion E. A. Lassen, who had won the title in 1908.

Harold Hilton, veteran champion player who had already won the title four times (1900, 1901, 1911 and 1913) scored the 99th victory in his British Amateur career but the experts, noting that he did not play well said "He is not in top form and must do better to stay in the tourney."

Brown defeated Allen Graham of the Royal Liverpool Club, 2 and 1. Brown was driving long and straight and his putting was even better. The match was all square at the 15th hole when Graham holed a "five-yard putt rather viciously," the report said, for a 3. Brown retaliated with a 30-footer at the sixteenth to win. Graham dubbed his third at the seventeenth. When Brown went boldly over the bunker and landed 15 feet away, and holed out for his 4, he won the match.

Wethered won easily, 7 and 6, over D. R. Cox and the newspapers reported "The champion is in fine stroke and showed again that he is one of the favorites to gain the final round." Cyril Tolley won easily over P. Clugh by 4 and 3 and "it was evident that he was not trying his hardest." Harry Hilton finally lost to Noel Layton, 6 and 5. Holderness, Major C. O. Hezlet (runner-up in the 1914 tournament) and Harry Braid also advanced to provide a "battle of giants" in the 4th and 5th rounds.

A heavy mist hung over the links in the morning of the fourth round and a strong wind whipped the course. Francis Brown, America's only hope to win the title, went out in a hard-fought battle against J. Birnie of Inverness, 2 and 1. Birnie had started "in excellent stroke" and three up at the 12th hole found Brown's long driving beginning to tell on him. Against the wind Francis won the 13th and the 14th when Birnie failed to carry "Hell's Bunker." He had to concede the hole to Brown at the 15th. The American squared the match when Birnie got a lucky break when his ball, heading directly for the "dreaded Principal's bunker" jumped the first ridge at the edge of the bunker. It escaped the second half of the bunker and rolled along the fairway. Then, to cap it all, Birnie, encouraged no doubt by the turn in his fortunes, sank an 18-footer for his 3. The match ended at the seventeenth when the wind blew Brown's ball into the heavy rough and he could not recover well enough to win the hole.

Roger Wethered had five 3s and eight 4s to win handily over C. P. Leese at the 13th hole. In the afternoon Roger was one under 4s as he sent Major C. O. Hezlet to the sidelines, 3 and 2.

In the meantime, Cyril Tolley, after having a comparatively easy time downing Major C. Campbell, was beaten in the 5th round by D. H. Kyle who needed a 5 and a 4 for a score of 69 but walked in with Tolley when the match terminated at the sixteenth hole. Kyle showed six 3s on his card. The final eight players were:

E. F. Storey	D. H. Kyle
John Caven	W. A. Murray
J. D. McCormack	Robert Harris
Roger Wethered	E. W. E. Holderness

Storey, a young man of twenty-three years, playing in his first championship, beat Caven and Roger Wethered and entered the finals against E. W. E. Holderness, who in his mid-forties was said to be "approaching middle age, and his past experience is thought to give him an edge on his younger opponent."

The twosome of Holderness and McCormack took 55 minutes to play five holes. McCormack, an Irish golfer, was an extremely slow player through no fault of his own, a war cripple who had spent six years in bed with disabling spinal injuries and who wore a steel "jerkin" to support his back and enable him to play golf. A rather remarkable individual, it must be said, and one who should be forgiven for playing slowly. Holderness not only defeated the Irishman but he also played a brilliant round against Bristowe in the 4th round and had nothing but 3s and 4s on his card.

The young Storey started the final match against the veteran Holderness with a birdie 3 and was four holes up on him by the 12th hole. At the 5th hole, as the Scots say, "The weather completely broke down." The players continued in steady rain and cold, driving winds. Holderness had gotten some of his lost holes back by the time the pair reached the home hole of the first round. Holderness was then only 1 down but had regained some of his confidence from his comeback.

The first round scorecards were:

Holderness	Out:	4 5 5 5 5 4 4 3 4	39	
Storey	In:	3 5 4 4 5 5 5 4 3 3	36	
			Storey leads 3 up	
Holderness	Out:	4 5 4 4 6 4 5 5 4	41	80
Storey	In:	4 4 6 5 6 4 5 5 5	44	80
			Storey leads 1 up	

In the afternoon round, the weather worsened, if that were possible, and the experience of Holderness began to tell. Storey visited several bunkers en route to a 7 at the second hole.

Holderness seized the lead at the 4th when Storey was short on both drive and approach shot. Storey got back even at the 11th hole but lost the 12th and 14th and was obviously beaten. The match ended at the 16th when Storey took a bogey 5 to Holderness's par 4. Champion for the second time and joining a distinguished list of great golfers who had won the British Open Championship more than one time was E. W. E. Holderness.

The cards on the last round of the thirty-six hole final were:

Holderness	4 5 4 5 5 4 3 3 5	38
Storey	4 7 4 6 5 4 5 3 4	42
	Holderness leads 1 up	
Holderness	4 5 4 5 5 4 4	
Storey	4 4 5 5 6 4 5	
	Holderness wins 3 and 2	

THE OPEN CHAMPIONSHIP
OF 1927

*Robert T. Jones, Jr., United States	68 72 73 72	285
Aubrey Boomer, France	76 70 73 72	291
Fred Robson, England	76 72 69 74	291
Joe Kirkwood, United States	72 72 75 74	293
E.R. Whitcombe, England	74 73 73 73	293
C.A. Whitcombe, England	74 76 71 75	296
A.G. Havers, England	80 74 73 70	297
T.H. Cotton, England	73 72 77 76	298
P.H. Rodgers, England	76 74 73 77	300
R. Vickers, England	75 75 77 73	300
*T.P. Perkins, England	76 78 70 76	300
Tom Williamson, England	75 76 78 71	300
Percy Alliss, England	73 74 73 80	300
Alex Herd, England	76 75 78 71	300

*Amateur

Twenty-five-year-old Robert T. Jones, Jr. became the fifth player to win the Open championship two years in a row when he won at St. Andrews this year with a record score of 285, six strokes ahead of his nearest competitors, Aubrey Boomer, an Englishman who was representing St. Cloud Country Club of France, and Fred Robson, of Britain, who tied for second place at 291.

In June of 1927 Jones had entered the United States Open championship at Oakmont, Pennsylvania and had played badly. He had not scored better than a 76 on any one of his four rounds and eventually finished in eleventh place at 309 strokes, a long way from the winning score of 301 which Tommy Armour and Harry "Light Horse Harry" Cooper managed to return to tie for the title, (Armour won in the playoff with a 76 to Cooper's 79).

In spite of his mediocre showing at Oakmont, Jones came to the international golf wars with a marvelous record behind him. He had already won the Open championship the previous year at Royal Lytham-St. Anne's. He won the U.S. Open twice, first in 1923 at Inwood, New York and then again in 1926 at Scioto Country Club near Columbus,

Ohio. He had won the U.S. Amateur championship twice, in 1924 and 1925, and had been runner-up twice in that event as well.

So when the English sports writers filed this international dispatch regarding Jones' challenge for the title, it must have been "a little whistling while passing a darkened cemetery." Here's what they said: "Mr. Jones, golfer, arrived here to defend his title at St. Andrews. Following his defeat at Oakmont, we believe that he will have a desperate time retaining the British crown, although we still regard him as a dangerous contender." Jones' chief opposition in "homebred" professionals would come from George Duncan and Archie Compston, it was thought. Abe Mitchell was at this time regarded as England's best player but would not be able to compete because of ill health.

Going into the tournament, the veteran Scottish sports writers were writing, "No amateur ever has won the British Open championship at St. Andrews since it became a 72-hole event in 1892, and only twice in all the years before 1926 has an amateur won it anywhere. Both times it went to Harold Hilton, at Muirfield in 1892 and at Hoylake in 1897. Not for more than twenty years has any golfer accomplished what Jones is attempting to do, namely, to win the title twice in succession. James Braid did it in 1905 and 1906. One can get heavy odds that Bobby Jones won't do it in 1926-1927."

Bobby Jones was staying at Rusack's Hotel, which is just across the roadway, alongside the eighteenth hole of the Old Course at about the three-hundred-yard mark. The hotel was in such a dangerous position that many a slicing drive had hit the road and taken the long bounce through the first floor windows which overlook the fairway and monstrous green. Jones, of course, had been given a "room with a view" on the second floor. Moreover, he was also being treated as visiting royalty by the hotel management, which, of course, was only proper in view of his unofficial role as a sports ambassador of good will. The hotel was proudly flying the American flag over its entrance in honor of Jones' presence.

A new cinema had been opened recently in the heart of the small town of St. Andrews. The movie house was enjoying great popularity with the large tournament crowds. The moviegoers would cheer loudly at the Pathé Newsreel pictures of the Jones entourage coming down the gangplank on his arrival in England. He was truly a popular idol in St. Andrews, so popular that the local newspaper noted that "Bobby Jones gets almost as much exercise trying to escape from the crowds which follow him, especially the 'flapper' autograph hunters, as he does from playing golf."

The qualifying rounds of the championship were played in a steady downpour but little wind. Jones qualified handily with a first-round 76 and a second-round 71 and showed a few flashes of the brilliance which he would exhibit in the next few days when "the lights would go on." Cyril J.H. Tolley, veteran campaigner and twice former amateur champion, led the qualifying with a 73 and 71 for a 144 total. His 73 score was even more remarkable considering the fact that at the eighteenth hole he was only six feet from the hole and needed the putt for a 70. He missed the hole with his first stroke, back-handled the ball at the hole and missed again. Then he back-handled it once more, only to miss for the third time. Then he took a proper stance and holed the putt for a 6 and his 73.

The weather cleared for the first day of the tournament proper. Bobby Jones settled down to the business at hand, winning this championship. He parred the first hole but got into trouble at the second when he bunkered his second shot, wasted a stroke and finally got on the green with his fourth stroke seventy-five feet away from the flagstick. Down went this tremendously long putt. He had "saved a bogey," but more than that, he had restored his confidence in himself. From there on, it was said that his putting was simply "uncanny." He holed a ninety-foot putt for an eagle 3 at the fifth hole, 520 yards long, afer reaching the green with his second shot, a mere 260-yard average for two successive strokes. He birdied the sixth hole, scoring another 3, and then sank a twenty-four-foot putt at the eighth hole for a deuce. At the ninth hole, he again holed a good putt for another birdie and was out in 32 strokes, four under par on this card:

Jones Out: 4 5 4   4 3 3   4 2 3   32

Coming in, Bobby drove only fifty yards short of the 316-yard long tenth hole but pitched weakly, twenty-five yards short of the hole. His first putt was nine feet short of the hole but he sank that putt for his par 4. The eleventh and twelfth holes were normal pars for him. At the thirteenth he finally got into trouble when his drive, although in the fairway, came to rest in a bad lie. His second shot was not a good one. At last he got onto the putting surface, but he was forty-five feet away from the flagstick with his third shot on this par four hole. Today he could do no wrong, it appeared, for the long putt found the hole and he

had saved his par streak on the second nine.

The fourteenth, the nasty par five, fell in routine fashion for Bobby. Then, at the fifteenth, he missed the fairway with a drive. The ball was found in an apparently hopeless spot in heavy rough. Out came "some magical instrument" from Jones' bag and, after a mighty swing, the ball soared out of trouble and reached the heart of the green, 160 yards away. The newspaper report of this round says "The fact that his swing didn't break his shaft speaks well for the American club-makers." The fact of the matter was that Jones' clubs had been made at Tom Stewart's forge only a few hundred yards away from the first tee at the Old Course. With steady pars the rest of the way in, Jones tucked a sound 36 on top of his 32 and waited to see who might catch him. No one else did. Joe Kirkwood's 72 came closest and left Bobby a comfortable four-stroke lead on the field.

O.B. Keeler had this say about Jones' 68 on the first round of the 1927 Open championship: "I have never seen nor hope to see another such round as Bobby played on the first day of the tournament. His score of 68 was the first time he had ever broken 70 in an open championship in twelve starts and was a record score for St. Andrews in competition, shot from the tournament tees. He was leading the chase from then on, a rare achievement for one man to set the pace of a tournament at the beginning of a tournament and still be in front at the finish."

Jones himself said later on in discussing this record round, "It was the hardest decent score I ever shot. I have never scored so well in so hard a round. Stewart Maiden (Jones' golf tutor) was right. He said if I ever got to missing my big shots, I might sink some putts. I sank some today." Jones was right. He had had 28 putts, six of them of more than 100-foot length and did not miss one under twelve feet. He played nine straight holes in 30 strokes, the Loop from the eighth through the twelfth in 3-4-4-3-4 and opened a gap between himself and the field which was never to be closed.

Jones' second round was a 72 which, coupled with his 68 of the first day, gave him a 140 total and a two-stroke lead over B. Hodson of England, who checked in with a fine 70 after a first-round 72. Hodson's principal occupation was clubmaking and he told reporters that he had "very little time for golf," he was so busy with his customary work. Regrettably, Hodson's third round was an 81 and he was no longer a factor in the tournament, finishing twelve strokes back of Jones. The third place behind Jones was taken by Joe Kirkwood on two 72s for 144 and after him came the relatively un-

"Old Alick" Caddie at Blackheath. Painting at Black-heath.

Mr. Henry Callander, Esq., Blackheath Golf Club, 1812.
Courtesy Blackheath Golf Club.

A Scottish foursome putting on the 17th green.

Looking southeast from the 17th hole right-hand rough. The Royal and Ancient clubhouse can be seen on the left.

known (at that time) "T.H. Cotton" on scores of 73 and 72 for 145. Henry Cotton, a "public schoolboy," was then only twenty years of age. He had recently become a professional golfer and was just beginning his long, successful career.

Jones' third round was a 73 with 36 putts and the only player in the field who made up any ground on him was Fred Robson of England, who brought in a 69 to move to 217 strokes, only four strokes behind Jones' total of 68-72-73-213.

Bobby started his last round rather badly and found himself three over fours at the long fifth hole. He missed a three-foot putt on the three-par eighth and appeared to be in serious trouble, although no one was really burning up the course in pursuit of him. This time Jones took the ninth through the twelfth holes of the Loop in four straight threes and the tournament was settled right then and here.

When Bobby putted out on the eighteenth green a roaring mass of people crowded in on him and he had to be rescued by six stalwart Scottish policemen. Enormous crowds had followed him all week and on the last day, Bobby was playing his shots through narrow lanes of solid humanity from tee to green. On many occasions he did not even see his shot come to an end because the crowds would close in on him immediately after he had struck the ball.

When Jones rapped the putt of three inches into the hole that made him again British Open champion there occurred an astonishing, almost a "terrifying scene," according to the reports of the event. There were about twelve thousand people encircling the last green. As soon as the putt went down the stewards were tossed aside and the entire crowd stormed the slope up the eighteenth green to get their hands on the beloved Bobby. In a flash, he disappeared and then, a few seconds later, was seen, borne aloft on the willing shoulders of his friends. He still had his hands on his precious putter. For several minutes the crowd surged this way and that with their load until the eventual rescue of their hero by the team sent out to get him by the Royal and Ancient golf club.

When Bobby accepted the cup symbolic of his victory, he made a magnificent gesture, greatly in keeping with his innate sense of good taste and sportsmanship. Bobby knew how much the Scots valued their trophy, that "old piece of silver," and as he accepted it he said to the assembled spectators and officials: "I would rather win a championship at St. Andrews than anything else that could happen to me. You have done so many things for me that I am embarrassed to ask one more, but I will. I want this wonderful old club to accept the custody of the cup for the coming year." And, graciously, the Royal and Ancient did accept the cup and kept it carefully in "the treasury" throughout that year, 1927. It was said that in that same year Robert T. Jones, Jr. was the "Unofficial King of Scotland." We can well believe it.

THE BRITISH AMATEUR OF 1930

Bobby Jones and Cyril Tolley were great friends and avid competitors, each one determined to beat the other if he could possibly do so. Cyril had already won the championship for a second time the year before. As defending champion he had great prestige in Great Britain and no doubt felt a great responsibility to keep the Cup on the Scottish side of the Atlantic. Tolley was a big man, a very powerful player and an especially long driver. Jones himself felt that in the entire field Tolley would be his most dangerous opponent, the one most likely to upset his chances for the first leg of the four championships. Jones and Tolley had to win two matches apiece in order to meet in the upper bracket of the draw. Jones got past Roper and won his second match, to fulfill his part in the destiny of Jones and Tolley. Tolley had a narrow squeak, however, in his first round, almost lost but did not and then came through with his second win handily. The stage was now set for the con-

Bobby Jones receiving the British Amateur trophy at St. Andrews from Col. Skene, Captain of St. Andrews Club, 1930.

The famous shot Bobby Jones ho!ed out of Cottage Bunker on the 4th hole in the 1930 Amateur Championship.

frontation between Jones and Tolley. Jones did not particularly like eighteen-hole matches, and much preferred to battle over the thirty-six hole route, feeling that he had more room to maneuver, more of an opporunity to make a few bad shots and yet recover and win. He had beaten Tolley very badly, 12 and 11, in the thirty-six hole singles match of the Walker Cup matches of two years before over the same Old Course. Any golfer hates to be "disgraced" by being beaten in "double figures" and Tolley just might have been harboring a grudge along with an even increased desire to win this particular match and avenge his earlier trouncing by Jones.

Furthermore, on the morning of the match it was soon apparent that Tolley would have another advantage, that of familiar "St. Andrews" weather and course conditions. Jones was far less experienced than Tolley in strong wind and rain. Strong winds were blowing at half gale force, coming in off the sea. The fine seaside sand was being whipped out of the bunkers and off sandy patches of the turf and driven into the faces, sometimes the eyes of the golfers when they played into the teeth of the wind.

The match between Jones and Tolley was followed by a gallery of thousands. Tolley began like a duffer with a topped drive off the first tee, an unbelievable shot from so good a golfer. It is to his great credit that although the bad stroke cost him a 5 at the first hole to go one hole down to Jones's 4, Tolley came right back with a strong 4 at the second to an equally weak second hole on Jones' part.

Tolley one up at the 4th, Jones and Tolley even by the 7th, Jones one up at the 8th, all even at the 9th when Tolley drove the 306 yard green and got a 3 to Bobby's 5. The scores were 39 for Jones and 38 for Tolley, not very good under ordinary conditions but remarkably good for the horrible wind and rain the two golfers were forced to undergo.

Scores of other leading players in the same wind, incidentally, were much worse in comparison.

Here are the first nine scores:

Jones	Out:	4 5 4 5 5 4 4 3 5	39	
Tolley	Out:	5 4 4 4 5 4 5 4 3	38	Match even

At the short eleventh hole, after both golfers had tied in 4s at No. 10, Tolley's driving iron was seen to fly as far as the putting surface in the air and then be blown backward into the fairway short of Strath bunker. Jones's shot was even stronger from the tee, caught a lull in the gusting wind and sailed over the green onto the bank of the Eden river. Cyril dubbed his next shot, did not even hit it as far as Strath bunker and then dumped the ball into Strath. Jones pitched onto the green safely, took 4 to Tolley's 5 when Tolley had a great recovery out of the bunker on his fourth shot. Jones, one up. Most incredibly, the next five holes were traded in succession, first one and then the other golfer making the superlative shot to win. Tolley eagled the 14th with two monstrous shots which reached the 5-par green, and a putt that went down to outscore Jones's equally beautifully played birdie 4.

The greens were "blown out" by the winds, dry and slick as glass. There were spike marks on them, too, which had not healed since the play of the day before and these irregularities added to the uncertainty of the players' putting. The effects of the wind itself had to be taken into consideration in calculating the line of a putt and that is most difficult when the wind is an unsteady one.

By the time the players reached the seventeenth hole, the match lead had been traded from one up to even or one down to even six separate times. Jones was one up at the end of the first and at the eighth, one down at the end of the fifth, sixth and seventh and even on the other four holes of the nine. On the back nine Jones took a one up lead at the eleventh, thirteenth and fifteenth only to see Tolley take it away each time at the twelfth, fourteenth and sixteenth holes.

Both Jones and Tolley had very long drives on the seventeenth. Jones's ball was to the left side of the fairway while Tolley's, a little bit longer, was in the center. Jones would be forced to play to the dangerous green first. The flagstick was directly behind the Road Bunker from Jones's position while the hole opened slightly for Tolley since he was more to the right.

In order for Jones to reach a position in front of the green from which he could chip to the hole it was necessary for him to land his ball very close to the road itself. If Jones hit the ball a shade too hard he would be in the road, a shade too softly and he might still be blocked from the pin by the Road Bunker. He decided to attempt to play intentionally past the Road Bunker on its left side with the idea that once past the hazard he could chip back to the hole with a better chance for a 4 than he would have if he should get into trouble in the road or by being blocked out by the bunker. Jones tried to get the massed galleries to move away from his intended target area. They moved slightly and begrudgingly. The stewards were doing their best but excitement was running so high that the people were unreasoning. They would chance being hit by a Jones shot and proudly show the bruise, no doubt, the next day.

Jones finally made the stroke, a 4-iron that caused the ball to land even with the bunker and then bound into the side of the roped gallery and there be stopped on the back edge of the green some forty or fifty feet away from the hole, but a most satisfactory shot under the circumstances, one which now threw great pressure on Tolley to equal or surpass it order to hold the match all square.

Tolley knew he had to "go for the flag" in order to save his half on the hole. Knowing the danger in letting the ball get to the right and into the road, Tolley instinctively guarded against any kind of a "push." As a result, the shot was slightly pulled to the left, safely away from the road, it is true, but it came to rest to the left of the Road Bunker with that dreaded sandy hole between Tolley's ball and the flagstick. Moreover, the ratio of distance between Tolley's ball and the bunker, and the bunker and the flagstick was so unfavorable that it appeared probable that Tolley would not put the ball onto the putting surface and still stop it anywhere near the hole because the hole was cut extremely close to Tolley's side of the green.

O. B. Keeler, the great reporter who followed Jones's career so avidly, witnessed the shot. He said that he felt that "no man alive could execute so deft a pitch that it would clear that bunker and stop anywhere near the hole in that absurdly narrow plateau green with the road just across it." He thought Tolley would be most likely to put the ball into the road, would never be able to get it near the flag. In one minute Jones had the hole "won" and in another minute Jones was putting an eight-footer for his life because Tolley would go one up should Jones miss his putt. But Jones did not miss the putt and the history of golf was better served as a result. Without that putt in the hole at seventeen it is fairly certain there would have been no "Grand Slam" for Jones.

At this crucial moment, Tolley was able to make what he later said, some twenty-eight years afterward, "was the finest shot of my life." He was able to loft his ball off the closely cut grass of the fairway onto exactly the right spot at the green's edge where it should hit and get enough underspin on the ball to cause it to stop within inches of the hole for a certain 4. Jones, startled no doubt by the excellence of Tolley's recovery, made his run-up shot from the back edge of the green. To his horror he saw the ball sliding farther and farther away from the hole, coming to rest at least eight feet away. Now the tide had really turned. From a probable 4 for Jones and a possible 5 for Tolley at the moment before Tolley had made his approach to the green, Jones now faced the certainty of Tolley's 4 and a very possible 5 for himself if he should not sink this wicked slippery eight foot putt.

Jones once more exhibited his silken putting stroke under pressure, holing the putt to tie Tolley. The two great golfers headed for the Home Hole with the wind now at their backs, all tied. The galleries lined both sides of the fairway and surrounded the back of the eighteenth green.

Both players drove to within ten yards of the green, helped by the powerful tail-wind. Jones was to the left and played his run-up shot first. His shot was too strong and ran up through the Valley of Sin about twenty-five feet past the hole. Tolley's shot was better than Jones's and stopped about twelve to fifteen feet away, also on the high side of the hole. Jones, of course, putted first. He missed the hole but was close enough to assure his par. Now the door was open for Tolley and Jones could do nothing about it. If Cyril downed this birdie putt he had won the match and put Jones out of the Amateur Championship.

Tolley missed. Jones, in mental agony waiting for the verdict, had another "life" in the match. They would go to extra holes.

The nineteenth hole was anti-climactic. Tolley

A practice round for Bobby Jones before the 1930 Amateur Championship drew crowds of thousands. The eminent professional to the Royal and Ancient Golf Club can be seen at the left. The gentleman with the shooting stick in typical Scottish golf garb is William Norman Boase, who himself was a winner of the silver club and Queen Adelaide Medal in 1935.

100

missed the green on his second shot and chipped weakly short of the hole by seven feet.

Jones, in the meanwhile, had hit a fine drive and a superlative second shot only ten feet away from the flagstick. The stymie rule was still in effect at that time. Since both balls were on the same side of the hole it was entirely possible that if Jones did not hole his putt it might stop on Cyril's line and block his line to the cup. That is exactly what happened. Jones's ball was only a couple of inches short of the hole but Tolley had a complete stymie which he could not possibly negotiate. So, it was Jones one up in nineteen holes over Cyril Tolley. Another piece of the jig-saw puzzle, the four championships of 1930 for Jones had fallen into place, reluctantly it is true, but it had fallen.

Roger Wethered, the tall, distinguished gentleman-golfer famous as much for his own golf as for the golf swing of his famous sister, British Women's Champion, Joyce, would meet Jones in the final thirty-six hole match.

Roger had had three very easy matches to start and then had had four equally tough ones. He was hitting his irons and pitches to the green in brilliant fashion. His driving, often erratic, remained good for the first nine holes of the match with Jones and then began to get him into serious trouble from which he never would recover.

These two golfers had recently played a preview of the match at Sandwich in the Walker Cup only a few weeks before. Wethered and Jones had each shot 35s to make the turn even. Then, Roger's game went to pieces and Jones took six of the next seven holes. The same thing happened at St. Andrews. Jones won five of the first seven holes on the second nine. Although Wethered birdied the Road Hole brilliantly, Bobby, having missed a two-foot putt after recovering so close to the pin that it appeared he would make his 4 there, too, was four up at the start of the second eighteen. Roger made as good a fight as he could, battling to the turn, trying not to get any further behind, but the result was a foregone conclusion. Jones played superb golf and was two under 4s for the thirty holes of the match, for Wethered was congratulating Jones at the twelfth hole on his great victory in the championship, the first crown of the four he would gather together for his Grand Slam of 1930.

THE OPEN CHAMPIONSHIP
OF 1933

"At Southport in 1933 our Ryder Cup team had

Denny Shute, Open Champion of 1933, right. Craig Wood, runner-up, left.

its first real chance to win on British soil. Denny Shute was our last man on the course and I was in the clubhouse with my host, the Prince of Wales. When Denny came onto the eighteenth green, if he made his putt in 1 we would win the cup; if he got down in 2 we would keep it; if he took 3 we would lose it to Great Britain. Of course,

A view of the great "follow-through" of Walter Hagen. Photo taken in 1933.

101

Walter Hagen, "The Haig," Open Champion in 1922, 1924, 1928, and 1929, but never a winner at St. Andrews. Scene is of the Open of 1933.

Denny, not knowing how some of our players had finished, did not know this. I was wondering if I shouldn't be down there putting him wise to how things stood. If I were at the green I could whisper in his ear . . . tell him to play safe . . . not to take three putts. But I knew it would be discourteous to walk out on the future King of England just to whisper in Denny's ear and tell him how to putt.

"Denny played it bold and much too strong. His ball rimmed the hole and went three feet past. He missed coming back and three-putted for a 5. The British had taken the Cup from us 6 to 5 with one matched halved. Two weeks later Denny and Craig Wood came through for a tie for first place in the British Open at St. Andrews. Denny beat Craig Wood in the play-off, and became British Open Champion for the first time in his career."

This article first appeared in Walter Hagen, *The Walter Hagen Story.*

Densmore Shute, United States	73	73	73	73	292
	Play-off 75-74				149
Craig Wood, United States	77	72	68	75	292
	Play-off 78-76				154
Gene Sarazen, United States	72	73	73	75	293
Leo Diegel, United States	75	70	71	77	293
Syd Easterbrook, England	73	72	71	77	293
Olin Dutra, United States	76	76	70	72	294
Abe Mitchell, England	74	68	74	78	294
Ed Dudley, United States	70	71	76	78	295
Henry Cotton, Belgium	73	71	72	79	295
Alf Padgham, England	74	73	74	74	295

In one of the fiercest and most exciting battles ever waged for the title of Open Champion, no less than fourteen players found themselves within five strokes of the eventual winner, American Ryder Cup star, Densmore Shute, who tied with his teammate, Craig Wood, with total scores of 292. Shute beat Wood soundly in a subsequent 36 hole play-off with scores of 75-74 — 149 to 78-76 — 154. Shute scored four successive 73s, even par on every round, to register one of the most consistent exhibitions of steady golf ever witnessed at St. Andrews.

However, Shute almost did not make the starting field. His first round 75 in the 36-hole qualifying test was satisfactory enough but on his second round he skidded badly to an 81 and by one single stroke barely qualified for the tournament proper with his 156 total. All of the American Ryder Cup team members were present and every one of them qualified for the Open Championship.

A little-known Irishman, William Patrick "Pat" Nolan, thirty-eight years old at the time, a golfer who had never before won anything in the way of a "big tournament," was the sensation of the qualifying rounds. Nolan was described as "the worst dressed golfer with one of the most stylish swings." He wore old trousers, brown shoes, and a white dress long-sleeved shirt open at the neck as he "burned up the course" on one of the hottest days the Fifeshire coast had experienced in years. He was said to possess "a perfect putting touch" which helped him to "master the red-hot pace of the fiery greens." He lost a stroke at the nefarious Road Hole, the seventeenth, or he would have checked in with a 66. As it was, his 67 erased former course record scores of 68 by Robert T. Jones, Jr. and George T. Dunlap, Jr. Nolan took the qualifying medal with 71-68 139. Thirteen Americans qualified, including defending champion Gene Sarazen, who had won the year before at Sandwich. One lone American amateur qualified, George T. Dunlap, Jr. Horton Smith led the American contingent with two 71s. Notable failures in the qualifying rounds were James Braid 88-80 — 168 and Harry Vardon 87-88 — 175. When one contemplates the fact that Harry Vardon first won the Open Championship in 1896 at Muirfield and that James Braid was a runner-up for the championship at Hoylake in 1897, it is almost incredible to realize that Vardon and Braid, both born in 1870, were still capable of playing championship golf so many years later at sixty-three years of age.

Among the near-casualties in qualifying was Craig Wood. He was treading narrowly on the edge of the qualifying limit after a bad 82 beginning. Wood took Ryder Cup Captain Walter Hagen's advice and used his irons off the tees of the first nine of his second qualifying round. Craig continued to score badly, took 38 strokes on the first nine, and then, getting back his courage somewhat, went to his woods again and shot nine straight 4s for a 74 which together with his 82 squeezed him under the 157 qualifying line safely. It is interesting to see now in retrospect how im-portant that "comeback" on the last nine was, for without it, Wood would never have had the chance to tie Shute for the Championship.

Walter Hagen was playing as brilliantly as ever and had qualified comfortably. With his inimitably flamboyant style it might have been said he was "resting" until the tournament itself started. Four times in the previous eleven years Hagen had won the championship, 1922, 1924, 1928 and 1929. He was the favorite to win this year.

On the first day of the tournament, played in ideal sunny weather with mild breezes, "The Haig" jumped into the lead with a brilliant 68. He found himself at the day's end with a stroke edge on the closest of the field Cyril Tolley, Tom Ferrier and Ed Dudley, three strokes on Nolan, the medalist who continued to show great golf ability, four strokes on Gene Sarazen and five strokes on Henry Cotton, who was considered to be the strongest of the defending forces in the British Isles. Denny Shute was in with the first of his 73s and was also five strokes behind Walter Hagen. Craig Wood trailed badly with a 77 beginning. Hagen's style was described as "far and sure" as he put together a 32 and 36 for his 68. He got tremendous distance from the tees, his pitch and runshots worked beautifully and his putter was said to have been "as finely tuned as a piano string." He picked up two strokes on 9-footers for birdies on the first and third, added two more precious strokes on a twenty foot eagle 3 at the fifth and sailed along serenely in straight par until he reached the seventeenth, which gave him a scare. Hagen banged his second shot straight for the flagstick which was placed near the rear of the plateau green. His ball almost over-ran the putting surface into deep trouble but hung on the edge and stayed safe. Walter putted carefully for fear the ball would move as he stroked it, saved his 4 on the hole and finished comfortably with another 4 at the eighteenth, a 68 which tied the old Bobby Jones course record.

On the second day of play, Hagen returned a sound 72 which, added to his opening 68, gave him 140, but his lead had shrunk to only one stroke. Ed Dudley had narrowed Hagen's lead by a fine 71 on top of his 70 of the first day and now rested in second place at 141. Sarazen was starting to show flashes of his normal brilliance and electrified the galleries with a dazzling 33 front nine. Then he got into Hell's Bunker on the 14th, took 6 for a 40 on the second nine, ending with a 73 and 145 for the two rounds.

The gallery was estimated at 8,000 people on this second beautiful day in Scotland. There was a veri-table army of stewards, police, caretakers and gatekeepers to avoid the mob scene which occurred at the end of Bobby Jones's last amateur triumph at St. Andrews in 1930; but the crowds were well-behaved and mannerly. For the first time the course was roped off and an admission fee was charged.

The scoreboard at the end of the second day read:

Walter Hagen	68	72	140
Ed Dudley	70	71	141
Fred Robertson	71	71	142
Abe Mitchell	74	68	142
Cyril J. H. Tolley	70	73	143
Henry Cotton	73	71	144
Gene Sarazen	72	73	145
Syd Easterbrook	73	72	145
George T. Dunlap. Jr.	72	74	146
Horton Smith	73	73	146
Craig Wood	77	72	149

Abe Mitchell, 46 years old, renowned as the private tutor to Samuel Ryder, the originator of the Ryder Cup trophy, had a sensational second round 68, five under par for a total of 142. His round with 33 strokes on the first nine looked like a certain 67 until Abe took 5 at the eighteenth hole. He had seven birdies and found himself tied at 142 with young Fred Robertson, the British "dark horse" of the tournament.

Then came the final day with its brutal thirty-six hole physical endurance test. Bernard Darwin, in his colorful reportage, said, "St. Andrews had its revenge on golfers who had been beating par over its hummocks, dunes and famous bunkers earlier in the week. With an easterly wind driving across Eden peninsula the long hitters were mostly in trouble in the bunkers. Sarazen and Hagen who saw their hopes die in its deep bunkers will not forget the fourteenth. Hell bunker and Kitchen bunker cut them down."

When the day was over, the great Hagen had taken 79 strokes and 82 strokes to go down in ignominious defeat to an eventual tie for nineteenth place in the field. His 82 included a 7 at the fourteenth.

In the meantime, Denny Shute was playing golf ahead of both Easterbrook and Sarazen. Easterbrook was a deliberate player and had been the star of the recent Ryder Cup matches, defeating Shute in the deciding match at Southport.

Sarazen, Diegel and Easterbrook had the best chances to catch or surpass Shute and Wood but each one failed by a single stroke to do so. Gene lost his opportunity to win two championships in succession when he took a horrible 8 on the 14th. Gene could not get out of Hell bunker. Easterbrook took 7 at the 14th and the stroke he saved there

over poor Gene he wasted on the eighteenth when he could not drop a putt of about six feet. Leo Diegel of the famous "spread-eagle" putting stance found it impossible to hole a three-foot putt that would have tied him for the coveted lead.

Shute reported his third 73 and had started his last round after Craig Wood startled the crowd with a superb 68 on his morning round. No one was paying much attention to Shute, who went out in 33 and stumbled a bit for a 40 on the second nine, a 73 and a 219 total at the start of the final round. Wood, in the meantime, with his marvelous third round 68 on nines of 34 and 34 appeared to be moving into the forefront of the field. His second nine 34 against heavy wind which had now risen was the work of a true master golfer. At the start of the third round, the scoreboard showed a four-way tie between Leo Diegel, Syd Easterbrook, Abe Mitchell and Henry Cotton at 216 strokes. All four of these leaders would vanish in the winds of the afternoon with 77s for Diegel and Easterbrook, a 78 for Mitchell and a 79 for Cotton. Ed Dudley, who was only one stroke back at 217, would also soar to a 78 and out of the championship.

Thus it came down to a stretch battle between Denny Shute and a "revived" Craig Wood. Shute had the disadvantage of starting about half an hour after Wood and although he began shakily with bogies on the first and second hole he retrieved them by shots dead to the pin for birdies on the fifth and sixth. His second nine was similarly steady with a birdie obtained at the tenth hole, offset when he took three strokes to get down from the edge of the sixteenth.

Denny Shute very nearly came to grief at the 18th hole. His first putt was weak and his second looked "hopeless." His playing partner threw up his hands in despair and at that moment the ball fell in the back door of the cup, a fraction of an inch away from second place behind Craig Wood.

Densmore Shute shot his fourth successive 73, 292 strokes for the four rounds. Before the tournament Bernard Darwin had seen Denny Shute practicing certain pitch and run shots which "though unfamiliar to him might prove profitable" and had remarked, "Here is an eminently dangerous man." Shute was about to prove Darwin right.

Wood knew what he had to do on his last round. He was now only one stroke back of the four-way cluster of Diegel, Easterbrook, Mitchell and Cotton. He had to hope to out-score them and still keep his eye on the ever-dangerous Sarazen who was only one stroke behind him. Wood knew also that Denny Shute might give him trouble should he falter.

As Wood played the first nine of his last round, word reached him about the various blow-ups behind him and the steady scoring of Denny Shute behind him. Wood was now driving confidently, extremely long and very straight. Hole after hole fell to him in par, a bogey at the seventh was offset by a boring-into-the-wind deuce at the dreaded eleventh. Standing at the 15th tee Wood knew he needed 4-4-5-4 to win by two shots over Shute, who was apparently on his way into the clubhouse with a 282. Suddenly Wood was in trouble. His drive had gone awry and his ball had lodged in a hateful whin bush. Another stroke got the ball out of danger but did not advance it. Wood salvaged a 6 on the fourteenth and knew then that his work was really cut out for him. He knew he had to par the last three holes merely to tie Shute. Beating him in the strong wind was out of the question. Making these three holes in par alone was a job only for champions. He then learned about Sarazen's misfortune behind him in Hell bunker. Sarazen was out of it, Craig felt, and it turned out he was right.

Craig Wood made those three pars. The seventeenth alone came with difficulty. A delicate chip shot saved the day. Wood almost drove the eighteenth with his great power, made his 4 there, scored a final 75 and had tied Denny Shute for the Open Championship.

Densmore Shute, not yet in his thirties, although of fairly good stature, weighed only 135 pounds. He was the son of a Scottish-born professional, Herman Shute, who had been brought up not far from St. Andrews and had even caddied at the famous course in his youth. He had aimed his son Denny at a golf career all his life. Herman had even constructed a special set of "Tom Thumb" golf clubs for Denny when the child was only three years old. Herman had migrated to the United States and was a practicing professional golfer in Huntington, West Virginia.

Denny Shute came to the world of professional golf after an excellent amateur career which included amateur championships in West Virginia and Ohio. He became a professional before the 1929 United States Open and although Robert T. Jones, Jr. won that tournament after a playoff with Abe Espinosa, Shute's fine swing brought him to the attention of the golf world as a possible future star.

Craig Wood, thirty-one years of age, was a speed skater in his youth. He was one of the first of the "collegians" to enter professional golf, having studied at Clarkson Tech in New York before he decided to "turn pro." He, too, had distinguished himself in golf thus far, had finished in third place in the U.S. Open Championship held the month before at North Shore Golf Club in Glenview, Illinois. Although there was at this time in American professional golf only a rudimentary "tour," Wood was the leading money-winner of the "winter tour," the total being a paltry $7,000 in prize money.

So the scene was set for the thirty-six hole playoff between these two American rivals.

Wood started off badly with a 6 on the first hole to Shute's 4. Craig's second shot, into the wind which was still blowing in his face, though not so strongly as on the final day of the championship proper, found Swilken burn. Wood took off his shoes and got into the stream in an attempt to salvage his par. He could not do it, settled for a drop behind the water and the eventual double-bogey six.

At the second hole Wood hit a "vast" drive but hooked a simple pitch into a bunker and after three putts on the green was four strokes behind Denny Shute, who followed with a second steady par 4 at the second hole.

After four holes, Shute was five strokes ahead. Shute appeared to be running away from Wood but the match regained some interest when Shute three-putted two greens in a row, the 9th and 10th, while Wood had helped his cause by getting a 3 at the sixth. The 11th hole was a "comedy of errors full of sandy fun" as the two golfers halved in bad double-bogey 5s.

At the 14th with Wood only two strokes away, Shute played a great pitch out of the bunker ominously called "The Grave" and holed his putt for a 4. Wood's 5 left him three strokes behind and the first round ended that way with Shute at 75, Wood a 78. Not very good golf from the tired competitors, especially in view of the fact that they had been helped all the way around by the wind which switched, most fortunately, as the golfers made the turn back home.

On the second round, Shute played with relentless steadiness and accuracy. The 7th hole was the final blow to Craig Wood's hope of making a comeback in the match. Craig had a bad lie on broken sandy ground and "fluffed the ball only twenty yards into the Shelly bunker of many bitter memories."

Shute was seven strokes ahead with only four holes left to play. Denny continued to play with an "outward frozen calm in perfect figures, taking no risks and yet never giving way to the cowardly or cautious."

And so, in methodical fashion, he got his par 4 at the last hole. Andrew Kirkaldy, the distinguished honorary Professional to the Royal and Ancient

Golf Club held the flagstick in the traditional manner for Denny as he holed his last putt on his sound 74 to Wood's 76, giving him a five stroke winning margin, the winner of The Open Championship of 1933.

1st Round Out	Shute	4 4 4	4 4 4	5 4 3	36		
	Wood	6 6 4	5 4 3	5 3 3	39		
1st Round In	Shute	4 5 4	5 4 4	4 5 4	39	75	
	Wood	4 5 4	4 5 5	4 4 4	39	78	
2d Round Out	Shute	4 4 4	5 4 4	4 3 4	36		
	Wood	4 5 4	4 4 4	6 4 4	39		
2d Round In	Shute	3 3 5	4 5 5	4 5 4	38	74	149
	Wood	3 4 4	5 4 4	4 5 4	37	76	154

When word of Denny Shute's victory reached his father back in the States, the latter said, "That certainly makes up for that putt the boy missed on the last green of the Ryder Cup match, doesn't it?"

THE BRITISH AMATEUR OF 1936

Hector Thomson, stylish golfer, 22 years old, a home-bred Scot, the son of a professional and the hope and pride of Scotland in this tournament, turned back the considerable threat of giant foreign invader James "Jim" Ferrier of Australia to capture the crown for Scotland for the first time in eleven years.

By turning professional, Lawson Little, Jr. had relinquished his right to contend for the Amateur Championship of Britain in 1936. Thus it was felt that the field was wide open for some new face to move into the headlines. Veterans Cyril Tolley and Roger Wethered were again contending and would mount a great threat to Thomson. But it was Jim Ferrier who burst onto the international scene in this tournament and while he was not the eventual winner it was clear that an eminent golf career was ahead of him.

Robert Sweeney, the transplanted American who had lived in America for years, was the lone American hope. He truly could not be considered a "real" American in the sense that his game had been so developed and practiced in England that he was more of an English stylist than an American one.

The round of sixteen found Bob Sweeny beating Jock McLean, another one of Scotland's great hopes at the twentieth hole in a very thrilling match. For fourteen holes Sweeny had played well, easily and comfortably. He had drawn steadily ahead of Jock and at the 14th hole, with five holes to play, found himself 4 up on McLean. Then the tide turned, it seemed. McLean played brilliant golf and Sweeny

Hector Thomson, Amateur Champion of 1936.

played erratic and bad golf at the fourteenth and fifteenth. At the sixteenth, Sweeny recovered with a fine second to make him dormie 2 going to the seventeenth tee. Then Bob three-putted both the

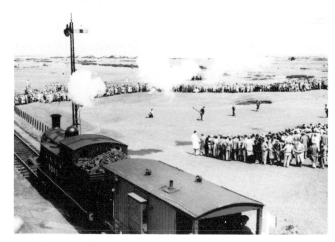

Putting on the 16th green with the distraction of a locomotive going by. This photo was taken in 1936.

106

seventeenth and eighteenth to lose both holes to Jock and throw the match into overtime. Both players holed "nasty" putts at the nineteenth to tie there, and at the twentieth Sweeny made a great chip from the bunker behind the green and holed a five-footer to win the match eventually. It was without any question a thriller and both players deserved to win.

G. Alec Hill defeated former Champion Cyril Tolley at the first extra hole in another overtime match. It, too, was a heart-breaker for both players. Hill played magnificently, and yet, after doing the seventh through the fourteenth holes in no less than 25 strokes, one over 3s was only three up on Tolley with four holes to play. Tolley made a 3 at No. 15 to win. Hill over-played the green at the sixteenth and lost another hole to Tolley. Tolley one down and two to play. A half in 5s at the Road Hole brought Tolley to the home hole one down. A monstrous drive from Tolley, a good pitch and Tolley had his 4 at the last hole. Hill played weakly to the green and then, under much pressure, three-putted for a 5 and a tied match.

At the first hole Tolley putted for his birdie to win at last, as he hoped he would do, and sadly left himself stymied by Hill's ball. Hill made his 4 and took the match. Bernard Darwin in his account of the match said, "All that magnificent effort (by Tolley) had been thrown away. There are moments when the word 'tragedy' is not misapplied to this game of golf."

Although Hill had been through the grueling match with Cyril Tolley, he was able to come back in the afternoon and again play a strong game against Jim Ferrier. But his 73 to Ferrier's 72 was not good enough to win. Ferrier had beaten Morton Dykes, the player whose main claim to fame was that he had beaten the South African "golf prodigy," Bobby Locke, in one of the early matches of the tournament.

Ferrier had had a tough "squeak" past Bob Sweeny, going twenty-one holes before dropping a 12-foot birdie putt to win. At one point in this match Ferrier struck one of the most colossal drives ever seen at the twelfth hole. It was reported to have gone more than 350 yards and he had to pitch back to the 316 yard hole for his 3 to win that hole and square the match. Ferrier won the thirteenth, halved the fourteenth and fifteenth and won the sixteenth. So with Ferrier two up with two to play it looked as if he would win, especially in view of his spurt of winning holes. The end was far off, however, for Ferrier drove out-of-bounds twice at the seventeenth and Sweeny canned a short putt for a birdie 3 at the eighteenth, a score which Fer-

rier could not match. The overtime play was exciting, with both players parring the first two holes. Ferrier's final twelve-foot birdie putt won it all at the third extra hole.

In the final match, Ferrier against Thomson, Thomson played the better golf and deserved to win. The weather was bad and the players had to fight driving rain and even hail-stones at times. Thomson was down three holes by the time they reached the twelfth hole of the morning round but rallied to win three holes in a row, the fourteenth, fifteenth and sixteenth, to end all even at noon-time, for Thomson a medal score of 74, for Ferrier a 77 (mainly on a bad 7 at the 14th where Thomson made a birdie 4).

The Scot moved out in front in the first nine of the afternoon round scoring a 35 to Ferrier's 36. Thomson's birdie 3 on the 6th hole and par at the 8th put him 2 up at the turn.

Ferrier got back one of the holes with a par at the tough eleventh hole but a birdie by Thomson at the fourteenth left him again 2 up, a margin which held until the seventeenth where Ferrier, now desperate, two down with two to play, played a courageous second shot to the green and won the hole with a birdie 4 to Thomson's 5. The eighteenth was anti-climactic, however, when Thomson's beautiful pitch to the green nearly went into the cup at the home hole, stopping only inches away from an eagle 2. Ferrier graciously conceded the match without even attempting to make his own birdie. Scotland again had a home-grown champion, Hector Thomson. Eleven years later, the crowning achievement of Jim Ferrier's golf career would occur when he would win the Professional Golfers Association's Championship of America, defeating Melvin Harbert 2 and 1 in the match play final of that event.

Bob Sweeny came back the next year to win the British Amateur Championship at Sandwich, England, defeating L. O. Munn 3 and 2 in the final. But undoubtedly the highlight of Bob's long and distinguished golf career came a number of years later when he returned to the United States and attempted to win the United States Amateur Championship of 1954 which was being held at the Country Club of Detroit, Michigan. Bob again got as far as the final round but there he encountered a strong slope-shouldered young amateur who trounced him by one hole in the thirty-six hole match play final round and soon afterward turned professional to make his own career in golf. The name of Sweeny's conqueror? Arnold Palmer.

THE OPEN CHAMPIONSHIP
OF 1939

Richard Burton, England	70	72	77	71	290
John Bulla, United States	77	71	71	73	292
S. L. King, England	74	72	75	73	294
Jock Fallon, England	71	73	71	79	294
W. Shankland, England	72	73	72	77	294
Reginald Whitcombe, England	71	75	74	74	294
Alf Perry, England	71	74	73	76	294
Martin Pose, Argentina	71	72	76	76	295
E. W. H. Kenyon, England	73	75	74	74	296
Percy Alliss, England	75	73	74	74	296
A. D. "Bobby" Locke, South Africa	70	75	76	75	296

Richard "Dick" Burton, Open Champion of 1939.

Richard "Dick" Burton, Cheshire professional with "iron nerves and steel wrists," turned back the final challenge of the American professional, Johnny Bulla, to win the Open Championship of 1939 by two strokes, 290 to 292.

Although tradition said that "an American golfer shall win at St. Andrews" ever since Jock Hutchison came in ahead in the tournament of 1921, Dick Burton ignored the prophets and set about playing his very hot game in the hope that he could break the old jinx and be the first native golfer in years to win at the Old Course.

Henry Cotton, Champion at Sandwich in 1934, came into this tournament playing stellar golf. At 5 to 1 odds, Cotton was the choice of the bookmakers for the title. Henry was known for his "cautious and cool" game and was described as hitting the ball like a "bloomin' automaton."

Another player who was to be watched carefully was the South African "schoolboy wonder," Arthur D. "Bobby" Locke, who was second choice in the pre-tournament betting at odds of 6 to 1. Everyone else in the field was held at 100 to 8, although there were several potential challengers in the American contingent, notably Lawson Little and John Bulla. James Bruen of Eire was looked upon as another juvenile miracle player in a class with Locke. Bruen had had a great 66 in practice on the New Course and exhibited a delicate touch in his short game. One old gnarled Scot who watched the practice rounds was heard to say "Those scores mean little on Monday. The wind will be blowing one way today, another tomorrow. Then we'll see what scores they can do on the Old Course."

Two hundred and forty players struggled in the two qualifying rounds over both the Old and the New Courses. At the end of the first day there was a tie at 69 between three players, Jim Bruen, the Irishman, Percy Alliss, an experienced British campaigner, and veteran American Lawson Little, Amateur Champion of the United States and Britain, who would win the United States Open Championship the next year at Canterbury Golf Club in Ohio after a playoff with Gene Sarazen. Bruen and Little played their first rounds on the Old Course and tied the amateur record of 69 previously set by Robert T. Jones, Jr. Little, now playing as a professional, was two strokes over the professional record of 67 which had been set by Bill "Pat" Nolan, the Irishman, in 1933.

John Bulla had a 72 on his first round and was well regarded by the galleries as one of the possible winners. The "Schenectady" or center-shafted putter had recently been banned from play by the Royal and Ancient and Bulla was rather upset to find that he would not be permitted to use his favorite putter. He took another club and for a while seemed to putt just as well as he did with the old one.

Lawson Little drove the twelfth hole 316 yards long and sank his putt there for a great eagle 2. His card read:

Dick Burton, Open Champion of 1939, plays from a shallow bunker. Courtesy H. W. Neale, London.

Par	Out:	4 4 4	4 5 4	4 3 4	36	
Little	Out:	4 5 4	4 5 4	4 3 4	37	73
Par	In:	4 4 4	4 5 4	4 3 4	36	
Little	In:	4 2 2	4 5 4	4 4 3	32	69

Henry Cotton, understandably, drew the largest part of the gallery, an estimated three thousand persons.

On the second day of qualifying, Jim Bruen, "with the greatest display of consistent golf the ancient St. Andrews golf course has seen since the days of R. T. Jones, Esquire," shot his second straight 69 to lead one hundred and twenty-nine qualifiers into the first day of the tournament.

Henry Cotton and Lawson Little were the early qualifying leaders at 142 strokes until Bruen came in at nightfall with his remarkable score of 138. Cotton had made a comeback from his beginning 73 and was four under par with 69 for his 142. Little reversed these scores and fell off to 73 on the New Course. Reginald Whitcombe, defending champion, having won at Sandwich in 1938, was in with a steady pair of 72s for 144. Martin Pose, the Argentinian and Jock McLean, amateur hope of Scotland, were at 145 after second round 73s. Bobby Locke checked in with 147 and was quoted as saying that he was "confident he would be in the first five from now on."

The first day of the championship brought awful weather. There was wind and rain and even sleet at times as the field battled to finish respectably on the Old Course. The top four players at the end of the day were all members of the British Empire, "Bobby" Locke, of South Africa, Dick Burton, Max

Faulkner and J. H. Busson, all of England, who set the early pace with 70s. One stroke behind were Whitcombe, the defending champion, Alf Perry, Open Champion in 1935, Martin Posé of Argentina and the diminutive Welshman David "Dai" Rees. Whitcombe was the most sensational of these golfers when he scored six straight 3s in "making the loop" from the seventh hole through the twelfth.

Lawson Little came to disaster at the long 14th. He had taken a 6 at the 13th hole and then drove into the "Beardies" bunker, just got his ball out, played his third shot to the left, was short on his fourth, chipped onto the green and two-putted. Just as Sarazen had lost his chances at the 14th hole in 1933, so, too, did Lawson Little see his hopes "go aglimmering" in this tournament in 1939. Lawson never recovered from the blow and failed to qualify for the final day of play.

But the 14th hole hadn't finished its dirty work for the day. It was waiting for Locke to come and give it a test. Bobby was steaming along in his customary "deadpan" deliberate fashion. He had been scoring remarkably well and was no less than six strokes under 4s when he came up to what the caddies call "that old De'il." An immense gallery of close to five thousand avid golfers was following him. Locke was certain in his own mind that he was "Destiny's own darling boy." Suddenly, "Destiny" deserted him. He staggered to the 15th tee after taking eight strokes on the 14th and, although he was ashen-faced and undoubtedly sick at heart to have blown such a glorious round, it is a tribute to Locke's control and golfing temperament that this horrible experience did not cause him to lose his game completely as he completed the round. He kept his temper under control and shot straight 4s for the last four holes. This exhibition of composure and lack of golfing "nerves" led many of the experts to think that Locke, not Bruen, Cotton or Burton, was the man to beat.

John Bulla with "new putter blues," began with a mediocre 77 and was far off the pace. It would be remarkable if he could yet make a run for the title but John did accomplish a fine second round, a 71 for a 148 two-day total which left him six strokes behind the pacesetter, Dick Burton, who added a decisive 70 to his first day 72 and took the undisputed lead at the halfway mark.

Meanwhile, Lawson Little had really "blown up" and put himself out of the tournament for good. He played badly, scored an 80, and at 159 was nine strokes away from the 150 qualifying score which sent thirty-four golfers into the third day of play. Lawson's wife was seen to console him as he came down the seventeenth hole. A number of eyebrows were raised at this scene. It just "wasn't done" at St. Andrews.

So, going into the final "double-round" day the scoreboard showed Burton leading the field of 142, Martin Posé one stroke behind at 143 after a steady 71 and 72, and unknown James "Jock" Fallon third at 144 after a second round 73. There were six other players bracketed at 145, including Locke and Alf Perry. Bruen, the "boy wonder" was in at 147 for his first two scores but would finish unspectacularly with a 75 and 76 for an eventual eleventh place in the tournament list.

Jock Fallon sprang into the lead at the end of the third round with a fine 71. He had played unspectacular golf after a 71 and 73, 144, two strokes behind Burton's 142. However, Fallon was able to gain six strokes on Burton as Burton slipped to 77 on his third round and Fallon came to the front of the massed group challenging for the title. John Bulla was also making his threat known as he came in with his second successive 71 for 219.

The end of the third round found the scoreboard reading:

Jock Fallon	144	71	215
W. Shankland	145	72	217
Alf Perry	145	73	218
Martin Posé	143	76	219
Dick Burton	142	77	219
John Bulla	148	71	219
Bobby Locke	145	76	221

Another relatively obscure player, W. Shankland, started to make his challenge known with a surprising 72 in his third round. He had started late and finished behind the other leading players rather unnoticed. With no gallery other than a few personal friends, he was in with a lovely 72 and had moved into the second slot behind Fallon as the fourth round began.

On the last day of the tournament the wind was blowing strongly from the west. One by one the various challengers fell off the pace. For Alf Perry and Martin Posé 76s, Posé's an unfortunate one in that he had to take a two stroke penalty for grounding his club in a hazard. Locke and Whitcombe could do no better than 75 and 74, while Shankland stumbled in with 77. Fallon blew to a 79 that most certainly cost him a tournament "he might have won" with a "mere" 74.

It was apparent that when Johnny Bulla posted his excellent finishing round of 73 for a total of 292 that Bulla's score might stand up as the winning score, inasmuch as all the others, with the exception of Dick Burton, were either in with higher scores or clearly headed for them as a result of where they stood in relation to par.

John Bulla took up a position on the Royal and Ancient clubhouse porch and sat back to await the arrival of his other challengers, notably Burton, who had the best chance, it was thought, to turn the trick. News of Burton's progress was trickling back to the clubhouse and it didn't look good to Bulla. Burton had turned the first nine in a one under par 35, and had made successive 3s at the seventh, the eighth, and the ninth holes.

Remember that Bulla and Burton had started their last rounds in a dead tie at 219 strokes. Bulla had scored a 35 on the first nine and had returned in 38 strokes, one over par on the back nine, but even par for the round. So, it was obvious that for Burton to squeeze under Bulla's 73 and 292 total he had to do 37 or better on the second nine, which would let him win by one stroke.

Burton parred the tenth hole and when he drilled a 3-iron into the wind at the "short" eleventh hole and saw the ball nestle some ten feet away from the flagstick he gained some further courage about his chances. Down went the putt on the slippery sidehill and Dick was now two under par for the round. The thirteenth fell in par, and at the fourteenth he got past Hell Bunker in two strokes to score a "normal" par 5. He parred the fifteenth and then, showing some signs of the pressure, hit a "slack second" to the sixteenth hole, chipped short and bogeyed the hole for a 5. Now, only one under par for the round, Dick knew he had to par the 17th and 18th holes to win by one stroke over Bulla. He played the seventeenth hole bravely, drove to the left, put his second in front of the green and ran up a nicely rolling shot onto the plateau and within eighteen feet of the hole. His putt was a cautious one, close to the hole; he had the first of his two badly needed pars.

The crowds sensed they were at last bringing home a winner who was "one of their own boys." "Come on, Richard, show that American that we can play golf, too!" Dick's drive at the home hole was long and straight almost into the Valley of Sin. The crowd closed around him as he got close to the green to make his approach to the flagstick. The crowd was nearly hysterical now. Dick could win by a stroke with a simple par.

Again, a delicate run-up shot from Burton much like the one at the seventeenth. The ball climbed the slope of the Valley and at last gained the flatter plane of the green, headed beautifully toward the hole. Then it slowed and stopped a pleasant ten or twelve feet away from that necessary 4. Two putts from twelve feet to win the Open Championship.

Dick Buron was cautious. He didn't want to over-run this cup in his anxiety to win. Bulla waited at the back of the green, hoping against hope he might see a three-putt and a tie for a play-off tomorrow.

Burton stroked the ball at last and wonder of wonders, it headed straight for the hole, neared it and ducked right into the cup for a miraculous birdie and the Championship. "Iron-nerved" Dick Burton had out-lasted the field and won for the honor of the Empire the first Open Championship in twenty-eight long years.

Burton's card on his final round was:

5 4 4	4 5 4	3 3 3	35
4 2 4	4 5 4	5 5 3	36	71
		Total	290

Bulla's card was:

4 4 4	3 5 4	4 4 3	35
5 3 4	4 5 5	4 5 3	38	73
		Total	292

THE OPEN CHAMPIONSHIP OF 1946

Sam Snead, United States	71	70	74	75	290
John Bulla, United States	71	72	72	79	294
A. D. "Bobby" Locke, South Africa	69	74	75	76	294
Henry Cotton, Great Britain	70	70	76	79	295
Dai Rees, Great Britain	75	67	73	80	295
Charles Ward, Great Britain	73	73	73	76	295
Norman Von Nida, Australia	70	76	74	75	295
Joe Kirkwood, United States	71	75	78	74	298
Fred Daly, Great Britain	77	71	76	74	298
Lawson Little, United States	78	75	72	74	299

As Samuel Jackson Snead accepted the trophy emblematic of the Open Championship of 1946 he was wearing his customary broad-brimmed straw hat. He smiled and said, "This is my happiest moment in golf. I told the folks at home I made my entry at the last minute just for the ride."

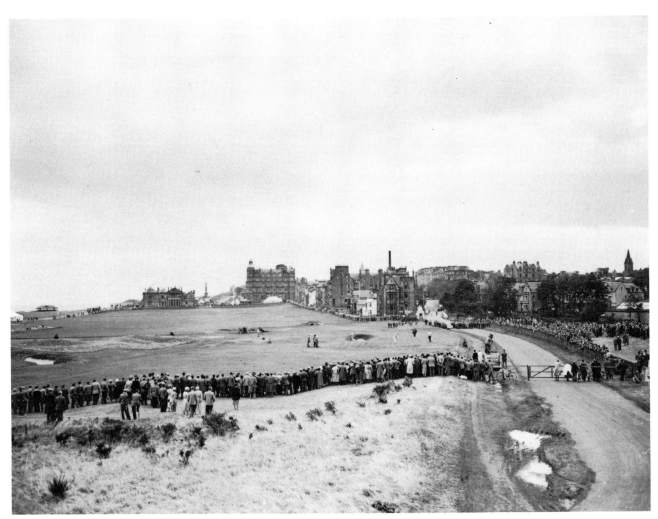

1946 Open. View of the crowd and 17th green looking north up to the 18th fairway.

111

Sam Snead with Open trophy, 1946.

tournament to be held in Great Britain since Richard Burton had won the prized cup there on the same links in 1939.

There were huge crowds to watch the golfers this year and "as one of several unprecedented measures to insure clear passage for the golfers" spectators were not to be allowed on the Old Course fairways during the play. The tournament committeemen no doubt were reminded of their horror at seeing the figure of Robert T. Jones, Jr. being engulfed by the unruly crowds of 1930.

Sam Snead was accompanied from America by Johnny Bulla and Lawson Little. These three American golfers would make the strongest "foreign threat" so the English book-makers had posted them as individual 10 to 1 "long-shots" to win the tournament.

Arthur D. "Bobby" Locke was thought to be the hottest man in British golf in 1946. He was the favorite to win at 7 to 1 odds while Henry Cotton and Dai Rees were at 8 to 1.

As was customary, the qualifying rounds were conducted with one round of eighteen holes to be played on the Old Course and one to be played on the New Course.

But "Slamming Sam" Snead really came to play. He had had a sparkling career in the United States since 1937, when he first broke into the golf world spotlight with a victory at the Bing Crosby Invitational Tournament played at the renowned Pebble Beach, California. Snead was the leading money-winner of the American professional tour in 1938 and had been named The Vardon Memorial Award winner of that year, an honor which recognizes the professional golfer who has the lowest scoring average of the year.

After twice being runner-up in previous years, Snead in 1942 finally broke through his apparent "jinx" and won his first so-called "major title," the championship of the United States Professional Golfers Association. He would win the Vardon Trophy once more in 1949 but he never would win the most coveted title of all, the United States Open Championship. Only one stroke away from victory several times, Snead would manage to botch a final hole or miss a crucial putt and let that championship elude him.

Now that the War had finally ended, the world of golf was ready to resume its international activity. The famous Old Course at St. Andrews was chosen as the site for the first Open Championship

John Bulla, twice runner-up for the Open title, in 1939 to Dick Burton and in 1946 to Sam Snead. John always had trouble with the Road Hole, it seemed.

In the qualifying, Snead started out slowly with 75 on the Old Course and 74 on the New. Snead already had a reputation as a tremendously long driver and the owner of one of the "sweetest" swings in golf. At St. Andrews with the small 1.62 ounce English ball he was driving even farther than usual. (The Royal and Ancient had recently reaffirmed its intention to stick with the 1.62 size ball for the foreseeable future.) In his qualifying round Snead drove the 312-yard 10th hole, for example, but three-putted the green for par. He had some caddie trouble, too, and took a different caddie on his second round when the first caddie displeased him. Lawson Little and Bulla had totals of 151 as the Australian star, Norman Von Nida, took the qualifying medal with an unspectacular 73 and 72 for 145. There was a strong west wind which swept the course. Scores soared as a result of the difficulty in judging the effect of the gusts on the shot-making.

The qualifying mark for the low one hundred players was 158 strokes or an average of two 79s so one may well understand the problems the field had in scoring. One interesting qualifier was Gabriel Garcia, a colorful Spaniard professional who gained a spot in the tournament proper while "playing with only four old battered clubs," a remarkable achievement on any course, not to mention St. Andrews's Old Course in a strong wind.

Bobby Locke started out as if he would win the tournament in prompt fashion by scoring a record-setting 69, four under the 73 par for the course. Locke was in trouble only once on his great round when a drive landed in a fairway bunker at the twelfth hole, but even then Bobby was able to play the ball onto the green from an awkward position in the sand and save his par. On three greens his birdie putts were no longer than five feet. His fourth birdie, at the seventeenth hole, came on a fifteen-foot putt and except for the four birdies he dropped Bobby played the course in straight par figures. His card was:

Sam Snead, Open Champion of 1946, a classic swing.

| Locke | Out: | 4 4 4 | 4 4 4 | 4 3 3 | 34 | |
| | In: | 3 3 4 | 4 5 4 | 4 4 4 | 35 | 69 |

With rounds of 70 each, one stroke back of Locke, were veteran Henry Cotton, now trying for his third Open crown, and Norman Von Nida, the qualifying medalist. Then came Sam Snead and Johnny Bulla at 71. Bulla and Snead were paired together in the first round. Both were driving the ball sensationally straight and far. Bulla's 71 could easily have been a 68 or 69 because he came to the seventeenth hole four under 4s, needing a 4 at the 17th, a birdie, but reasonably obtainable by a good player such as Bulla.

Bulla's second shot at No. 17 faded into the treacherous road and the ball "nestled among stones as big as the ball itself." John swung once and the ball came out of the road, almost climbed the slope to the green, stopped short of the top and then trickled back onto the road once more. Another swing and the ball was still short of the putting surface. A fifth shot and the ball was on the green but a long way from the hole. Two putts brought a 7 to Bulla's card, which up until that point had nothing but 3s and 4s on it. A bad break for a fine golfer. Since he finished only three strokes behind Snead, the eventual winner, we are able to see in retrospect, how costly that seventeenth hole was to Bulla.

Lawson Little was off to a bad 75 and when he followed that with an even worse 78 he ceased to be a factor in this tournament.

So the scoreboard showed these leaders at the end of the first day of play:

Bobby Locke	69
Henry Cotton	70
Norman Von Nida	70

113

Sam Snead	71
Johnny Bulla	71
Joe Kirkwood	71
Reg Whitcombe	71
Dick Burton	74
Dai Rees	75

On the second day, Henry Cotton, twice winner of the cup, sprang into the lead when he scored his second successive 70. Henry, an Englishman, had first won in 1934 at Sandwich, England and broke a long streak of successive victories by the American "invaders," Jones, Hagen, Armour, Sarazen and Shute. He had taken his second crown at Carnoustie, Scotland, in 1937 and moved strongly into contention in this tournament one stroke ahead of Snead, who scored a sound and steady 71 for his total of 141. Diminutive Dai Rees, a Welshman, provided the fireworks on the second day with a great 67 which was considered to be the new course record for the "extended" Old Course. Note: The lengthening of the course amounted to only two hundred and thirty-one yards, from 6652 to 6883 yards but it caused the authorities to consider it a different course, an "extended course," not the same one on which the earlier record of 67 had been set by Nolan in 1933 at 6572 yards or the 69s of James Bruen and Lawson Little in 1939 when the course was extended to the 6652 yard distance.

Locke slipped a little bit on his second round, scored a 74 and fell into a tie for fourth place with Johnny Bulla at the halfway mark. Kirkwood faded to a 75 and although he continued to play steady golf, he, like Little, was never again a contender in this championship.

The second day of play was once more afflicted with driving rain and strong westerly winds. Snead again changed caddies, taking his third one in four days. This one would remain until the cup was in Sam's hands and the caddie would be rewarded by Snead giving him the entire winner's purse, one hundred and fifty pounds, worth $600.00 in American money at the exchange rate of 1946.

And, thus, heading into the strenuous double-round, thirty-six hole final day, the scoreboard showed the leaders to be:

Henry Cotton	70	70	140
Sam Snead	71	70	141
Dai Rees	75	67	142
Johnny Bulla	71	72	143
A. D. "Bobby" Locke	69	74	143

After the group of five players were Reginald Whitcombe, seven strokes behind at 147, Fred Daly, the Irishman and A. J. Lees of Yorkshire at 148. Surely it could be expected that the eventual winner would come from the five front-runners, Cotton, Snead, Rees or Bulla or Locke.

The final day brought strong winds but sunny skies. Snead was still driving well, hitting long, low tee-shots under the wind. He had a difficult battle with the Old Course, as did every other player. This was one of those tournaments which was ready to be captured by the golfer who could "outlast" the rest of the closely-bunched field, the golfer who could win on sheer physical endurance and continued concentration on the task at hand.

Snead's morning round was a 74 but he lost ground only to Bulla who had 72 and thus came into a tie with Sam at 215, and Dai Rees whose 73 also gave him 215. Locke lost one stroke to Snead on his morning round with a 75 and slipped from being down two strokes to three strokes with his total of 218. So the leading players remained in a close contest right on into the last eighteenth-hole round.

Johnny Bulla had 39 strokes on the first nine of the last round and, when Snead took 40, Bulla took the momentary lead, 254 strokes to 255 with nine holes to play.

Snead himself said later on, "I didn't know I had a chance to win until the sixteenth hole this afternoon. In every championship round there is a point where you're either going forward or going back. Well, that happened during this round at the tenth hole. I got a three there with a nice putt and I just missed getting another birdie at the eleventh. After that I was on my way." Bulla, playing ahead of Snead, had scored a bogey 5 at the tenth hole, thus losing two strokes to Snead's eventual birdie 3.

Snead had heard the groans of the gallery surrounding Bulla at the short 4-par tenth and surmised that John was in difficulty but the scoreboard system used today was not in effect in 1946 so all Sam could do was continue to play "in the dark" on the back nine, play as well as he could and hope for the others to falter.

Sam proceeded to play the last nine holes in 35 strokes, a score which, coupled with his outgoing 40, gave him 75 and a total of 290. He continued to gain on Bulla with the wind now helping him considerably. Sam reached the green in two strokes and got a remarkable birdie 4 at the 14th against Bulla's par at that hole. The rest of the field had fallen down badly under the pressure of the desire to win and the increasingly stronger winds which were now switching more toward the northwest. When Snead made his par 5 at the wicked Road Hole, the seventeenth, he gained another stroke on John Bulla, who had had trouble for the third time in a row with the demanding short 5-par. Locke with a 76 did not pick up any ground on Snead.

He had some putting troubles, unusual for him. Rees ballooned to an 80 for 295. The great Henry Cotton, a marvelous wind player and experienced champion shot, made a miserable 79. Henry's first nine looked like a duffer's, showing five 5s and a 6 on his card. He did get a deuce at the 8th hole, however, to stagger in with a 40. Cotton was all through, Locke was finished, Rees had fallen far behind, and Bulla, the one who might have withstood Sam's last charge, lost his chance to do so with hurtful bogies on the tenth, another one on his nemesis hole, the 17th, and, sadly, a bad five at the home hole before the massed galleries.

Snead finally became aware that he was truly in the lead when he was playing the sixteenth hole. He came in this time in smashing fashion, shaped a beautiful low 3-iron onto the seventeenth green and two-putted for a birdie 4 which put him three strokes ahead of Bulla, who was then in the clubhouse, tied with Locke at 294 strokes. Sam needed a 4 at the eighteenth to win by four strokes. His drive was long, low and straight, almost to the front edge of the green. He played a Scottish run-up 4-iron through the Valley of Sin to a comfortable place twenty feet from the flagstick. Two putts later, Sam Snead had won the first "major championship" of his long career, "the happiest moment of his life" thus far.

Snead's cards on the last two rounds were:

Morning						
Out:	4 5 5	4 5 3	4 3 4	37	141	
In:	4 4 4	4 4 4	4 5 4	37	74	
Afternoon						
Out:	5 4 4	5 6 4	4 4 4	40		
In:	3 3 4	4 4 4	5 4 4	35	70	290

Bulla's cards were:

Morning						
Out:	3 4 5	5 4 4	4 3 4	36	143	
In:	4 3 4	4 4 4	5 4 4	36	72	
Afternoon						
Out:	4 5 4	4 6 5	4 3 4	39		
In:	5 3 4	4 5 4	4 6 5	40	79	294

THE BRITISH AMATEUR OF 1950

Frank Stranahan won his second British Amateur championship by a smashing 8 and 6 victory in the 36-hole final match over his countryman, Richard D. "Dick" Chapman. For Stranahan there was a measure of revenge in that he was able to conquer big Sam McCready, the champion of the previous year, in a preliminary match. McCready had knocked out Stranahan the year before in his way to the title. For Chapman, the loss was a great disappointment and he went into the Amateur record books as the first man to be runner-up twice without winning the coveted cup. Dick would recover, however, and beat Charlie Coe of the United States in the Championship the next year at Porthcawl.

There were thirty-two American amateur golfers in a tremendous field of 324. This entry was the largest ever and would not be surpassed in size until 1958, when the tournament would again return to St. Andrews. Among the contenders and favorites to win this championship were William P. "Willie" Turnesa, British Amateur Champion of 1947 and United States Amateur Champion of 1948, and Joe Carr, famed Irish golfer, who had not yet won this event but would do so in 1953, 1958 and 1960. The big smiling Irishman, Sam McCready was also well regarded by the odds makers. There were two sentimental entries in this field, also. In one of his last strong challenges for the crown, Cyril J.H. Tolley was appearing. Tolley had won the Amateur Championship in 1920, three years before Frank Stranahan was born, and here he was, thirty years later, still a great golfer and capable of reaching the semi-finals of this difficult tournament. Unfortunately, he would run out of steam and fall before young Frank, 4 and 3. The other was Francis Ouimet, United States Open champion of 1914, who was also playing in the event and won several matches before going down to eventual defeat.

The first rounds of the championship were played in poor weather. Most of the 4,000 people in the gallery followed Harry Lillis "Bing" Crosby, the American crooner and entertainer, who played respectably well, only to lose in his first match at the sixteenth green to James K. Wilson of St. Andrews. The crowds were delighted to see Bing and pleased to note his excellent golf game.

On the first day, William "Dynamite Bill" Goodloe, of Valdosta, Georgia, startled the gallery as he eagled the 374-yard first hole and finished four under par in defeating Sir John Craddock-Hartopp by a 7 and 5 margin. The strongest favorite to win, Frank Stranahan, used only 36 strokes in ten holes in winning his second match over his unfortunate victim, A.C. Gibson. Frank was straight and long off the tees, accurate with his approaches and deadly with his putting.

Sam McCready won easily, 5 and 4, over F.G. Dewar and Willie Turnesa advanced into the fourth round to meet William Campbell of the United States. Campbell would eventually win the United States Amateur Championship fourteen years later, in 1964 at Canterbury, Ohio. Campbell stopped Turnesa's chances of winning a second British Amateur championship by scoring a sensational eagle 3 on the "world's finest hole," the "Road Hole" seventeenth. Bill's second shot left him only three feet from the hole for the deciding putt. McCready, in the meanwhile, had two close squeaks winning by 2 and 1 over S.B. Williamson of Britain, and by only 1 up over Cecil Ewing, also of Britain.

Stranahan barely won over Bob Neill, veteran Scottish international player. Frank was three holes up at the tenth tee but started to play raggedly and lost holes until he was one down at the sixteenth. Frank was fortunate to win the seventeenth when Neill three-putted. The players went to the eighteenth all even and then Neill once more failed to hole a short putt on the monstrous eighteenth green and the match was over, Frank the winner by 1 up.

Turnesa was eliminated by Bill Campbell when Willie's drive went out of bounds on the 16th. Campbell hung on to win at the eighteenth, 2 up.

Dick Chapman was coming along steadily, won easily by a 6 and 5 margin over W.S. Whitelaw and then by 3 and 2 over E.S. Nugent-Head, both of Britain. Joe Carr downed Bill Campbell in an exciting extra-hole match, holing a 10-footer for a birdie three at the nineteenth hole. Campbell made a valiant try for his birdie there, too, and barely missed holing a twenty-foot putt that would have kept the battle alive.

In the round of sixteen, Chapman came close to losing to Jack Mitchley of Britain. If Mitchley had been able to sink a three-foot putt on the eighteenth hole, he would have been able to send the match into overtime. Unfortunately, the ball refused to drop and Chapman proceeded on the way to his final rendezvous with Stranahan.

John McHale of America fell before Chapman, 1 up in one semi-final match, while Stranahan easily defeated the tiring Cyril Tolley in their match. All in all, it was a remarkable showing for Tolley, going so far in the select field of this tournament thirty years after his first championship in 1920.

The golf of Stranahan and Chapman in the final rounds was undistinguished. The weather was cold, in the low 50s, and windy. A cruel rain set in about noon and did not let up until the players were three holes from the end, when the sun finally consented to appear.

Stranahan was 3 up at lunchtime and then won five of the next twelve holes to end the match on the 30th green, for the most lopsided margin in a final in sixteen years. Stranahan's scores were 40 and 38 for a 78 morning round against Chapman's 41 and 39 for 80. In the afternoon, Frank, consistently outdriving Dick by forty yards at a time, needed 38 strokes on the first nine while Dick required 42. Stranahan was 6 over par in winning,

Chapman 14 over par in losing.

Frank Stranahan thus won his second British Amateur championship. Three years later in the Open at Carnoustie Frank would register a remarkable total of 286 strokes, a score good enough to win seven of the previous eleven Open Championships. But, unfortunately for Frank, Mr. Ben Hogan, also in the 1953 Open field, would be four strokes better than Frank with his winning total of 282 and Frank would end in a tie for second in that tournament.

THE OPEN CHAMPIONSHIP OF 1955

Peter Thomson, Australia	71	68	70	72	281
John Fallon, England	73	67	73	70	283
Frank Jowle, England	70	71	69	74	284
A. D. "Bobby" Locke, South Africa	74	69	70	72	285
Antonio Cerda, Argentina	73	71	71	71	286
Ken Bousfield, England	71	75	70	70	286

Henry Cotton, left, and Peter Thomson. Cotton was Open Champion in 1934, 1937, and 1948. Thomson won in 1954, 1955, 1956, 1958 and 1965. Thomson's 1955 victory was accomplished at St. Andrews.

Henry Cotton, left, with Peter Thomson.

it for three straight years now but had had only moderate success. His low hooking drives, while tailored for the hard-baked Scottish links, were just not suited for the American fairways, which had grasses cut much longer than in Scotland. However, his international record was already sensational and, as we shall see, Peter not only won this Open Championship to put his name alongside the other double-winners of the Cup in years past, Braid in 1905 and 1906, Jones in 1926 and 1927, Locke in 1949 and 1950, but he would go on and win the Open Championship again in 1958 and once more in 1965. He would also finish second in the Open less than three times, besides. All in all, an incredible performance and one that may not be duplicated.

Thomson's 70 in the morning round (the tournament was still being finished in a grueling thirty-hole final day of play) put him into the undisputed lead at 209 strokes. Jowle at 210 on a third

round 69 was his closest threat. Harry Weetman on a 70 for 212 and Locke, also on a third round 70, were, at 212 and 213 respectively, within shouting distance if Peter slipped at all in his afternoon eighteen holes.

Peter Thomson had two bad holes in his final round, a 6 at the fifth and ominously a 7 at the fourteenth. In the meantime, John Fallon started out with a great 31 on the first nine, a score which picked up four strokes on Thomson as Peter turned the nine in 35. So going down the stretch the two players were in a momentary tie. But the pressure started to tell on Fallon and he staggered in with a ragged 39 for a 70 and a 283 total.

Peter Thomson's second nine showed

In: 4 3 3 4 7 3 4 5 4   37

and coupled with his first nine 35 gave him a 72 for 281 and his second Open Championship by two strokes over the field.

THE OPEN CHAMPIONSHIP
OF 1957

A. D. "Bobby" Locke, South Africa	69	72	68	70	279
Peter Thomson, Australia	73	69	70	70	282
Eric Brown, Scotland	67	72	73	71	283
Angel Miguel, Spain	72	72	69	72	285
David Thomas, Wales	72	74	70	70	286
Flory Van Donck, Belgium	68	72	74	72	286
Tom Halliburton, Scotland	72	73	68	73	286
*Richard Smith, Scotland	71	72	72	71	286
Anthony Cerda, Argentina	71	71	72	73	287
Max Faulkner, England	74	70	71	72	287
Henry Cotton, England	74	72	69	72	287

*Amateur

There were 290 entrants in this Open Championship, with much of the pre-tournament speculation centered on Arthur D'arcy "Bobby" Locke's chances to win his fourth Open title and make himself the first four-time Open Champion since the immortal James Braid accomplished the feat in 1909. Remember that it was here at St. Andrews in 1936 when "Bobby" missed that tiny but slippery putt

Arthur D'Arcy "Bobby" Locke, Open Champion of 1957.

on the eighteenth green to put himself out of the Amateur championship he was hoping, "expecting," to win. "Bobby" had almost obtained his revenge on the "Old Lady" in 1946 when he nearly caught Sam Snead for the Championship of that year but ended four strokes off the winning score in a tie with Johnny Bulla. Since then Locke had returned from Sandwich, England with the Open Cup, in 1949, again from Troon, Scotland, in 1950 and a third time from Royal Lytham and St. Anne's, England in 1952. Ominously enough, as far as this tournament and Bobby's chances of winning again were concerned, Peter Thomson was entered as well and came in on a three year winning streak in which he had won the prize at Royal Birkdale, England in 1954, at St. Andrews in 1955 and at Hoylake, England in 1956. This championship might see these two wonderful golfers, Locke and Thomson, go down to the wire in a tight finish. The crowds knew their fine records and were waiting impatiently to see them battle, hoping they might even be paired for a head-to-head match.

There was a very modest American contingent entered this year, a mere ten golfers, of whom only three were other than "unknowns:" Cary Middlecoff, Frank Stranahan and Gene Andrews. They did not distinguish themselves in this Open Championship. Middlecoff and Stranahan alone made it to the final day of play.

Cary Middlecoff, the American dentist-turned-professional golfer, had not only won the cherished Masters title in America in 1955, but he had also twice held the National Open Championship of the United States in 1949, when he won at Medinah, Illinois and in 1956, when he won at Rochester, New York. Cary was an especially straight, long hitter and possessed a delicate putting touch as well. This year Cary intended to add to his extensive trophy collection by taking the Open Championship away from St. Andrews. Then he would truly be called an "international champion of golf."

So Cary Middlecoff came to the qualifying rounds rather confident that he would at least "do well," if he did not win the prized trophy itself. Other than Middlecoff, there were ten American challengers in the 1957 event, the most prominent of whom was Frank Stranahan. Frank, as well as Cary Middlecoff, was considered a prime prospect to win the tournament, for hadn't he had one of the most important triumphs of his amateur career right here at hallowed St. Andrews in 1950 when he buried R. D. "Dick" Chapman in the British Amateur thirty-six hole final match by the monumental score of 8 and 6? Frank, an experienced international golfer, member of several Walker Cup teams, had

A match about to end on the 17th ho'e. Notice how the road to the right remains in play while the gallery waits politely behind the stone-wall fence.

come within a hairsbreadth of winning the Open Title twice, once at Hoylake, when he was runner-up to Fred Daly (Frank's pitch to the final green rimmed the cup or he would have tied) and again at Carnoustie in 1953 when Ben Hogan's great final round took the cup out of his grasp.

The qualifying rounds were again played over both the Old and the New Courses. When the firing was done the American contingent had been reduced to only four players, Middlecoff, Strana-han, Andrews and Lieutenant Frank D. Keck, a good amateur golfer, an Air Force officer, stationed in Germany, for a "golf vacation and some fun."

The handwriting started to appear on the wall. The qualifying leader, winner of another shiny medal in his illustrious career since the "boy won-der" days of 1936 was none other than Arthur D'arcy "Bobby" Locke with 137 strokes. Bobby had to share the preliminary honors with Bernard Hunt who also had 137. Locke was now a hardened com-petitor accustomed to winning and resisting the pressure of the final rounds. Bobby fully expected to win this Open Championship, which would give him an outstanding total of four championships and place his name where Bobby had intended to put it since his "prodigy" days in South Africa, alongside the "other" true golf immortals who had proven their ability by winning more than one important championship.

The first day of the championship was a "miser-able" one, cold, windy, rainy at times, gusty, and all in all, unpleasant. In spite of the weather and its added problems there were some fireworks out of golfers who always seemed to start off with a rush but seldom fulfilled their promises coming down those last nine holes of the seventy-two hole contest. At dusk of Wednesday, both Eric Brown and Lawrie Ayton had posted beautiful 67s, Brown on a 30-37 card and Ayton on a 34-33. Brown's 30 equaled the first nine record set in 1950 by Charles Ward. Furthermore, both scores of 67 equaled the course record at that time. Bruce Crampton of Aus-tralia, just starting his long and very successful pro-fessional career, was in with a 68 (33-35) and Mr. Locke was in a comfortable position just two strokes off the Brown-Ayton pace with a 69. That Bobby was in a crowd with Keith McDonald, Nor-man Sutton and Jimmy Hitchcock did not trouble him. He knew that he was on his way and that the others probably would never be heard from again. Nor were they.

Middlecoff, as usual, suffering from symptoms of hay fever in mid-summer, was greatly bothered by the dust being raised by the crowds following the golfers. The course had been dry until the morn-ing of the first day and the winds had been blowing the normal pollen and dust into Cary's watery nose and eyes. He hadn't slept well either and had risen at 4:00 A.M. to go out on the practice putting green in an attempt to "get the hang of these slick St. Andrews greens." Cary not only had hay fever, it seems, he had putting woes as well. The greens were to be mowed "short," and that means "short" at St. Andrews, and were not to be watered again during the rest of the tournament. So while Cary was practicing on moderately slow practice greens he was perturbed because in his mind he knew he had to prepare for much faster greens on the mor-row.

Middlecoff played a scrambling 72 on his first eighteen on nines of 35 and 37. He was taking more pills to stop his watering eyes and he was slightly in a daze from a sleeping pill "hangover." Cary really played good "scrambling" golf to score 72 under these circumstances.

Frank Stranahan stayed in contention through the first two rounds. Frank had a 74 on his first round and a 71 on his second and was six strokes away from Brown's lead at the half-way point. However, he was not really in serious contention as he finished with a 74 and 72, well off the pace of the leaders.

Anthony Cerda of Argentina was Middlecoff's playing partner in the first round. As usual, Cary played slow golf. He is noted for his deliberate style and for his ten to twenty "waggles" before he strikes an important shot. There were official pro-tests to the committee from the players who were behind Middlecoff and while the protests were dis-missed it was reported that he was given an unofficial request to "hurry it up tomorrow." Three hours and twenty-five minutes for the first round was much too slow at St. Andrews in the Open Championship. Cary nodded and went back to his hotel room on the Course and took another sleeping pill and another hay fever pill. Tomorrow would be another day.

Now a little bit about the wonderful first round scores of 67 by Ayton and Brown. Lawrie Ayton was a 240-pound forty-three year old native of the city of St. Andrews itself, part of a remarkable dynasty of great golfing Aytons. He had grown up there and then, having decided on golf as a career, found himself employment as a professional in Evanston, Illinois. He was back to show the home folks he could still play golf and with one error, a three-putt at the 4th hole, he did show them in this fashion:

```
Ayton's card
Out:   4 4 3  5 3 4  4 3 4    34
In:    3 2 4  4 5 4  3 4 4    33    67
```

Eric Brown, at thirty-two years of age, was a former locomotive fireman, a strong man and a powerful golfer. His card showed a remarkable seven 3s on the first nine, *nine* out of the first twelve holes in 3, and although he took a nasty 6 at the 13th when he got into the rough and then three-putted on top of that trouble, he managed to recover and score a sound final five holes for his 67.

Brown's card:

```
Out:   3 3 3  3 5 3  4 3 3    30
In:    4 3 3  6 5 4  5 4 3    37    67
```

Bruce Crampton also had an excellent beginning score on this card:

```
Out:   3 4 4  4 4 4  4 2 4    33
In:    4 2 4  4 5 4  4 4 4    35    68
```

The largest gallery, one thousand spectators, followed Middlecoff on the second day of play as the skies cleared, the sun blazed and mild cooling breezes took the place of the wicked winds of the day before. Cary still could not putt the St. Andrews greens. He said, later on in a press interview, "I have it in my mind that the greens are fast, they look fast and yet they are not fast. I just can't figure them out." Cary's second round was a respectable but scrambling score of 71, and when Frank Stranahan also reported a second round 71 (his first was a 74) the two major American contenders found themselves four and six shots behind the pace-setter at the half-way mark, Eric Brown, who was off to a spectacular start with his 67 and 72 for 139 strokes.

Lawrie Ayton, unfortunately, had a bad 76 on his second round and never again was in contention for the title.

Peter Thomson was in good position behind Brown, only three strokes away as Flory van Donck, veteran professional from Holland, moved up into contention with a marvelous 68 on top of his first round 72 for a two-day score of 140. Thus the scoreboard at the half-way mark read:

Eric Brown	67	72	139
Flory Van Donck	68	72	140
A. D. "Bobby" Locke	69	72	141
Peter Thomson	73	69	142
Bruce Crampton	73	68	141

Again the largest gallery followed Cary Middlecoff but Cary's golf was mediocre for a champion such as he. Cary failed to sink a long putt on his final round after starting his first nine with an excellent 34 to remain close to the leaders. Then he three-putted the thirteenth from 18 feet, missed a four-footer on No. 14, putted short at both No. 15 and No. 16, and sadly chipped short at the seventeenth. Middlecoff was "through" at that point and later on said that he was "bitterly disappointed" at his failure to emulate Ben Hogan's victory at Carnoustie in 1953 and at his inability to "read the greens" successfully. Cary finished at 289 in 14th place in the field. Bruce Crampton also finished badly after his great start, scored 78 and 79 on his last day's play and ended at 298, far down the list. Lawrie Ayton ended at 295 on final scores of 75 and 77.

In the meantime, "Bobby" Locke was making his move while Peter Thomson, very much aware of where the threat lay, was doing his best to keep up with Bobby's pace. Locke blistered the course on his morning round with a great 68. His first nine, alone, was enough to frighten off his competitors:

Here was Locke's morning card:

```
Out:   3 4 4  4 4 3  3 3 4    32
In:    3 3 4  5 5 4  4 4 4    36    68    209
```

Notice that "Bobby" successfully got past his former "jinx hole," the 14th, in par.

In the meantime, Peter Thomson was trying to keep up with Locke. His first round card was:

```
Out:   4 5 4  4 4 3  4 3 4    35
In:    4 3 4  4 5 3  4 4 4    35    70    212
```

There were two other threats that appeared in the third round, Angel Miguel of Spain shot a 69 and Tom Halliburton of England a 68, which brought each one to 213, or four strokes away from Locke's 209, but neither one could make any further advance in the afternoon round.

Bobby Locke finished his fourth round with a 70 for 279 and tied the low score for the Open Championship which he himself had set at Troon in 1952.

Locke began his final round with three 4s and then birdied the fourth and fifth holes with 3s. Thomson, in the meantime, was able to match Locke's first four holes, getting his 3 at No. 4 as well, but when Peter bogied the fifth hole and did not match Locke's birdie on No. 5 the race was practically over.

Both Locke and Thomson had 34 first nines but, with the exception of a birdie at No. 10, which narrowed Locke's margin to two strokes, they matched scores exactly until the eighteenth hole which Locke, finishing comfortably ahead was able to birdie on a beautifully stroked fifteen-footer. Locke tipped his little white hat, flashed a rare smile and the tremendous gallery gave him St. Andrews cheers. Even if one of their own boys hadn't been able to win the crown at least one of "our" boys had done so. Put Locke's name down in golf history alongside that of Jim Braid, now fellow golf immortal.

THE BRITISH AMATEUR OF 1958

Former British Amateur Champion Joseph B. Carr of Ireland won his second championship in five years when he defeated fellow Walker Cup member, twenty-eight year old Alan Thirlwell, 3 and 2 in the thirty-six hole final of the tournament. Carr had won his first crown in 1953, beating Harvie Ward of the United States in the finals at Hoylake, England. Carr defeated Michael Bonallack of

Joe Carr, Amateur Champion of 1958 at St. Andrews. Joe also won in 1953 at Hoylake and in 1960 at Portrush.

Joe Carr.

England in a semifinal match, 4 and 3. Bonallack went on in subsequent years to win the Championship four times: in 1961 at Turnberry, Scotland, in 1965 at Porthcawl, South Wales, at Troon, Scotland, in 1968 and at Hoylake, England, in 1969. In 1968 he would defeat Joe Carr in the finals for a measure of revenge for his loss in this tournament.

A cold rain and a sea mist shrouded the Old Course in the round of thirty-two on Tuesday, June 3, 1958. Nor did the weather improve much during the next few days.

Tim Holland of Long Island, New York made the best showing of a small American group that included Jimmy McHale of Philadelphia, Gene Andrews, former U.S. Public Links Champion of 1954, Frank Strafaci of Miami Beach, Florida, U.S. Public Links Champion of 1935, and Ed Meister of Cleveland, a U.S. Walker Cup team member.

Holland won by 4 and 2 over Stuart Wilson of Scotland as Andrews lost his match to South African Reginald Taylor, 2 and 1. McHale called the weather conditions the "worst he had ever seen" and retired to the sidelines. Frank Strafaci advanced with a 6 and 4 victory over D. H. Jamieson of Scotland, in spite of playing to the wrong flagstick at the 5th hole. He put his second shot close

to the hole and then discovered he had played to the wrong flag, that he had left himself a 100-foot putt to the 5th hole on the other side of the green. This was the only hole Frank lost in a 2 over par performance.

Tim Holland was four under par in his quarter-final match in defeating Stuart Murray of Scotland, but Holland strained his ankle in a deep bunker and a result played badly in his semi-final match against Alan Thirlwell, the British Walker Cup star and eventual finalist. Holland won the first three holes against Thirlwell but three-putted seven times subsequently to go down to defeat and put Thirlwell into the finals against Carr. The semi-final matches were played at thirty-six holes.

Joe Carr said he was disappointed in not having the chance to play Tim Holland, that he'd "like to have a go at that fellow who hits the ball as far as I do."

Carr's semifinal match against Michael Bonallack, who was then only 23 years old, was a thriller. Carr was 2 down at the ninth hole on his own 35 against Michael's 33 but Joe went to work and produced a methodical 36 second nine for a round of 71 while Bonallack was in with 41 and 74 to be 2 down at noon-time. In the afternoon Carr again was steady with 36 out and led 4 up at the 27th. Mike got the eleventh hole back, but when he lost the 13th it was all over for him. The next two holes were halved as Carr was able to protect his lead successfully.

The final, Carr against Thirlwell, was a dramatic match watched by less than a thousand spectators. The weather had moderated a bit but remained cold and generally unpleasant with lowering gray clouds painting a dreary scene.

Thirlwell started off strongly with a 3 on the 4th hole which won it for him, a 4 on the 6th, and a 4 on the 7th as Carr had some putting problems. Alan went 3 up at the 11th hole but then Carr made a comeback, holed a few putts on the way in, evened the match at No. 16 and birdied the home hole to be 1 up at the end of eighteen.

The morning round cards were:

Thirlwell	Out:	4 4 4 3 5 4 4 3 4	35
Carr	Out:	4 4 4 5 5 5 5 3 3	38
Thirlwell	In:	4 3 5 4 6 5 5 4 4	40	75
Carr	In:	4 4 4 4 6 4 4 4 3	37	75

Carr leads 1 up

Although Thirlwell battled hard in the after-

1958 World Amateur Team champion Bruce Devlin studies his putt on the 17th green from a vantage point in the Road Bunker. Dr. Frank Taylor is on the right side of the green. Courtesy U.S.G.A.

noon round he never quite caught up. Carr used the first five holes to build his lead to three up in this fashion:

Thirlwell	Out:	5 4 4 4 5
Carr	Out:	4 4 4 4 4

Then Alan birdied the sixth and took the seventh, a 4 to Joe's 5, and Carr's lead had shrunk to only one hole. The next three holes, the eighth, ninth and tenth, were halved in par and Joe won the eleventh with his par 3.

Then came one of the most sensational shots ever seen in British Amateur history. In a real battle with the younger player, Joe Carr, now 36 years old, had seen his lead build up and then slip away. He needed to win another hole badly as he came to the twelfth tee. The putting surface was 312 yards away, the wind now slightly helping his tee-shot as it blew in from the right quarter. The sun broke through and the green was clearly seen, like an emerald behind the bunkers on the left side of the fairway.

Joe Carr cracked a tremendous drive which, it appeared to the spectators and the players, might even carry far enough to reach the green slightly downhill from the tee. The direction was perfect; the ball had missed the bunker, which is slightly left of the line Joe took to the green, a courageous shot because it flirted with trouble in the whins and heather to the right side of the putting surface.

Thirlwell drove well, too, but his ball ended definitely short of the green. Carr's ball could not

be seen until the players and gallery came considerably closer to the green. Then, there it was, well on the green and level with the flagstick but a monstrous, estimated eighty-foot distance, from the hole.

Alan Thirlwell was seen to gasp audibly when he saw Carr's ball on the green. Alan approached the pin with a satisfactory pitch which would give him an opportunity for a tieing 3 if Joe made his birdie, as it certainly appeared he would do.

Carr's ball had to be putted up the slope of a good-sized mound and be struck with great accuracy in order to cause the ball to get close to the hole, a very difficult and challenging situation, especially with the pressure increasing in the final holes of the match. Thirlwell was not out of the hole yet. Carr might easily three-putt for a 4, Thirlwell could hole his eminently makable birdie and the match would be square.

Carr struck the putt. It climbed the mound successfully, made the properly calculated turn toward the cup, rolled straight on and on and fell dead in the cup at the last second for an incredible eagle 2. The crowd roared its approval. Thirlwell shrugged his shoulders as if to say, "What can I do after a shot like that?"

The last four holes were halved in pars as Joe Carr, once more in the lead by three holes, "ran out the string" for Alan Thirlwell at the sixteenth hole, victor by 3 and 2 and for the second time British Amateur Champion.

The cards of the last eighteen holes were:

Thirlwell	Out:	5 4 4 4 5 3 4 3 4 36
Carr	Out:	4 4 4 4 4 4 5 3 4 36

Carr leads 1 up

Thirlwell	In:	4 4 4 4 5 4 4
Carr	In:	4 3 2 4 5 4 4

Carrs wins 3 and 2

THE WORLD AMATEUR TEAM CHAMPIONSHIP OF 1958 FOR THE EISENHOWER TROPHY

The first World Amateur Team Championship Tournament was held at St. Andrews in October of 1958. A handsome new trophy had been created by the famous designer, Mr. Gordon Lang of Spaulding and Company of Chicago, Illinois and executed in silver by silversmith craftsmen in England. It was to be called "The Eisenhower Trophy" in honor of President Dwight D. Eisenhower of the United States, an avid golfer himself

*U.S. World Amateur Team, 1958. Left to right: Billy
Joe Patton, Dr. Frank Taylor, Bill Hyndman, Charlie
Coe, and Bobby Jones, the non-playing captain.*

and beloved soldier to millions of Europeans.

The invitations to compete were sent to nations all over the world. Twenty-six were accepted. Teams of four members, all amateur golfers, would enter the contest for what would come to be known as the "Eisenhower Cup." The format of the play called for each member of the various teams to play four successive eighteen-hole rounds over the Old Course. The best three scores of each four would be added together to give a daily total and eventually a four-day final total. This meant that the score of one man might be used one day and not the next.

Bobby Jones (non-playing Captain) and the other members of the American team arrived by plane at Prestwick airport in Scotland and were chauffeur-driven to St. Andrews in a convoy of cars loaded with the players' clubs and baggage. Accompanying Jones were Charles Coe, 1949 U.S. National Amateur Champion as well as Champion in 1958 (Coe had won his latest title only two weeks previously at Olympic Country Club, San Francisco, California beating Tommy Aaron 5 and 4 in the 36 hole final match). Coe had had a distinguished career so far in Amateur golf, having been selected for the Walker Cup Teams of 1949, 1951 and 1953. In two years he would miss winning the Masters of 1961 by only one stroke, the year that Arnold Palmer blew up on the 18th hole to lose to Gary Player.

The second and third members of the team were Dr. Frank M. Taylor, runnerup for the U.S. Ama-

The Australian World Amateur Team, winners of the 1958 World Amateur Team Championship. Left to right: Peter Toogood, Bruce Devlin, Doug Bachli, and captain Robert Stevens.

teur Championship of 1957, also a Walker Cup Team member (1957), and William Hyndman III, another Walker Cup Team member (1957) and runnerup for the 1955 U.S. Amateur Championship. The fourth member of the United States Team was colorful William Joseph Patton, more familiarly known as "Billy Joe," the other Amateur golfer who had "almost" won the U.S. Masters Championship of 1954 when Snead and Hagen managed to slip by him by only one stroke. Patton was another experienced Walker Cup player having been named to the team in 1955 and 1957.

There was a morning mist. After all, it was October and a little late to expect really good weather at St. Andrews. But the worst had not yet

been seen. By mid-morning the mist had become slashing rain as raging northeast winds raided the field of golfers with gusts up to 50 miles per hour. Fred Tupper, the golf reporter and a most discerning observer of the scene, said, "For those out early or late, golf was possible. In between, it was chaos."

The early individual leader was Reid Jack, a former Commando, the only Scot in the field. Jack teed off early and scored sixteen pars, one bogey, and one birdie for a wonderful 72, considering the adverse weather. Jack had ten straight pars, three-putted the 11th which was "like glass" and then pitched to within two feet of the cup for a birdie 3 at the 12th hole. He then came in in straight par. Jack had won the British Amateur Championship

127

the year before at Formby, England, and was the "hope" of the large Scottish galleries at this tournament.

Only fourteen out of the eighty players "broke the 80 barrier." Raul Borges of Argentina took an 11 at the 5th hole and reported a total of 99 strokes for the round. Fortunately, the scores of the other three Argentinians were better and were used in their team total.

Dr. Frank Taylor's score of 81, not used in the U.S. total, included two penalty strokes suffered when the wind blew the ball back against his putter. Charlie Coe, from Oklahoma, said that the quartering wind behind him "reminded him of the "Dust Bowl" at home. He said, "I'm used to it." Coe had one of the better scores of the day, a 74.

So, at the end of the first day the leading team scores were:

British Isles:
United States:

British Isles:

Joseph Carr	79	
Reid Jack	72	
Guy Wolstenholme	76	
Arthur Perowne	—	(81)
Total	227	

United States:

Charles Coe	74	
William Hyndman	79	
William J. Patton	80	
Dr. Frank Taylor	—	(81)
Total	233	

Since Australia made a magnificent showing in this tournament it is interesting to note that the Australians at this time were seventeen strokes off the lead on these scores:

Doug Bachli	81	
Bruce Devlin	81	
Robert Stevens	82	
Peter Toogood	—	(84)
Total	244	

Reid Jack continued his race for individual scoring honors, had an unusual round in which he was seven over par through the twelfth hole but recovered to score three birdies on the way in, one of which was accomplished before a huge gallery with a 24-foot putt at the home hole. His score was 77 and put him in second place in the individual scoring with 149. His team member, Guy Wolstenholme, played beautifully from tee to green but three-putted seven times for a 79.

Irishman Joe Carr, who had won the British

Roger Wethered in a friendly match with General Dwight Eisenhower (1947).

Amateur Championship at St. Andrews earlier in the year, had a "woeful" 84 including a 7 at "Hell Bunker." He was quoted as saying: "There'll be no Irish jigs danced by me tonight."

On the third day, the Australian team made another move toward the lead. From seventeen strokes behind on opening day to nine behind at the end of the second day, the Australians shot the best daily aggregate (221) to move into a tie for third place with the British Isles at a total of 691. New Zealand now held a mere three stroke lead at 687 over the United States's 690. Peter Toogood's 71 on the third day was the best score recorded in the first three days of the tournament. Devlin had 74 and Bob Stevens had a 76, which completed the trio of Australian scores for their 221 total.

In the meanwhile, the United States team was also making a run for the top position. From six strokes behind, the margin had closed to only three. Bill Hyndman, who had not had a birdie in two days, scored a startling eagle on the third hole of the third day. A tremendous drive on the "Cartgate hole" left him only a wedge-distance away from the flag. His second shot sat down on the green, turned over once and dropped into the cup for a 2. Bill was even par at the seventeenth tee but indecision

Putting on the 18th green of the Old Course. The Royal and Ancient clubhouse and the first tee can be seen in the background.

A view of Swilken Burn and the old stone bridge. The Old Course Hotel is in the background.

The scene at the 10th hole as it was dedicated to Bobby Jones.

on his second shot, a change of mind from a 7-iron to a 6-iron, cost him two strokes. Bill took a 6 on the hole when he overplayed it. However, he dropped a ten-foot birdie putt on the last hole and marked down a 73 for the day.

Peter Toogood's round of 71 on the third day was said to have been a "classic one." He made only one mistake, a run-up shot at the 11th hole that fell short of the hole. Peter holed putts of 35 feet for a 4 on the 5th hole, 10 feet for a 3 at the 7th and 15 feet for a 3 at the 12th hole.

Thus, at the end of the third day, the battle for the championship narrowed down to these four teams:

New Zealand:					
Robert J. Charles	74	74	76	224	
J. D. Durry	81	(78)	77	236	
S. G. Jones	81	75	(80)	236	
E. J. MacDougall	(83)	77	72	237	
Total	236	226	225		687
United States:					
Charles R. Coe	74	77	76	227	
William Hyndman	79	77	73	229	
William Patton	80	78	76	234	
Dr. Frank Taylor	(81)	(79)	(76)	236	
Total	223	232	225		690
Australia:					
Doug Bachli	81	(77)	78	236	
Robert Stevens	82	77	76	235	
Bruce Devlin	81	76	74	228	
Peter Toogood	(84)	76	71	231	
Total	244	226	221		691
British Isles:					
Joseph B. Carr	79	(84)	78	241	
Reid Jack	72	77	74	223	
Arthur Perowne	(81)	78	(79)	238	
Guy Wolstenholme	76	79	78	233	
Total	227	234	230		691

The fourth day of play brought a hint of good weather at last. After an overnight downpour which left pockets of water on the course, the sun finally broke through at noon and bathed the scene in brightness for the rest of the day. There was also some very dramatic golf to be seen by the tremendous galleries. The partisan Scots, of course, were pulling hard for their own Reid Jack to win individual honors and hoped that he could bring the British Isles team along with him to victory. In his excellent third round 74, Jack had not missed a putt under eight feet in length, had one-putted six times. Furthermore, Joe Carr was overdue for a good round and, as a matter of fact, did produce it.

On the last day, the Australian team posted its final score first. It was a good one. Although Peter Toogood had taken a horrible four putts on the 17th hole, three of them from within a foot of the hole, the last a stab from three inches that missed,

the scores were in for Australia as Devlin, 73, Stevens 75, and either Toogood or Bachli who had 79s a piece for a total of 918 strokes and the early lead. The British Isles team had fallen short by one stroke and were on the scoreboard at 919 as Carr had a sound 76, Arthur Perowne a 75 and E. J. MacDougall a 77 for a 288 daily score but unfortunately one stroke from the top.

The word concerning the Australian finish at 918 and the British finish at 919 was sent out on the course where the Americans had yet to play the last few holes. Apparently, the chance to catch the Australians was all up to Bill Hyndman. All the other American players were on their way to scores in the high 70s and, in fact, did come in with two 78s (Coe and Taylor) while Patton scored a 79. Hyndman was playing brilliantly. Later, he said, "This was the best round of golf I ever played."

Bill was heading for a low 70s score, which conceivably might win for the United States or, if it didn't win, might at least bring about a tie.

At the sixteenth tee, Hyndman knew that he must birdie all three holes to tie the Australian score. On the 351-yard 16th hole Hyndman drove so far that he needed only a "half" 8-iron to the pin. He opened the face of his club and plunked the ball down six feet away from the hole. But, Bill's putt spun out of the cup and now he needed an eagle and a birdie to win for the team. An eagle on the seventeenth at St. Andrews? Never in a million years under those circumstances. The treacherous crowd surged to the sides of the Road Hole to watch the demise of the United States team.

But Hyndman was equal to the task. His drive was a long one, 275 yards right in the middle of the fairway. This time his club selection was correct and a 6-iron put the ball only eight feet from the cup. The crowd went wild. Could Hyndman do it after all? His putt was dead in the center of the cup and he had the eagle 3 on the seventeenth. One more birdie, at eighteen, would win it all for the United States. The sun had sunk now behind the row of hotels and clubs to the west of the eighteenth hole. A wild crowd hurtled down the sides of the fairway in the gloom. Bill's drive was 260 yards off the tee and slightly left of the center of the fairway. Only the white flag and shadowy outline of the green were visible to him.

His pitch was a courageous one to within twenty feet of the cup but his putt went a foot wide and when it failed to drop it meant that the United States and Australia had tied at 918 strokes. He had made a valiant try for the victory only to fail by inches. The crowd roared its applause in tribute to a remarkable golf score of 72 strokes under that incredible pressure.

So, here were the four day total scores of the Australian and United States Teams which tied and the British Isles team which came so close to tying as well:

United States:

Charles Coe	77	77	76	78	305	233
William Hyndman	79	77	73	72	301	232
William Patton	80	78	76	(79)	313	225
Dr. Frank Taylor	(81)	(79)	(76)	78	314	228
				Total		918

Australia:

Doug Bachli	81	77	(78)	79	315	244
Peter Toogood	(84)	76	71	(79)	310	236
Bruce Devlin	81	73	74	73	301	221
Robert Stevens	82	(77)	76	75	310	227
				Total		918

British Isles:

Joseph B. Carr	79	(84)	78	76	317	227
Reid Jack	72	77	74	(78)	301	234
Arthur Perowne	(81)	78	(79)	75	313	230
Guy Wolstenholme	76	79	78	77	310	228
				Total		919

The New Zealand team finished fourth with a score of 234 as MacDougall scored a 75 but Bob Charles fell off to an 81 and S. G. Jones to a 78.

Since there was no organized sport in Scotland on a Sunday, the play-off between the Australian and United States teams was arranged to take place on Monday.

Australia won the play-off by two strokes over the United States with a score of 224 to 226. The margin was closer than the two stroke difference might indicate. The Australians started off brilliantly with 35, 35 and 36 on the first nine to be two under par going out. The Americans, on the other hand, started off badly as Hyndman took 6 at the first hole while Taylor and Patton took 5s. So, the "Aussies" were four strokes to the good immediately.

At the 14th, Bob Stevens had an unusual stroke of luck himself. He scuffed a 7-iron shot, rifled it apparently well on its way into the deep heathery rough beyond the green. Suddenly the ball was seen to hit the top of the flagstick and then drop down right into the hole for an incredible birdie 4.

For a while it appeared as if Charlie Coe might help in catching the front-running Australians. Coe was out in 38, one stroke down to Doug Bachli. But Coe came back with 3s at No. 10 and No. 11 and straight 4s down to the 17th. But there, sadly, an erring drive into the rough cost Coe a precious stroke as he scored a 5 in a round of 73 which was the best score of the day for the United States.

Here are the cards of the play-off:

Toogood	Out:	4 5 4	6 5 4	4 3 4	39	
Hyndman		6 5 4	5 5 4	5 3 3	40	
Toogood	In:	4 3 4	4 5 4	4 4 4	36	75
Hyndman		4 3 5	4 6 4	4 4 4	38	78
Devlin	Out:	4 4 4	4 6 4	4 3 4	37	
Taylor		5 4 5	5 5 4	4 3 4	39	
Devlin	In:	4 4 4	4 4 4	4 4 3	35	72
Taylor		3 4 4	4 6 4	4 4 4	37	76
Stevens	Out:	4 4 5	5 6 4	4 4 4	40	
Patton		5 3 4	5 5 4	5 4 3	38	
Stevens	In:	3 3 4	4 5 4	4 5 3	35	75
Patton		4 4 4	4 5 4	4 4 4	37	75
Coe	Out:	4 5 4	4 5 4	5 3 4	38	
Bachli		4 3 4	4 5 5	5 3 4	37	
Coe	In:	3 3 4	4 4 4	4 5 4	35	73
Bachli		4 3 5	5 6 4	5 4 5	41	79

The winning team scores were:

Australia:

Bruce Devlin	72
Peter Toogood	75
Robert Stevens	75
	222

United States:

Charles Coe	73
William J. Patton	75
Dr. Frank Taylor	76
	224

THE OPEN CHAMPIONSHIP
OF 1960

Kel Nagle, Australia	69	67	71	71	278
Arnold Palmer, United States	70	71	70	68	279
Roberto DeVicenzo, Mexico	67	67	75	73	282
Harold Henning, South Africa	72	72	69	69	282
Bernard Hunt, England	72	73	71	66	282
Guy Wolstenholme, England	74	70	71	68	283
Gary Player, South Africa	72	71	72	69	284
*Joe Carr, Ireland	72	73	67	73	285
Peter Thomson, Australia	72	69	75	70	286
Eric Brown, Scotland	75	68	72	71	286
*Major David Blair, Scotland	70	73	71	72	286
Syd Scott, England	73	71	67	75	286
Dai Rees, Wales	73	71	73	69	286
		*Amateur			

Kelvin D. G. "Kel" Nagle, the imperturbable and steady Australian golfer, fought off a "patented Arnold Palmer charge" on the last eighteen holes of the 1960 Open Champion to win by one stroke over Palmer, 278 to 279. Nagle's score was a new record for the championship at St. Andrews, breaking Bobby Locke's record total of 279 set only three years before in 1957.

The qualifying rounds were highlighted by some remarkable golf from former Open Champion, Gene Sarazen. Sarazen, fifty-eight years old, scored a 69 and a 72 on the two St. Andrews courses to take the qualifying medal and show the world that he was still capable of great golf.

Roberto de Vicenzo, the genial and suave Argen-

Kel Nagle, Open Champion of 1960.

Peter Thomson, five-time Open Champion, driving from the 10th tee (1960).

Arnold Palmer.

The monstrous double green, the 5th and 14th, where the dramatic confrontations between Tony Lema and Jack Nicklaus occurred during the "double-round" last day of the 1964 Open Championship.

The cascade of water down the steps in front of the Royal and Ancient clubhouse in 1960 on the third day of play.

"Lake Valley of Sin" during the third round of the 1960 Open Championship.

The "Valley of Sin" at the 18th green became a lake during the third round of the 1960 Open.

tinian, representing Mexico in this event, took the first day lead and some of the attention away from Arnold Palmer, the great American National Open and Masters Champion.

The year 1958 saw the beginning of the "Era of Arnold Palmer." Not since the days of the flamboyant Walter Hagen had such a charming personality exploded on the golf scene with as much attention and commotion as did Arnold Palmer once he turned professional in 1954, after having won the U.S. Amateur Championship of that year. Blessed with a burly physique and the arms of a blacksmith, Arnold rifled his straight, long drives and equally long accurate irons right at the hole with a daring and audacity that caused the galleries to take him immediately to their hearts. Not ashamed of showing emotion, Arnold would wince in pain as a putt refused to drop, smile broadly when an especially dangerous shot came off successfully, hitch his trousers up and stride forward with a determined face that said to the world, "No one can stop Arnold Palmer when he's playing golf like this!" And very frequently, during the "Palmer Era," no one could stop him. Here, at St. Andrews, as we shall see, he was stopped under pressure of the marvelous golf of Kel Nagle and by the wicked seventeenth "Road Hole," which Palmer played in 19 strokes while Nagle was able to conquer the hole in 14.

Palmer was on a "hot streak" when he arrived at St. Andrews for this Open. He had just seized the U.S. Open Championship at Cherry Hills Country Club in Englewood, California, on an incredible final round of 65 strokes which projected him out of the "pack" into a two stroke victory over such notable golfers as Jack Nicklaus, Ben Hogan, Julius Boros and the third-round leader of the tournament at the time, Mike Souchak, who rather thought his seven stroke lead over Palmer would be more than sufficient to enable him to win.

While Palmer took the attention of the huge galleries, De Vicenzo was making the score. Roberto, a long accurate driver in his own right, was on his game. Although he was bundled up in a heavy crew-necked sweater and short-visored wool cap in an attempt to mitigate the bone-chilling crosswinds, his swing remained fluid, his putting stroke delicate and accurate. Putting with his customary aluminum mallet-headed club on slick greens which the experts say require a blade putter, Roberto went out in 32 strokes on the first nine, birdying three holes in a row, the third, fourth and fifth, the last one on a two-putt from thirty feet after reaching the 5 par hole in two strokes. On the second nine Roberto made a 3 at the twelfth when he almost

drove the 360-yard green with the wind behind him and got past the Hell Hole with a great 4, slipped at the fifteenth to a bogie 5 but was able to make 4 on the seventeenth, once more helped by a long drive with the wind.

The cards of Palmer and De Vicenzo for the first day were:

De Vicenzo

Out:	4 4 3 3 4 4 3 3 4	32	
In:	4 3 3 4 4 5 4 4 4	35	67

Palmer

Out:	3 4 3 5 5 4 4 3 4	35	
In:	4 3 3 5 4 3 4 5 4	35	70

In the meantime, while attention was focused primarily on Palmer, the rest of the field, in spite of the miserable biting cold, was scoring extremely well. At the end of the day there were no less than nine golfers with scores of 72 or less in close pursuit of De Vicenzo. Here is how the scoreboard looked:

De Vicenzo	32	35	67
Fidel De Luca	38	31	69
Kel Nagle	38	31	69
Arnold Palmer	35	35	70
Ken Bousfield	33	37	70
Peter Shanks	36	34	70
*Major David Blair	35	35	70
Gary Player	36	36	72
Peter Thomson	36	36	72
*Joe Carr	35	37	72
*Amateur			

Arnold Palmer missed only two greens in regulation figures on his first round. He birdied the first hole with a short putt and dropped a 25-footer at the third hole. Then he went into a streak of "almost holing birdies" when his putts hit the cup at the fourth, sixth, seventh and eighth holes. Arnold showed his great driving strength by putting his ball on the 316-yard twelfth hole only ten feet from the flagstick. But another rimmed putt resulted and he had to settle for a birdie 3. He got into the heather at the thirteenth and lost a shot to par but immediately recovered with birdies at the fourteenth and fifteenth, the latter on a 20-foot curling putt that caused his gallery to explode with great cheers of encouragement. Arnold three-putted the seventeenth hole, as we shall see, for the first of three successive times. He drove so far that he needed only a 6-iron to the green 466 yards from the tee.

On the second day De Vicenzo kept up his fine golf and brought in his second straight 67. He held the lead for the second day in a row on his total of 134. Meanwhile Kel Nagle was starting to make his move. Kel also reported a great 67 and stayed in the same position relative to DeVicenzo, two strokes off the pace of the first day. Palmer fell behind even further on his second round 71 and was seven strokes behind De Vicenzo, five behind Nagle going into the hectic thirty-six hole final rounds of the tournament.

There were other good scores on the second day, too. One came from Peter Thomson of Australia, four-time winner of the championship, who showed strength with a 69 to go into a tie with Palmer at 141, seven strokes behind the leader. The other belonged to Sebastian Miguel of Spain, who had a beautiful 68 in spite of lack of attention from the galleries, who concentrated their attention on their favorites, Palmer, their new favorite De Vicenzo and the always surprising Kel Nagle.

The second day of play was warm and windless. Palmer played well from tee to green but once more was unable to get the ball into the hole. Arnold had only one bogie on his card when his tee-shot caught a bunker at the 11th and he exploded poorly to about 12 feet from the hole. He missed the putt. His driving was flawless. He hit seventeen greens in regulation figures or less. Four of his putts lipped the cup and two others stopped "dead center," one revolution short of holing. Palmer three-putted the 567 yard 5th hole from 60 feet after leaving himself a 4-footer for the birdie. Again, he was done in by the Road Hole, reaching the green with another 6-iron and then taking three putts to get down.

Here are the cards of Roberto de Vicenzo and Kel Nagle for the second round of play:

De Vicenzo

Out:	4 4 4 4 4 3 4 3 4	34	
In:	4 3 4 4 4 4 3 4 3	33	67-67-134

Nagle

Out:	3 4 4 4 5 3 4 2 4	33	
In:	4 3 3 4 6 4 3 4 3	34	67-69 136

Finally, conceding to the demands of the television audience, the tournament committee had at last done away with the strenuous "double-round" last day. The four rounds would be conducted over a four-day period this year.

On the third day, Arnold Palmer appeared to be starting his customary tactic of closing in on the leaders. He improved his position by three strokes when he carded a 70 for a 54-hole total of 211. At that point he went into a tie with Syd Scott of England, who shot a "career round," a 67, only to fade away with a final 75 on the next day.

De Vicenzo started to show signs of the pressure and slipped to a 75 for a 209 total, still two strokes ahead of Palmer's 211 but ominously two strokes behind Nagle, who had really moved into the lead with a steady 71 for a 207 total. Others down the line were Joe Carr, whose excellent 67 put him at 212, Gary Player at 215, and Peter Thomson with a bad 75 after his 72-69 start for 216. The margin was too much for either Player or Thomson to catch the leaders. Player dropped from the top ten entirely while Thomson's good last round of 70 did not help him enough to make up the difference on Nagle's 71 or Palmer's remarkable closing round of 68.

Palmer's third round started off in a typical Palmer "rush," with Arnie sinking birdie putts of 8 feet and 6 feet at the second and fifth holes. He picked up two more strokes on par with a 12-foot birdie at the thirteenth and safely got past the dreaded fourteenth with another great display of golf skill, a delicate chip on his third shot to 10 feet from the hole, with the result another birdie on his card.

Palmer had many distractions during this third round as, no doubt, did all the leading golfers, but it did seem that Fate was working against Arnold in spite of his best efforts to play well and score well. Jet planes from nearby Leuchars Air Base screamed overhead during his first nine holes. At the fifteenth hole he had to step away from his putt after addressing it when the steam locomotive puffed and tooted alongside the putting surface. Then, to cap it all, a bee attacked him in furious fashion at the sixteenth hole. Arnold took all the troubles with his customary equanimity but there is no doubt his concentration was upset, especially by the bee episode because he came in with bad 5s at the seventeenth and eighteenth to rob himself of a 68 that certainly would have been on his card had he gotten past No. 17 in what should have been for him a "normal" 4.

Once again, his caddie, the famous "Tip" Anderson, suggested a 6-iron to the green after another long Palmer drive to the identical place in the fairway he had reached on the first and second days. The wind was not as helpful on the third round as it had been the previous two days. Arnold's shot fell short of the green, close to the putting surface but in the grassy dip in front of the green. He putted the ball up the slope and saw it come to rest 6 feet away from the hole. For the third time in a row Arnold took 5 on this treacherous Road Hole that should normally, for him, have been returning birdie 4s or even an occasional eagle 3. Kel Nagle, in the meantime, was playing this hole well, had already birdied it once, had two other pars and, as we shall see, was able to birdie it on the last day for a most critical gain of one stroke on Palmer.

A heavy rain swept the Old Course from late evening of the third day until late in the morning of the fourth. Play was postponed for the day. The course was absolutely flooded. Fortunately, the rains ceased and the winds helped to dry the links into playable conditions so that the golfers might continue on the fifth day.

On the last day the final battle was strictly between Nagle and Palmer. There were other fireworks, however, when Bernard Hunt, British Ryder Cup star, blazed in with a course record-tying 68. But Hunt was obviously unable to make up the full nine strokes he needed to catch Nagle and settled for a respectable finish, a tie for third place at 282 with Robert de Vicenzo, whose final 73 was outscored by both Nagle and Palmer with their rounds of 71 and 68. Harold Henning, of South Africa, on a good finishing 69, also moved into a three-way tie for third place.

Palmer was playing directly in front of Nagle. The scoreboards were keeping both players aware of each other's progress. They were both out in 34 strokes apiece on the first nine. Remember that Palmer started four strokes behind Nagle. When Palmer picked up two immediate birdies on the first and second holes, the gap narrowed to two strokes. Nagle matched Palmer's pars on the third, fourth, fifth and sixth holes and then got two birdies in a row himself with a 3 at the seventh and a fifteen-foot putt for a deuce at the often troublesome eighth hole. Nagle managed to save his par at the sixth, incidentally, in spectacular fashion. The hole was played at 405 yards and Nagle's second shot was on the green but a long, difficult 60 feet from the hole. His first putt was struck much too strongly and Nagle found himself faced with a return putt of 8 feet. Two strokes of his lead had already slipped away; would another one go here? Kel calmly surveyed the situation. At least his outward appearance was a calm one, it was said, but he must have been in an anxious state of mind under that placid face. He made the putt and undoubtedly breathed a great sigh of relief at keeping the two-stroke margin over Arnie.

The back nine was once again agonizing for Arnold. The "charge" was there, the great swing under pressure was getting the ball close to the hole for those required birdies, but the ball just wouldn't go in the hole. At the tenth hole, for instance, Arnold's short wedge shot, after a tremendous drive, was within 5 feet of that birdie 3. He missed the putt once more for a par 4, but no ground was gained on Nagle, who followed right after Arnold finished the hole with his "normal" par 4. Palmer was still four strokes behind Nagle. The crowds around the 3-par eleventh hole witnessed Palmer's 4-iron shot, perfectly struck, as it had to be, into the wind, saw it bounce once and come to rest only ten feet from the hole. Surely, here would be another birdie. The putt was close but the score was another par, not the 2 he needed so badly. For Nagle, steady pars, 4, 3, 4 on the tenth, eleventh and twelfth. If Kel could help it he would not give up ground to Palmer by his own mistakes. He would force Palmer to win it by his own better play.

Then Palmer got his 3 at the thirteenth after a great drive, an excellent wedge shot, and a putt that finally stayed in the hole. The margin was down to three strokes when Nagle followed Palmer at No. 12 and made par there, not the matching birdie. Both players parred the 14th and then Nagle, showing signs of cracking, took a bogey on the fifteenth. There was nearly a swing of two strokes here but Palmer could not sink a makable putt there and thus had narrowed the margin between Nagle and himself to two strokes.

Both players made 4s at the sixteenth, with Palmer in birdie range again but unable to get the ball in the hole.

"Tip" Anderson, the famous caddie who always "carries" for Arnie when he plays in the Open Championships, the Ryder Cup event or Piccadilly tournament in Great Britain, tells about Arnold's mental block on the seventeenth hole at this moment in the fourth round. Remember that Arnie had three-putted it three times in a row and here he was only two strokes down to Kel Nagle with this hole, a killing one for Palmer, yet to be played in par or, if at all possible, in a birdie so as to put unbearable pressure on Nagle behind him.

Tip tells us that three times in a row Arnold had driven well on the seventeenth and then asked Tip what club he would suggest to get the ball home on the slanted, plateaued green. Three times he had advised Arnold to take his 6-iron and each time Arnie successfully reached the green, or at least putting position, as he did on the third day.

Tip said, "You know it's a 6-iron again."

Arnold shook his head and said, "Give me my 5-iron."

Tip told him, "If you take your 5-iron, you'll be over in the road."

Arnold insisted, "Give me my 5-iron."

Sure enough, when Arnold made the shot the ball went "through the green" over the back of the putting surface down the slope and came to rest in long grass at the edge of the road. Arnold

The two famous "career" caddies, "Tip" Anderson, senior and "Tip," junior. "Tip," senior is now dead, but "Tip," junior has carried for Arnold Palmer in Scotland, Ireland, and England for years.

elected to putt the ball. He made a sensational recovery under the circumstances, ran the ball through the tall grass to within a couple of feet of the hole. Much pleased with the result of the shot, Arnold sank the putt for the birdie 4. Then, with a broad smile such as Arnie alone can muster in such a situation jokingly he scolded Tip by saying, "See there, Tip, what you've been doing? Giving me the wrong club all week." It is interesting to consider the fact that at this critical juncture of the tournament, with one hole yet to play and under great stress to produce sub-par performance, Arnold could relax in such a delightful fashion and tease "Tip" Anderson about his club advice. So, to the eighteenth tee.

Palmer had again narrowed Nagle's lead to two strokes and would force Nagle to birdie the seventeenth in order to hold his edge. Now Arnold was

really "charged up." Perhaps he could do it once more, win it with a birdie at the last hole which might cause Nagle to "choke" at seventeen and eighteen.

Palmer crushed a 300-yard drive right down the middle of the eighteenth fairway. Nagle was now nearing the seventeenth green. He, too, had put his second shot near the green, but it was a long way from th flag-stick. Nagle's approach left him 10 feet away from his urgently needed 4 to match Palmer's 4 there.

At that moment there came a tremendous roar from the vicinity of the eighteenth green. Palmer's second shot at No. 18 had come to a stop only 3 feet from the hole. Palmer—Birdie 3.

Another great noise from the eighteenth reached Nagle just as he was surveying his tough 10-footer at the seventeenth. Kel says he thought to himself,

"I must get this birdie or a birdie at the last hole." Kel sank the putt, kept his lead on Palmer. Now, with Palmer's 3 at the eighteenth Nagle needed a par to win the title outright, a bogie to tie.

Nagle's drive at the eighteenth was not as long as Palmer's had been but it was satisfactory, just beyond "Granny Clark's Wynd," the road which crosses the fairway from left to right about 280 yards from the tee. Nagle then played a great shot to the flagstick at the home hole, placing the ball just two feet short of the hole. The crowds surged in around the green, completely surrounding it. Nagle had to battle his way through the massed throng in order to finish his round.

Although his putt was only two feet long, Kel was understandably nervous. He jabbed at the putt and moved it to within nine inches of the hole. That putt he downed and the championship was his. Kel Nagle had beaten the great Palmer, 278 strokes to 279 strokes, and had finished like a champion under great pressure. For Kel it was the first Open Championship, a sweet victory. For Arnold Palmer, it meant more determination to win this coveted title, a determinaion which culminated the very next year. Arnold Palmer returned to the British Isles, this time to Royal Birkdale in England, and won his first Open Championship with a score of 284, one stroke ahead of diminutive Dai Rees, the Welshman. Where was Nagle in 1961? Five strokes behind Palmer at 299. Then, in 1962, Arnold Palmer came back to Scotland once more, this time to Old Troon. His 71, 69, 67, 69—276 set a new Open record score. Who was runner-up to Palmer at Troon? Kel Nagle, six strokes behind.

THE BRITISH AMATEUR OF 1963

Since 1826, the year Jess Sweetser won the British Amateur Championship at Muirfield, Scotland, an American golfer had taken the title in every Walker Cup year. The team match, of course, is played every four years in Britain. This year was to prove an exception to the rule when an "all-Empire" final developed and 28-year-old Michael Lunt, British Walker Cup player, defeated 48-year-old John Blackwell by a score of 2 and 1 to win the Championship at last.

Among the thirty-nine entrants from the United States there were eight members of the American Walker Cup team who qualified for the tournament, among them Richard "Dick" Davies of Pasadena, California, the defending American Amateur champion and Labron Harris, Jr., American Amateur champion of 1962.

Michael Lunt, Amateur Champion of 1963.

By the time the fourth round was over, only four Americans had survived. Davies, Dr. Edgar Updegraff and R. H. Sikes of Springdale, Arkansas, United States Public Links champion of 1962, and Dr. Ronald Luceti, of San Francisco, California.

In the final round Davies was forced to go nineteen holes to win over John Wilson of Scotland. In his afternoon match, he found himself four holes down at the eleventh tee to John Beharrell, now twenty-five years old, who had been one of the youngest golfers ever to take the championship when he won at Troon as an eighteen-year-old in 1956. Davies won five of the last nine holes. After he had managed to square the match at the seventeenth, he saw Beharrell miss a three-foot putt at the home hole which would have put the match into overtime. It was, thus, Davies one up over Beharrell. Updegraff, in the meantime, upset the established favorite, Ronnie Shade, British Walker Cupper, 3 and 2. Joe Carr, perennial champion, lost in the 5th round to Peter Green of England, 3 and 2. Michael Bonallack, British Amateur Champion of 1961 at Turnberry, Scotland had gone out in the fourth round.

In spite of the hard work and fine golf exhibited by Davies in his matches with Wilson and Beharrell, he found Michael Lunt too much for him and went down to defeat by a one-hole margin. When Updegraff beat Sikes 2 and 1 the draw put Lunt against Updegraff in one semi-final match. The other match shaped up between John Blackwell and a surprise entry, a non--Walker Cupper from the U.S., Dr. Ron Luceti, an Army officer and dentist on leave from duty in Italy.Very much an "outsider," Dr. Luceti had successfully reached the last four of the tournament and had beaten some good players along the way.

The Lunt-Updegraff semi-final match was an example of the fact that in match play the golfer needs to defeat only his own opponent, and fortunately for him sometimes, is not contending against the field. For, in retrospect, it is interesting to consider that the eventual 1963 champion was able to reach the final round and then win that match after a "bad" round of 76 against Updegraff's 77. Updegraff was 4 down at the turn and though he got back three precious holes he was never quite able to catch Lunt.

The match of Updegraff and Lunt was a thriller nevertheless. With the Doctor three holes down with three holes to play, Ed holed a 14-foot putt to win at the sixteenth, then took the seventeenth in par when Lunt was over to the left with his second shot at No. 17 and through the green with his third. Both players were on the eighteenth hole in two, with Updegraff needing to win the hole to "stay alive." Lunt putted first and the ball stopped a good five feet away from the hole. Ed putted safely to within one foot of the cup. Lunt's second putt just reached the cup, very much in doubt as to whether it would go down or not and then "slithered into the cup" for the half and the victory for Lunt.

Champions are made of such "breaks!"

Their cards were:

Michael Lunt	Out:	4 4 4 4 5 4 5 3 4	37	
	In:	4 4 4 5 5 4 4 5 4	39	76
	Lunt 4 up at 9 holes			
Ed Updegraff	Out:	4 4 5 5 6 4 4 4 4	40	
	In:	4 3 5 5 5 4 3 4 4	37	77
	Lunt wins 1 up			

The pressure was showing as well on John Blackwell and Ron Luceti in their semi-final match as they stumbled through the first nine holes in 40 and 42 respectively to make Blackwell 2 holes ahead at the turn. The players halved the tenth, eleventh and twelfth holes. Then, when Blackwell took the thirteenth and fourteenth on a 4 and a 7

against Luceti's 6 and 8, the match was Blackwell's at the sixteenth, by a score of 3 and 2.

John Blackwell was the scion of the well-known international food processing firm, Crosse and Blackwell. He was from Sandwich, England and was a member of the Royal and Ancient Golf Club at St. Andrews. He had been troubled all his life with a persistent slice which he could not seem to lose in spite of much professional instruction. At last, in desperation, he commissioned a set of golf clubs to be specially made for him with a three-degree anti-clockwise correction in the connection of the heads to the shafts so that he could "psych" himself into hitting a straight ball with an artificially square-faced club.

Strangely enough, the new clubs worked, to the point that Blackwell was able to play well enough to reach the final round of the prestigious Amateur Championship of Britain, and that in itself is a great golfing achievement for any one to accomplish in his lifetime.

So, an older (48) John Blackwell met the young (28) Walker Cupper Michael Lunt on a beautiful sunny day at St. Andrews for the Championship cup. There were fewer than a thousand spectators but the match was a very exciting one, even though the individual scores were not of true championship calibre.

The end of the first eighteen found the players all even after scores of 78 for Blackwell and 80 for Lunt. Blackwell had won the par 5 fifth hole with a 6 to a 7, for instance, and the seventh with a par 4 but Lunt's two 3s at the eight and ninth brought them to the 10th tee all even. They tied three more holes, this time in par, and then traded two holes apiece in the next four, with Lunt getting a bad 7 at the fourteenth. All even at the eighteenth hole.

The afternoon round continued nip and tuck, with the players trading the first two holes. Blackwell birdied the first, then they halved four straight in par. When Blackwell took 6 at the seventh to Lunt's birdie 3 and then lost the ninth with a 5 to a 4, Lunt went 2 up. Both players again found trouble at the par 5 Hell Hole and Lunt picked up, conceding the hole to Blackwell's bogey 6. Lunt came back, winning the fifteenth in par once more to go two holes ahead and they "ran the string out" at the sixteenth and seventeenth in mutual pars. So it was Michael Lunt, not only Walker Cup Member, but also British Amateur Champion of 1963.

The cards of Blackwell and Lunt in the final rounds were:

Morning
John Blackwell   Out: 4 5 5 5 6 4 4 4 4 41

Michael Lunt	Out:	5 4 5	5 7 5	4 3 3	41	
	Match even					
Blackwell	In:	4 3 4	5 5 5	3 4 4	37	78
Lunt	In:	4 3 4	4 7 4	5 4 4	39	80
	Match even					
Afternoon						
Blackwell	Out:	3 5 4	4 5 4	6 3 5	39	
Lunt	Out:	4 4 4	4 5 4	3 3 4	35	
	Lunt 2 up					
Blackwell	In:	4 3 3	6 6 5	4 5		
Lunt	In:	4 3 4	4 X 4	4 5		
	Lunt wins 2 and 1					

THE OPEN CHAMPIONSHIP OF 1964

Anthony "Tony" Lema, United States	73	68	68	70	279
Jack Nicklaus, United States	76	74	66	68	284
Robert De Vicenzo, Argentina	76	72	70	67	285
Bernard Hunt, England	73	74	70	70	287
Bruce Devlin, Australia	72	72	73	73	290
Christy O'Connor, Ireland	71	73	74	73	291
Harry Weetman, England	72	71	75	73	291
Angel Miguel, Spain	73	76	72	71	292
Harold Henning, South Africa	78	73	71	70	292
Gary Player, South Africa	78	71	73	70	292

If ever a comet had flashed on the golf scene before, there never was one to equal the brilliance of the star that was Anthony Joseph Lema, "Tony," "The Champagne Champion."

Tony burst into prominence in 1962 after five years of frustrating golf. He had been an also-ran, just barely scraping by, heavily in debt to a "backer" who would soon lose faith in his chances to ever recoup his investment. Tony had such putting woes ("I had started taking between 38 and 40 putts per round," he said in his book *Golfer's Gold*) and in desperation, after not qualifying for the 1961 U.S. Open Championship, presented himself to Horton Smith at Detroit, Michigan, who was known to be a remarkably good putter himself as well as a great teacher of golf. Horton watched his stroke and told Tony that all he had lost was his confidence and said, "We'll get that back for you!" Lema said, "I could feel my confidence ebbing back into me as we talked. It was a miracle. I can never thank Horton Smith enough for what he told me and what he did."

In 1963 Tony won his first Open Championship in the United States in a play-off with Bob Rosburg for the Orange County Open Championship. He tells of winning it on the third hole of the extra hole match this way: "It was my turn to putt first. As I got over the ball I suddenly felt certain that I was going to make the putt. My confidence was supreme and I stroked the ball straight into the

hole. Bob's putt hit the back of the cup and bounced out. I had won my first championship." Horton must have done his job well.

"I've won tournaments and I've won money," "Champagne Tony" said the day before he flew off to Scotland. "Now I want to win a major championship. It is on my schedule of things to do and I'm going to do it!"

So off to St. Andrews Tony Lema went. Arnold Palmer had decided not to enter this Open. After all, Arnie already had two Open Championships under his belt, the 1961 and the 1962 trophies, and he was physically tired from the long, hot Whitemarsh tourney. So, very thoughtfully, he had told Tony Lema that if he wanted to do so he might engage one of the greatest caddies of all time, James "Tip" Anderson, who had "carried" for Palmer and coached Arnie himself to his two victories at Royal Birkdale and Troon. Of course, Tony was much pleased at this turn of events. He would very much like to have "Tip" carry for him. He would need all the advice and help he could get in contending with the Old Course.

The weather forecast for the opening day of the tournament, Thursday, was ominous. On Wednesday a storm front had begun to move in from the Irish Sea, had already started to kick up whitecaps off the western shores of Scotland and was advancing into the highlands. The clouds hung dark and low over the North Sea, visible to the east off the St. Andrews links as if they were awaiting some help from the west before they would unleash their combined fury on the golfers. The pennants on the flagsticks around "the Loop," the 7th through the 12th holes, were whipping and snapping in the wind.

Fred Tupper, British golf correspondent, was writing this report for American consumption: "Wrinkles and bumps seam the Old Lady's countenance. The lies are tight, uphill and downhill and pot bunkers and deep caverns materialize out of the mist. The Old Lady, it is agreed, must be staunchly wooed."

The luck of the draw for pairings of playing partners and starting times for both Thursday and Friday rounds was posted by the Golf Committee of the Royal and Ancient Golf Club about midday on Wednesday. The players hurried to see the sheets and with the stormy weather obviously coming soon, hoped for early starts. Tony Lema would tee-off at 9:10 A.M. the first day and at 1:30 P.M. the second. On the other hand, as we shall see later on, an unusual twist of fate put Jack Nicklaus and Bruce Devlin, of Australia, in a late starting time the first day, at 1:50 P.M. and in an early time for Friday, 9:00 A.M.

*Tony Lema, Open champion of 1964. Provost of St.
Andrews, Tomas Fordyce, is at left.*

Arnold Palmer driving from the first tee in a practice round with Gary Player in 1964.

At 8:00 A.M. on Thursday, the meteorological officer at Leuchars Air Base, two miles northwest, took his usual hourly reading on his anemometer. Fifteen knots.

The field started off the first tee at St. Andrews at 8:00 A.M., driving into the face of the storm. The second shots to the first green were already 4-irons, where customarily, in calmer weather, the club might be an 8-iron or pitching wedge. By ten o'clock the wind had risen to twenty-two knots. 3-woods were now being used to "get home" on No. 1. Tony Lema was now on the fourth hole. At noon, the reading at Leuchars was twenty-nine knots. Lema was mid-way in "the Loop" and doing very well.

When Nicklaus and Devlin started their rounds at 1:50 P.M., the velocity of the wind was about to reach gale proportions. Leuchars' chart shows that a wind-speed of 40 knots was clocked at 3:30 P.M.

and that there were occasional gusts up to 60 knots.

Jack Nicklaus had a score of 76, a great round under the circumstances. Jack said, in a press interview, "I just couldn't get set to putt. My eyes watered, the sand flew into my face. I had great trouble trying to keep my balance. I've never had to putt like that before. I was afraid the ball would move on me so I would stroke it quickly." Jack drove the eighteenth green, incidentally, 358 yards away, with the wind at his back and two-putted from twenty feet. Jack's 76 put him three strokes behind Tony Lema's opening round of 73.

Scores of all the afternoon players on Thursday went skyrocketing. Kel Nagle had a 77 which included four putts on the seventeenth hole. Peter Thomson and Bob Charles of Australia had 79s as more than half the later field reported scores in the 80s.

Christy O'Connor of Ireland and Jean Garaialde

of France were early leaders of the Open as well as early starters with scores of 71 apiece. O'Connors round was especially sensational as "the leprechauns touched his putter with magic." Christy played the 7th hole through the 12th in 3, 3, 4, 3, 3, and 3. Included in this remarkable streak were a putt of about thirty feet over a series of "lumps" and a hole-out from a bunker. His good luck even extended to help from the wind when a twelve-foot putt stopped at the front edge of the cup on the twelfth hole and then, in kindly fashion, an extra strong gust blew the ball into the hole for Christy to give him his birdie there.

The scores at the end of the first day read:

O'Connor	37	34	71
Garaialde	37	34	71
Weetman	38	34	72
Devlin	35	37	72
Boyle	35	37	72
Lema	37	36	73
Hunt	36	37	73
Miguel	37	36	73
Faulkner	36	37	73

On the second day the winds continued to blow strongly but not quite so hard as the day before. By mid-afternoon the storm had almost blown itself out. With the reversed starting times in effect both Devlin and Nicklaus had to play through the tail-end of the bad weather, while Lema with his "late" start on Friday again had the good fortune to miss a good part of the difficult conditions of play.

Jack Nicklaus again had trouble in the wind. He couldn't get the ball in the hole on the slick wind-swept acres of greens, took 40 putts in a round of 74 which meant that four times he reached 4-pars in one stroke or 5-pars in two strokes to cut four strokes off the six he wasted on the putting surfaces. This total of 40 putts was the greatest number Jack had had in a single round since turning professional in 1961. He finished his round and went out to the practice green for two hours of intensive work on smoothing his stroke in an attempt to solve the hard, fast greens.

On the second day, the gallery started to "warm up" to the charming personality of Tony Lema. The golf-watchers are most knowledgeable in Scotland. They are slow to accept a new face or personality until they have had a good opportunity to watch what happens in bad times as well as in good times on the golf course. How does he take a bad bounce, for example, one that is truly not his fault? Hogan and Jones had both shown the "dour" nature the Scots themselves admire and often exhibit. Now, Lema, more outgoing than Jones or Hogan, it is true, but indeed a sweet-swinging golfer of

smiling, pleasant countenance, was starting to capture their fancy and their cheers. A tremendous yell, the loudest yet to be heard, went up at the 12th hole of Tony's second round when he drove the hole, 312 yards away and then smoothly stroked a 30-foot putt into the cup for a great eagle 2. Tony was winning their hearts more and more, hole by hole, as he fashioned a beautiful four under par 68 and seized a two stroke lead over the field at the end of the second day of play.

The last day, with its punishing thirty-six holes of golf, dawned clear and sunny. The wind had now died down to "reasonable proportions," less than ten miles per hour.

Jack Nicklaus, far back in the field, started long before Tony Lema on that last day. He had begun his round nine huge strokes behind the front-running Tony, with a total of 150 strokes (76-74) to Tony's 141 (73-68). Jack never gives up, however, under any circumstances and has become almost as famous as the great Arnold Palmer for his come-from-behind charges in the last rounds. Jack knew he had to do most of the work today. He couldn't count on an experienced Tony Lema giving up as much as a seven stroke lead on a fine golfing day such as this had turned out to be.

Jack rolled in an unbelieveable 60-foot putt on the 12th hole for a 3, went five under par at that point, needed pars in for a 67.

Lema had now started his third round. Some word of Jack's good scoring had trickled back to headquarters but Lema was not disturbed, resting on top of such a solid lead.

Tony made his par 4 at the first and then things started to go badly for him. A putt switched out of the cup and he had a bogey at the second hole. He made a shakey par at the third and then took a 5 at the 4th to lose another stroke to par. The 5th hole should have fallen to the long-driving Tony in two strokes to the 5-par green, two putts for a "natural" birdie. Tony took 5. Nicklaus had made a 3 on the same hole two hours earlier. The margin between Nicklaus and Tony was narrowing fast.

At this very moment on the monstrous 5th - 14th double green there came a strange confrontation between these two great players. Jack had just made his par at the 15th as Tony failed to get his birdie on the 4th, some ninety feet away on Jack's left. Jack's scoreboard carried proudly by a young teen-age Scot showed this report to the gallery: Nicklaus "+1."

Jack's figures had come down steadily from his "+6" start to the "+1" his score-keeper now exhibited. Tony Lema, on the other hand, had walked down the first fairway with his standard-bearer carrying a "—3" sign which had inexorably changed to "—2" at the second hole and "—1" at the fourth. Tony took a look at Jack's scoreboard, saw the "+1," gulped and swallowed hurriedly. Jack was now only two shots away from Tony and with the wind behind him at the seventeenth and eighteenth ought to pick up another birdie or two on the way home. Incredibly, Lema had lost seven strokes of his nine stroke lead over Nicklaus and Tony still had the tough "Loop" to play. The issue was squarely up to Lema. "Tip" Anderson, disappointed himself in "their" start, says that at this moment Tony Lema turned to him and said, "Tip, we've got a job to do, let's do it, shall we?"

Nicklaus did get his 4 at No. 16 and another sound 4 at the Road Hole. Then he cranked up another tremendous drive to the eighteenth green, calmly stroked a curling, slippery, sidehill putt from more than 90 feet away to within inches of the flagstick, dunked the simple birdie putt and reported his 66, six under par, for the third round. Jack knew very well what Lema's scoreboard showed when they passed each other at the fourteenth. He believed that with his sixth birdie he had climbed into a virtual tie with Tony, that if Tony should fall back at all, Jack might move into the lead or possibly a tie for the lead as the fourth and decisive eighteen holes began. Jack had a light luncheon and then sat down on the steps nears the eighteenth green to await the results of Lema's third round, to see whether Lema could stand the pressure put upon him by Jack's six-under-par "attempt to catch Lema" in one single round.

Lema's resolve to "get down to business" resulted in an amazing comeback on his part. He would forget about Nicklaus and play his own game, a daring and bold attack on the course. The newspapers said "Lema played like a man possessed." Tip Anderson says that all he did was tell Tony where to hit his drives, in the middle of the fairway usually, but sometimes to the left or right of some particularly dangerous bunker so as to make his approaches to the green simpler, and Tony "hit every shot where he was supposed to."

Jack Nicklaus started out in pursuit of Lema for the second time that day. He picked up his first birdie at the third hole but canceled that with a bad 5 at the 4-par fourth hole. Then he bungled the 4-par fifth hole, missed the green on his second and then three-putted for a nasty double bogey 6 which seemed to kill his chances right there of narrowing the margin between Lema and himself. However, Jack stormed back in typical Nicklaus fashion. He marked down 3, 4, 2, 3 on the last four

holes of nine. Jack dropped a 35-footer at the sixth and six-footers at the eighth and ninth. He was out, then, in a very respectable 34 strokes. Jack was now even par for the seven nine's or sixty-three holes he had played. He had one last nine to work with and he had to play it sensationally if he had any hope of winning from Lema.

In the meantime, Lema had begun his last round of play, his playing partner the Frenchman, Jean Garaialde, whose third round of 79 had destroyed his hopes of winning the tournament. His first two scores of 71 and 74 had put him five strokes ahead of Nicklaus at the time, but it was too late now for Garaialde.

Lema did not quite equal his five 3s in a row but he did do 4, 3, 3, 3, 4, 3 on the sixth, seventh, eighth, ninth, tenth and eleventh to turn in his own 34 and match exactly Jack Nicklaus's earlier 34. So, Tony had again been equal to the task.

Standing on the thirteenth tee, Tony Lema was aware that he had practically an insurmountable lead. Nicklaus had finished now, well ahead of Tony, with another excellent 34 on the second nine and an eighteen-hole score of 68 but his four-round total of 284 meant that Tony had a seven stroke lead over Jack at the start of Tony's final nine. Tony lost two strokes of those seven strokes, one when he parred the twelfth hole (Jack had birdied it) and one at the wicked fourteenth, once more with a par to Jack's birdie. Tony played the seventeenth in 5 strokes, missing a short putt which would have saved his par there, but now, on the eighteenth tee, with between 8,000 and 10,000 spectators lining the entire stretch between the tee and home green, Tony knew that he was "in." The gallery knew it, too, and became increasingly exuberant and boisterous.

Tony's drive at No. 18 was a good one, just short of the Valley of Sin. Then he saved his "shot of the day" for this moment. He rolled a 7-iron shot up through the huge dip in the green to within inches of the hole for a "sure par" and almost equally certain birdie. The crowd broke ranks and swarmed around Tony. The gallery marshals and police had to pull him from the clutches of the crowd before he would emerge, stride up onto the green and tap in his birdie 3 for the winning score, 279.

Tony Lema had achieved one of his great ambitions, the winning of a major championship, the Open Championship of 1964.

Roberto de Vicenzo of Argentina finished strongly for third place at 285 strokes with a great final round of 67. Bernard Hunt of England and Bruce Devlin of Australia finished fourth and fifth at 287 and 290 on scores of 70 and 73 respectively.

The cards of Lema and Nicklaus for the final day were:

Morning					
	Par:	4 3 4 4 5 4 4 4 4	36		
Lema	Out:	4 5 4 5 5 4 3 3 3	36		
	In:	3 3 4 4 4 3 4 4 3	32	68	208
Morning					
	Par:	4 3 4 4 5 4 4 4 4	36		
Nicklaus	Out:	3 4 4 3 5 4 3 3 3	32		
	In:	4 4 3 4 4 4 4 4 3	34	66	216
Afternoon					
Lema	Out:	4 4 4 5 4 4 3 3 3	34		
	In:	4 3 4 4 5 4 4 5 3	36	70	279
Nicklaus	Out:	4 4 3 5 6 3 4 2 3	34		
	In:	4 3 3 4 4 4 4 5 3	34	68	284

THE OPEN CHAMPIONSHIP OF 1970

Jack Nicklaus, United States	68	69	73	73	283
			Play-off		72
Doug Sanders, United States	68	71	71	73	283
			Play-off		73
Lee Trevino, United States	68	68	72	77	285
Harold Henning, South Africa	67	72	73	73	285
Tony Jacklin, England	67	70	73	76	286
Neil Coles, England	65	74	72	76	287
Peter Oosterhuis, England	73	69	69	76	287
Hugh Jackson, England	69	72	73	74	288
Tommy Horton, England	66	73	75	75	289
John Panton, England	72	73	73	71	289
Peter Thomson, Australia	68	74	73	74	289
Arnold Palmer, United States	68	72	76	74	290

The 99th British Open was undoubtedly the most dramatic golf tournament ever played at St. Andrews. In the presentation of the honored cup to winner Jack Nicklaus, William Whitelaw, Captain of the Royal and Ancient, said, "This was one of the great golf matches of all time."

But before we get into the dramatics let us set the scene. Jack Nicklaus, the incredibly powerful young golfer from the United States, had already won nine major championships in his short golf career, including the British Open itself when the tournament was played at Muirfield in 1966. And yet, as far as Nicklaus was concerned, he had been in a slump and was seeking his first major tournament victory since 1967.

His eventual opponent in the showdown was greying Doug Sanders, another American professional with a good but not great tournament record behind him as he neared his thirty-seventh birthday. In the eyes of the golf cognoscenti it might have been said that Doug was on his way down and

would eventually be out of the tournament picture. He had not won a Professional Golf Association championship in three years. He looked backed on runner-up finishes in the 1959 P.G.A. championship and the 1961 U.S. Open. He had, however, been second to Jack Nicklaus at Muirfield in 1966, so undoubtedly Doug Sanders had more than a slight hope of finishing well in this Open at St. Andrews. He was not eligible for an exempt spot in the field and thus Doug played the customary qualifying rounds for the British Open and did qualify handily with scores of 67 and 74 at nearby Panmure Golf Club. There is no doubt, however, that the physical and mental strain of qualifying rounds were harder on Sanders than the casual practice rounds then being played at St. Andrews by Nicklaus, Trevino, Jacklin, Coles and the other notable golfers who were entered in the field on their records and were exempt from qualifying. Any way the situation is viewed, it could be said that Doug Sanders was a remote possibility to win this British Open. A sentimental favorite, perhaps, because of his personal charm and gracious manners, but he hadn't much of a chance to win, it was thought.

The scoring fireworks began. By the end of the day, when only two-thirds of the field were finished, there had been twenty scores under seventy. The British Open record of 65 at this time was held by Henry Cotton, Eric Brown, Peter Butler of England and Leopardo Ruiz of Argentina. For the Old Course itself the Open record was 66.

The crowds had reason to hope that Tony Jacklin, British Open champion of 1969 and U.S. Open champion of 1970, was compiling an incredible round. A 3, 3, 3, start on birdie putts of fifteen, five and fifteen feet put Tony three under par at once. No. 4 fell in par and then two straight woods and two putts gave him birdie number four at the 5th hole. Tony flirted with trouble on the 7th hole when his tee-shot was almost bunkered. His ball hung on two clumps of grass on the edge of the bunker. A delicate chip-and-run shot came off successfully. Then a six-foot putt brought still another birdie, a 3, at the 7th. At the 9th hole, Tony made the most sensational shot of this already spectacular nine. He hit a wedge to the green for his second shot. After taking one big bounce the ball struck the pin soundly and then promptly dove into the hole for a startling eagle 2, but more than that, a score of 29 on the first nine of the Old Course.

The weather started to get worse. The winds began to rise and the temperature dropped noticeably. Tony continued his hot streak by getting

Barbara and Jack Nicklaus after Jack's victory in 1970.

another birdie on the tenth hole. His long drive brought him within wedge distance of the hole. Another six-footer went down for a birdie. Jacklin was now eight under par through ten holes. Could he keep it up? Pars came on the next three holes and, hoping for a birdie on the 5-par 14th, Tony made one of his few mistakes of the day. Later on he reported that just as he was stroking his second shot someone had yelled a loud "Fore!" and had distracted him in the middle of his swing. The ball went awry and ended up in a whin bush deep in the heavy rough.

It was at this point that the heavens opened up with a monstrous deluge. Play was halted and it soon became obvious that the flooding of the course was so serious that there was no possibility that it could begin again on this first day. One-third of the contestants had not yet completed their rounds. The Rules Committee had a serious problem in deciding whether or not to cancel the scores of the day. Finally, the ruling was announced. "The scores already in will be counted. Let the balls remain where they are overnight and let play begin at that point on the morrow."

Of course, Tony Jacklin was most pleased to know that his splendid effort would not be wasted, that he would still have a crack at that potential course record score of 64 if he could just play par figures the rest of the way in. Tony was rather pessimistic about his chances of saving par at the fourteenth hole, however, and said, "I'll have to take the penalty (for putting the ball in the unplayable spot in the bush, that is) and drop it out tomorrow. It looks unplayable. I'll be lucky to get a 6."

Tony was right about the fourteenth hole. The next day when the storm had passed and play began again for the last section of the field, Tony took his penalty on the hole and made a bogey 6 to lose a stroke of his edge on par. Then he

145

Jack Nicklaus accepts the Open Cup from the Right Honorable William S. I. Whitelaw in 1970.

stumbled in with a 4, 5, 5, 4 finish for an excellent total of 67, but still not the course record score he might have had if he had been able to recapture his torrid pace of the prior day.

When all the scores were in for the first day, another great golf round was posted. Lee Trevino, the colorful United States Open champion of 1971, breezed in with an excellent 68 to join the large group of golfers who scored under 70 on that first round. Lee was four under par after the 12th hole and matched par the rest of the way for his score. Trevino's 68 joined him at that figure with Arnold Palmer, Jack Nicklaus, and surprisingly enough, veteran Doug Sanders. The scoreboard at the end of the first day's play showed these players as the leaders:

Neil Coles, Britain	31	34	65
Tony Horton, Britain	33	33	66
Maurice Bembridge, Britain	34	33	67
Harold Henning, South Africa	35	32	67
John Richardson, Britain	34	33	67
Florentino Molino, Argentina	34	33	67
Brian Huggett, Britain	33	35	68
Arnold Palmer, U.S.	35	33	68
Doug Sanders, U.S.	34	34	68
Jack Nicklaus, U.S.	34	34	68

Photo taken during the 1970 Open Championship. Left to right: The Rt. Hon. Reginald Maulding, M.P., Secretary of State for the Home Department; Tony Jacklin, Great Britain; The Rt. Hon. Edward Heath, M.B.E., M.P., Prime Minister and First Lord of the Treasury; Lee Trevino, U.S.A.; The Rt. Hon. W.S.I. Whitelaw, M.C., M.P., Lord President of the Council and Leader of the House of Commons; Captain of the Royal and Ancient Golf Club.

A view of the tremendous gallery around the 18th green in the 1970 Open Championship.

Some past Open Champions. Back row, left to right: Arthur Havers, Gene Sarazen, Dick Burton, Fred Daly, Roberto De Vicenzo, Arnold Palmer, Kel Nagle, Bobby Locke, Henry Cotton, Peter Thomson. Front row, left to right, Denny Shute, Bob Charles, Max Faulkner, Jack Nicklaus, Tony Jacklin, Gary Player.

Although there was again wind and rain, the play on the second day went on without interruption. Jack Nicklaus was once more playing steady golf, got sixteen pars, one birdie and one eagle for a comfortable 69 to add to his start of 68. Nicklaus was in at 137 and was a distinct threat for the lead, which was taken at the end of the second eighteen holes by Lee Trevino with another excellent round of 68 for his halfway total and single stroke lead of 136 strokes.

Nicklaus's eagle came on the twelfth hole when he drove the 312 yard distance to the flag and dropped a fourteen-foot putt. Doug Sanders appeared to be on his way to a share of the lead with Trevino but got into trouble on the 17th Road Hole. A seagull distracted him on his second shot to the green and he pulled his iron to the

left. Then his pitch would not hold and he found himself deep in the Road bunker, as had so many thousands of other golfers. Doug exploded well to four feet but could not hole the putt. A nasty double bogey 6 spoiled his card and he completed the round with a 71 for 139 to enter a three-way tie with Nicklaus and Tony Jacklin (who was playing the "twenty-two hole" round this day, making up for his rain-out of yesterday).

Jacklin tacked a sound 70 onto his opening round score of 67 and late in the day entered the tie for second place one stroke behind Lee Trevino. Tony claimed that it was necessary to "improvise" a golf game on the second day. He said that the wind had been blowing the ball to the right going out in the morning and left coming back. Tony also made the observation that he didn't "adapt"

*Left to right: Doug Sanders, runner-up for the 1970
Open Championship, The Rt. Hon. W. Whitelaw,
Leader of the House of Commons, and Jack Nicklaus,
Open Champion of 1970.*

to the wind conditions in his morning round when he failed to continue scoring well.

Neil Coles fell off to a shaky 74 on his second round while a new face appeared in a contending position. Peter Oosterhuis, tall young smooth-swinging Englishman, came to the attention of the galleries for the first time when he reported an excellent 69 for his second score. Both Tommy Horton and Harold Henning, who had been in the 60s that first day, weakened a bit for 73 and 72 respectively.

So the leading scores at the end of the second round were:

Trevino	66	68	136
Jacklin	67	70	137
Nicklaus	68	69	137
Clive Clark	69	70	139
Neil Coles	65	74	139
Harold Henning	67	72	139
Tommy Horton	66	73	139
John Richardson	67	72	139
Doug Sanders	68	71	139

The end of the third day of play found Lee Trevino with a two stroke lead over Sanders, Nicklaus and Jacklin. Lee's round was a solid one, with twenty-five-foot putts into the hole for birdies on the first and the last holes to offset two bogeys along the way. A score of par 72 on top of two 68s and Lee was in at 208 to the 210s of the other three strong contenders.

Weather conditions were worsening day by day as the play continued. The Old Course was getting its subtle revenge on that covey of golfers who dared to shoot 60s on Wednesday. This day produced a real "howler." The wind veered from north to west directly across the course. While twenty-four players successfully broke 70 on the first day, only six were able to do so on Thursday.

This third day produced two scores in the 60s, one of them by Oosterhuis, who continued to make his presence felt with a great round of 69. There was increasing difficulty, not only getting the ball onto the green, but especially getting the ball into the hole as the wind buffeted and tossed the golfers and interfered with their balance and ability to execute the various demanding shots the "Old Lady" required.

The scoreboard now showed:

Trevino	68	68	72	208
Nicklaus	68	69	73	210
Jacklin	67	70	73	210
Sanders	68	71	71	210
Oosterhuis	73	69	69	210
Coles	65	74	72	211

Nicklaus considered himself fortunate to have scored his 73 in the third round. Remember that Jack, with his 68-69 start, had been four under par. He began to struggle for pars on the third round, as did the entire field, of course, in the bad weather. Burdened by sweaters and blown by the wind, Jack suddenly found his seven under par status slowly slipping away from his grasp. He ran into a straight string of bogeys at the short eleventh hole, then the twelfth and the thirteenth. At No. 11, for instance, he pushed his 5-iron far to the right and left himself a difficult sixty-foot putt over the crest for his par. Jack's first putt was five feet off and he missed the hole for the bogey 4. At No. 12 his wedge second shot was windblown or misjudged, or both. The ball hit the ridge on the front of the putting surface and rolled back down the wicked upslope, leaving Jack with a chip-shot to save the hole. Once more, the shot was short of the hole and another bogey ensued. Trouble continued at the thirteenth when he was in such obvious difficulty in a pit bunker that all he could do was get the ball out and then worry about saving his par. He blasted out and had to settle for 5 on the hole. He had lost three precious strokes with great rapidity and still faced the threatening long stretch in to the eighteenth.

But Jack Nicklaus is famous for not losing his composure when disaster is apparently striking him. He settled down to business on the par 5 fourteenth. He was, as usual, close enough to the green in two strokes to use his sand wedge for the approach to the flag-stick. The stroke was beautifully executed and the ball trickled to a mere ten feet from the hole. Jack gave a sigh of relief as he canned the putt for a most desirable birdie 4. Perhaps he had reversed the trend.

At the fifteenth, Jack used a 6-iron to put him-self twenty feet away from another possible birdie. But this time his well-stroked putt switched off the line just when it appeared ready to drop into the hole, a heartbreaker but still a sound par. At the sixteenth, a drive and 5-iron to twenty feet from the flag did bring about a hesitant birdie as the ball tried to stay on the rim of the cup but finally fell.

He saved his par at the Road Hole, when he appeared to be in trouble again after leaving himself an eighty-foot approach putt. However, he putted this one magnificently, laid it dead, six inches from the hole. Now he needed a birdie at No. 18 to save the round and get in with a par 72. He knew everyone else was having trouble today and Jack would be glad to settle for a par score if he could achieve it. With his awesome power, Jack almost drove to the putting surface of the eighteenth green. He was just short of the Valley of Sin and elected to use his wedge but could not close in on the hole. The ball ended twenty feet away. Jack did not drop the birdie putt, but took his 4 and breathed a sigh of relief. He had recovered well from what might have been a disastrous round.

So it looked as if there would be a mad rush for the title on the last day. Trevino, playing steadily with his two 68s and his par 72, giving him the two stroke lead, had to be considered the favorite to win. But there remained the threat of strong, tournament-toughened Jack Nicklaus and Tony Jacklin, experienced bad weather players and former champions accustomed to the pressure in the last eighteen holes of an important medal tournament.

While Doug Sanders was in the cluster two strokes behind Lee Trevino it certainly was thought that he would not be able to mount the strength and stamina needed to come down the stretch. He had done extremely well so far but after all those qualifying rounds and the physically strenuous play thus far he had to be considered an outside chance to challenge the front-runners in the final stretches of the last eighteen holes.

So the scene was set for a most dramatic finish for this 99th British Open. Although it seemed that it could not have been worse, the weather actually did get worse on the last day. The wind rose to gale force at times, the rains pelted the players' faces. And yet, in spite of the terrible playing conditions, the scores were most respectable, even sensational, as we shall see.

Remember that Jack Nicklaus had never won at St. Andrews. He coveted the championship cup avidly. Three times he had been runner-up, only a stroke or so away from the winning spot. At St. Andrews in 1964 he had been second to Tony Lema when Jack had unfortunately been caught in "St. Andrews weather" on the incoming nine while Lema had escaped the brunt of the storm.

Jack, moreover, had not won a major tournament since 1967 when he took the United States Open title. No one would try harder to win on this last day than Jack Nicklaus.

Nicklaus was scheduled to play ahead of Sanders and Trevino on the final day. Jack began his round auspiciously with a good par at No. 1. Then a beautiful and delicate pitch to within ten feet of the hole brought his first birdie at No. 2. At the long fifth hole, Jack's powerful swing put him close to the green in two strokes. He had only a short pitch remaining, and although he did not get the ball as close as he would have liked to, he holed his putt, a twenty-two-footer for his second birdie.

Now Jack had put himself eight under par. Sanders and Trevino had already started their rounds behind him, and with Jack's second birdie he knew, via the scoreboards strategically placed on the golf course to keep the spectators posted on progress of the play, that he was two strokes ahead of Sanders and startlingly, had picked up an extra stroke on Jacklin and Trevino, who were gradually falling back of him. He had taken the lead away from Trevino, and Trevino was never to regain it. Lee had suddenly lost his putting touch, even missing one putt of fifteen inches on the ninth hole. He stumbled all day, losing strokes to par until six strokes were gone. Lee got his only birdie on the eighteenth hole when a ten-footer fell, but Lee Trevino, after leading the field through the second and third rounds, was never in the battle for first place on the final day. Nor was Tony Jacklin, or for that matter anyone else. Tony carded a hard-fought 76 and so did Neil Coles, but 76s were not enough to close in on Jack Nicklaus, who was making his charge for the trophy he wanted so much.

Then Jack started to miss putts he customarily holes. A seven-footer at the sixth, a five-footer at the seventh. Already he had canceled the effect of his two early birdies and was even par for the round. Then, a great wedge shot at the ninth hole gave him another chance for a birdie. He cashed it and was through the turn in 35 strokes, a most commendable performance under the pressure of the final round, to say nothing of the buffeting winds and rain.

In the meantime, however, it began to appear that if anyone would challenge Nicklaus down the stretch, it might be Doug Sanders. Doug had started well and was putting beautifully. He had birdied the third and sixth holes and although he had taken three strokes to get down from the edge of the eighth green it was an understandable if not forgivable error.

When Sanders parred the tenth hole while Nicklaus ahead of him had racked up a bogey, the two players were in a tie for the lead. Nicklaus appeared to be weakening, missed a three-foot putt at No. 12, a six-footer at No. 14, again another three-footer at No. 16, and this putt at the sixteenth was for a bogey. In the meantime, Sanders had not been able to catch up as much as he might have. Doug missed a three-foot birdie at No. 14, too. However, Doug had taken the lead from Nicklaus now and was six under par to five under for Nicklaus playing ahead of him. Jack knew what he had to do, be careful with the dangerous seventeenth hole and hope for a birdie at the last hole. Perhaps Sanders would have trouble behind him and lose a stroke or two.

Jack played the seventeenth hole brilliantly under the circumstances of the vicious weather, which had moderated somewhat now to strong winds only, no rain. His 5-iron second shot rolled up to within twelve feet of the hole. He would birdie this hole and the last one and force Sanders into an impossible strategic position. But the putt refused to drop and Nicklaus had to settle for his par and remain one stroke behind Sanders, who was then about to drive on the seventeenth hole.

Nicklaus, with the wind strongly behind him but quartering a bit, took his time with his tee shot, stepped behind the teed ball to take careful aim on his target. He must make a birdie here or else he had lost the battle, he felt.

The tee-shot was a great one and a powerfully long one, right straight for the flag-stick and incredibly up onto the apron of the green. Two putts for the birdie now and he was in with a difficult score for Sanders to beat. After a careful study of the long uphill putt out of the Valley of Sin, Jack took aim and slowly, methodically took the putter away in a slow backswing. Then, aghast, Jack saw that he had overestimated the strength of the upslope. The ball raced past the cup most shockingly and came to rest some twenty feet beyond it.

Jack Nicklaus might have three-putted from there but he did not. He could not hole the twenty-footer downhill and, disconsolate, he felt that he had lost the tournament right there. With a two-putt birdie right in his hands he had three-putted for a par. Nevertheless, Jack was on the scoreboard at 283 strokes with his final round of 73.

Sanders, needing pars at the seventeenth and eighteenth holes to win by one stroke, had his work cut out for him. He knew, of course, what he had to do. On No. 17 he had miraculously saved his par. His second shot found him deep in the Road bunker. With great courage he blasted the ball out of the trouble to within eighteen inches of the cup. While it was not a "sure" par, Doug carefully made the putt and put down the 4 on his card.

All Doug Sanders had to do now to win his first major championship, the historic British Open Championship, and put his name alongside the long list of former winners, was to score a par 4 on the last hole, the eighteenth, with its monstrous slick green and its forbidding entrance through the treacherous Valley of Sin.

Doug drove carefully from the eighteenth tee. With his fore-shortened golf swing he did not pretend to have the power of a Nicklaus or a Snead. He placed his shot to the left, away from the out-of-bounds on the right and left himself a pitch shot of perhaps seventy yards to the plateaued green. With thousands upon thousands of spectators watching the scene, some of them hanging from the nearby roofs, Doug told himself not to be short on this shot, "Whatever you do get it up and out of the Valley of Sin."

The pitch shot at first appeared to be a good one, definitely up to the hole but then it lost its spin, if it ever had any, and rolled on and on past the hole, into a very dangerous position above it. The putt was on a very slick green, now much drier since the rains had ceased. Doug Sanders needed a two-putt from here to win. The slope was a little to his right and he overestimated the effect it would have on the ball. We'll never know what happened but the result was evident in that the ball pulled up almost hole-high but on the left side of the cup as you look backward down the fairway toward the tee. Now, Doug really had a problem. The putt was probably three feet long, perhaps three-and-a-half feet. It would break to his left but how much depended upon the way he stroked it. If he hit it gently it would break several inches and it took a great deal of nerve under these testing circumstances to stroke a putt gently that last few feet.

Doug stood up to the putt and then stepped away from it to pick up what he later said was a pebble near or on his line to the cup. That Sanders missed the putt was almost a foregone conclusion after that loss of concentration. He pushed the putt to the right, never touched the hole. 5 strokes, a bogey, on the eighteenth had lost the title for sentimental favorite Doug Sanders and thrown him into a tie for the championship with formidable Jack Nicklaus. Jack had a new lease on life. Fate had been unkind to Doug, good to Jack. The morrow would bring the final act to a close with an eighteen-hole play-off between the two fine golfers.

The last 36 hole play-off in the Open occurred in 1963 when Bob Charles and Phil Rodgers played 36 holes with Charles winning with a score of 140 to Rodgers' 148. Shortly after that time, the rules were changed to provide for an 18 hole play-off. Bobby Locke defeated Harry Bradshaw of Ireland, 135 to 147 in the last previous 36 hole play-off in 1949 in the Open Championship at Sandwich.

The play-off on Sunday at first appeared to be anti-climactic. The strength of Jack Nicklaus was soon apparent while Doug Sanders, undoubtedly let down by his failure to win the title outright, played so raggedly that by the time the golfers reached the fourteenth hole, Doug was four strokes behind Nicklaus. The chances of gaining four strokes on Jack Nicklaus in an eighteen-hole round are remote to say nothing of doing it in five holes. The gallery was giving up on the match, some drifting away, some merely waiting to be "in on the kill."

Suddenly, from some unknown depths of his experience, Doug Sanders was able to reach in and bring out more determination than ever before. He would not admit defeat, he would fight to the bitter end. On the fourteenth hole, the first daylight started to appear for him. In the bunker at greenside in two strokes he played a magnificent wedge shot out to within four feet of the hole. He made the birdie and gained one precious stroke back from Nicklaus. There was hope yet, three strokes behind with four holes to play. At the fifteenth, the great reporter Fred Tupper, tells us that Doug Sanders "shaped an iron to thirteen feet from the hole." Down went the putt. For Nicklaus a par but another stroke of the lead was gone.

Both drives were excellent, with Nicklaus as usual ten to fifteen yards beyond Sanders. However, Nicklaus would be "playing the odd" which means that Sanders had the first opportunity at the green and if he could put the ball in "tight," he would put even more pressure on Jack's second shot. Thousands of Scots were massed around the "infamous" green. The large bunker loomed on the left as monstrous trouble. And it was if the golfer got into it. The precipitous slope on the right side ran down to the wicked road. The "alley" to the hole is only eight yards wide and I am sure to Doug Sanders it looked like a needle's eye. He had to run the ball up and with the wind behind him; as it was, it was a most delicate shot to accomplish.

Doug fidgeted with his stance and grip for what seemed to be an interminable amount of time. The shot was good, the ball on line to the opening of the green. It struck the front part of the upslope, tried to head for the bunker, but then curved gently right and ran up onto the green up the slope to the plateau and settled down beautifully at last some eighteen feet from the hole. A magnificent effort on Sanders' part, one that put the final result of the match, now clearly slipping away from him, squarely up to Nicklaus.

Jack was more than equal to the task. His club was a 7-iron and he intended to loft the ball more than Sanders did and attempt to hold the green. The ball had to be "pinched" exactly right to accomplish this type of golf shot. Jack was equal to the task and stood up under the immense pressure he now had to be feeling. His shot was even better than Doug's. His ball came to rest inside of Sanders' only ten feet away.

The putting on No. 17 was excruciatingly tense. If either one holed his putt and the other did not the whole match would swing one way or the other. The pressure was too much, it seems. Neither golfer came close to holing. Sanders, as a matter of fact, left himself a short but testing second putt when he went by the cup but the hole was halved in 4s.

Sanders, with the honor, since he had last won a hole, drove first on the eighteenth. He placed his tee-shot 275 yards away and right in the middle of the fairway. Now it was squarely up to Jack Nicklaus. Here was his chance to "nail the door shut" on Doug Sanders. With the wind fairly strong at his back, Jack might conceivably drive the green. He had decided that he would try to do so. Off came his yellow sweater. He wanted no interference with this swing. Later on Jack said, "I almost hit it (the tee shot at No. 18) before I was ready. I told myself to wait for a second and make it right." The stroke was a prodigious one, over three hundred and twenty yards on the carry, onto the front of the green and then, like a scurrying rabbit, the ball shot past the flagstick and darted over the green into the greenside heavy fringe at the back of the green. Incredibly, Jack Nicklaus had driven too far. At a distance of sixty feet from the flagstick Jack now faced the formidable problem of a most delicate chip-shot off dry grass of questionable resistance to his club, downhill on a very fast icy green. Sanders was not out

of the picture now by any means. Doug played first. He could sense that a birdie from him would put intolerable pressure on Jack's pitch to the pin. Again, as at the seventeenth, there might be a two-stroke switch in the scores. Doug's 4-iron run-up shot was a great one and came to rest only five feet from the hole. The whole match was now squarely up to Jack Nicklaus at the back of the green. He must get down in two for his birdie to win by one stroke. Take three strokes, let Sanders hole his putt and the match is tied again awaiting another eighteen hole play-off the next day.

Now Jack, who had seen three strokes of his four-stroke lead taken away by the charging Sanders, studied his shot. He paced it off carefully trying to decide what to do with that very difficult shot. Finally, his mind made up, he popped the ball out of the heavy grass with a hooded wedge. The ball came out alright but was not struck hard enough. The fast green and the downhill slope helped it somewhat on its way toward the hole but at last it rolled to a stop an agonizing eight feet above the cup.

Most good golfers would say than an ordinary golfer's chances of holing that putt would be most remote in view of the great pressure, the panic that ensues when a large lead disappears suddenly, the speedy green and the considerable length of the putt, eight feet. Nicklaus made the putt, however, with a beautiful controlled stroke. The ball rolled at just the right speed and hit the center of the hole. A birdie three for Jack and no matter what Sanders did with his birdie putt now, Jack had at last won at St. Andrews the British Open Championship he had tried so hard to win in the footsteps of Robert T. Jones, Jr., his idol.

Doug Sanders made his birdie putt, but by then, of course, it was too late. The crowds roared their approval of the courageous play of both players. Soon the score-board was hung was a banner reading, "Well done, Jack!"

Later on, at the presentation ceremony, Jack Nicklaus said, "There's not a place in the world that I would rather win a championship than at St. Andrews." As he put his arm around Doug Sanders, the gallant runner-up, he said, "I have mixed emotions about this, Doug, somehow I really wish it had been you."

8

Walker Cup Matches

The Walker Cup competition began in the wake of the first World War with a view to stimulating golf interest on both sides of the Atlantic. It was born in an era of dawning internationalism and grew, at least in part, out of two informal international matches, one held in 1919 at the invitation of the Royal Canadian Golf Association and another in 1920 when representatives of the United States Golf Association met abroad with the Royal and Ancient Golf Club's Rules Committee. The conferees met frequently in England and Scotland and played many of the well-known links.

Among the participants was George Herbert Walker, of the National Golf Links of America, in Southampton, New York. Walker was President of the U.S.G.A. in 1920 and a keen advocate of the game. When the Executive Committee returned from Britain, the possibility of international team matches was discussed. The idea so appealed to Mr. Walker that he presented a plan for an international golf championship and offered to donate an International Challenge Trophy. To his chagrin, when the newspapers printed the news of the new event, they called it "The Walker Cup" and the name has stuck ever since that time.

The finest amateur players of both American and Great Britain and Ireland have made their appearances in the Walker Cup matches. There have been twenty-four matches in all, through 1973. Seven of these matches have been held at St. Andrews on the Old Course from the second match of the series in 1923 to the glorious victory of Great Britain and Ireland over the United States of America team in 1971.

1923

An invitation to send a team to St. Andrews, Scotland, to defend the cup was quickly accepted the following winter, and the Americans nearly received their comeuppance in May, 1923. There had been many changes in personnel. Robert A. Gardner succeeded William C. Fownes, Jr., as captain, and ten players were selected so that alternates would be available on the scene. In addition to Gardner, Francis Ouimet, Jess Sweetser and Max Marston continued as members. S. Davidson Herron, Harrison R. Johnston, J. F. Neville, George V. Rotan, Dr. O. F. Willing and Frederick J. Wright, Jr., replaced Evans, Fownes, Guilford and Jones, who was studying at Harvard.

In the British Amateur at Deal, which preceded the match, Ouimet, who had won the Gold Vase, went to the semifinals, along with Douglas Grant, a fellow American who was living abroad. Roger Wethered defeated Robert Harris, 7 and 6, in the final, and he remains the only Briton who has won a British Amateur in a year when a United States Walker Cup Team was playing abroad.

On the first day of the match at St. Andrews, with Cyril Tolley and Roger Wethered leading off, the British won three of the four foursomes so that the Americans went into the eight singles

1923 Walker Cup Team of Britain and Ireland. Front Row, left to right: Roger Wethered, Robert Harris (captain), Cyril Tolley. Back row, left to right: C.V.L. Hooman, William L. Hope, W. Willis MacKenzie, Ernest Holderness.

needing five victories to tie and six to win. The prospect became even more gloomy when most of the Americans were trailing in their singles matches at noon. At one point the team, collectively, had been 24 holes down. Then their competitive fire was kindled. Ouimet, 2 down with three to play, made 3s on the thirty-fourth and thirty-sixth holes, the latter by holing an eighteen-foot putt around a partial stymie, to halve with Wethered and equal the course record of 70. Rotan, who had been 6 down after fourteen holes, rallied to win eleven of the next twelve holes and defeat Mackenzie, 6 and 4. Marston, who had been 1 down at noon, came

back to beat W. L. Hope, 5 and 4. Wright, 2 down with three to play, won the last three holes, the final one with a seven-foot putt for a birdie 3, to defeat Holderness.

These comebacks, coupled with Gardner's 1-up victory over Harris, the British Captain, tied the match, and the decision rode on the contest between Dr. Willing and William A. Murray. They were last on the course, and with three holes to play, they were even. But Dr. Willing won the thirty-fourth and thirty-fifth to give the United States a 6-to-5 victory and retain the Cup.

1923 U.S. Walker Cup Team. Front Row, left to right: Max R. Marston, Robert A. Gardner (captain), Jess W. Sweetser, George V. Rotan. Back Row, left to right: Frederick W. Wrights, Jr., J.F. Neville, Francis Oui-met, Harrison R. Johnston, Dr. O.F. Willing; S. Davidson Herron.

1926

In 1926, the Americans, again captained by Gardner, went first to Muirfield, Scotland, for the British Amateur. Jess Sweetser, suffering severely from near-pneumonia, became the first American-born winner of that Championship. Then the team, comprising a nucleus of veterans, with George Von Elm and the two youngsters, Roland MacKenzie, who was only seventeen, and Watts Gunn, returned to St. Andrews for the match and defended the Cup by the narrowest of margins.

Robert T. "Bobby" Jones, who later that year was to win his first British Open, started his series of one-sided victories in singles play by defeating Cyril Tolley, 12 and 11. Jones was never defeated in five singles matches. But the Americans won only six contests against Captain Harris's side, and their 6 to 5 victory traced to Von Elm's tie with Major Charles O. Hezlet in a grim singles contest on the final day.

*1926 U.S. Walker Cup Team. Front row, left to right:
Robert T. Jones, Jr., Roland R. MacKenzie, Jess W.
Sweetser, Francis Ouimet, Watts Gunn. Back row, left
to right: Robert A. Gardner (captain), George Von
Elm, Jesse P. Guilford.*

*1926 British and Irish Walker Cup Team. Front row,
left to right: Cyril J.H. Tolley, Robert Harris, Roger
Wethered (captain). Back row, left to right: Edward F.
Storey, Hon. W.G.E. Brownlow, Sir Ernest W.E. Holderness, Major Charles Hezlet, Andrew Jamieson.*

157

Playing at St. Andrews in 1934, the Americans won their eighth successive victory, by 9 to 2. The British side was Captained by the Hon. Michael Scott, who had won the 1933 British Amateur at the age of 55 and the following year became the oldest competitor in the Walker Cup series.

1934 Walker Cup Team of Great Britain and Ireland. Back row, left to right: Harry G. Bentley, Roger Wethered, Hon. Michael Scott, captain, T.A. Torrance, Eric Fiddian, Cyril J.H. Tolley. Seated, left to right: Eric A. McRuvie, Jack McLean, Sam MacKinlay.

1938

1938—The American team had had a succession of nine victories, the last four by decisive margins. There was every reason for the Americans to be confident again when they went to Scotland in 1938.

The British, however, were most serious. Captain John B. Beck, conducted trials for a squad of players in an effort to end the American string of victories. When the teams met at St. Andrews, the British won two and halved another of the four foursomes to take a lead they never relinquished.

An indication of their excellence was the fact that James Bruen, Jr., and Harry G. Bentley, 3 down at noon, came back with an approximate 68 to halve John Fischer and Charles R. Kocsis.

The Americans needed five victories in singles to insure defense of the Cup. Ward played the Old Course in 67 in the first round and beat Frank Pennink, 12 and 11. Fischer, 4 down at noon, was six under 4s for 16 holes in the afternoon to beat Leonard Crawley. Yates also won. But their victories were not enough. Great Britain finally took possession of the Cup, 7 to 4.

1938 U.S. Walker Cup Team. Front row, left to right: Charles Kocsis, John Goodman, Charles Yates, Fred Haas. Back row, left to right: Harold Pierce (Vice-President U.S.G.A.), Marvin Ward, Francis Ouimet (captain), John Fischer, Reynolds Smith, Ray Billows.

159

1938 Walker Cup Team of Great Britain and Ireland.
Front row, left to right: Harry G. Bentley, Cecil Ewing,
John Beck (non-playing captain), Charles Stowe, James
Bruen, Jr. Back row, left to right: Gordon Peters, Hec-
tor Thomson, Leonard Crawley, Alexander Kyle, J. J.
Pennick.

Ray Billows putting on the huge 16th green in the
Walker Cup singles of 1938. His opponent, Cecil
Ewing, is not visible. Billows lost 1 down to Ewing
as the Great Britain-Ireland team won 7 to 4 in the
overall competition. Courtesy U.S.G.A.

Captain Michael Bonallack proudly exhibits the Walker Cup to his fellow team members after their victory in 1971.

The 1971 U.S. Walker Cup Team. Front row, left to right: Jim Gabrielson, Lanny Wadkins, John Farquahar, Tom Kite, Allen Miller. Back row, left to right: Jim Simon, Marvin Giles, Bill Campbell, John M. Winters, Jr., Bill Hyndman, Steve Melnyk.

Laurie Auchterlonie in his shop making a club.

1947

It took a decade for the United States to regain the Cup. The war intervened and no match was played until the U.S.G.A. sent a team to St. Andrews in 1947. Under normal circumstances, the match would have been played in this country, but postwar conditions would have made the trip difficult for the British.

The match was another close one, closer than the score indicated. Captain Ouimet's side won two foursomes, and Captain Beck's side won two. After eighteen holes of singles play, four British players were ahead and four Americans were leading. It was anyone's match, but the Americans were equal to the occasion.

Ward, 3 down at noon, played fifteen holes in three under 4s to beat Leonard Crawley, 5 and 3,

in the No. 1 contest. Frank Stranahan, 2 down at noon, went to the turn in 34 and defeated Charles Stowes, 2 and 1. The four Americans who had been ahead at noon held their advantages, and the United States regained the Cup, 8 to 4. The team stayed abroad for the British Amateur at Carnoustie, and Willie Turnesa won.

Only one member of this 1947 team had played in 1938—Ward. In the war decade, Ted Bishop, Dick Chapman, Fred Kammer, Smiley Quick, Skee Riegel, Stranahan and Turnesa achieved Cup status and took over from the veterans. In 1951 Turnesa replaced Ouimet as captain. These players were joined in the following two Cup matches by Billy Campbell, Charley Coe, John Dawson, Bobby Knowles, Bruce McCormick, Harold Paddock and Sam Urzetta.

American Walker Cup Team member, Smiley Quick, on crutches before the start of the 1947 Walker Cup match. Quick had stepped on a nail during a practice round. In spite of this injury, he was able to play and won his singles match by 8 and 6 over James C. Wilson as the American team won the cup by a score of 8 to 4.

161

The try-outs for the 1947 British-Irish Walker Cup Team at St. Andrews. Left to right: Max McCready, Charles Stowe, Joe Carr, James Wilson, Alec Kyle, Gerald Micklem, Leonard Crawley, Hamilton Mc-Inally, Laddie Lucas.

1947 U.S. Walker Cup Team. Back row, left to right: George Hamer, Dick Chapman, Frank Stranahan, Willie Turnesa, Fred Kammer. Front row, left to right: Marvin "Bud" Ward, Ted Bishop, Francis Ouimet (captain), Robert "Skee" Riegel, Smiley Quick.

1955

St. Andrews's Old Course, the site of the British Team's best showings in earlier Matches, was again the host course. Britain's only victory, in 1938, had come there. Twice the score at St. Andrews had been 6 to 5, with one match halved. Only one member of the 1955 American side had gone as far as the final of the United States Amateur—Dale Morey, runnerup in 1953. The United States's margin of victory in the 1955 match, 10 to 2, came therefore as something of a surprise. Harvie Ward, who was to win the Amateur Championship in both 1955 and 1956, played brilliantly to defeat Britain's Ronnie White, 6 and 5, in singles. It was the first defeat in Walker Cup competition for White, who had won three earlier single matches. William C. Campbell, Captain of the United States Team, declined to put himself in the lineup for either day of the Match, even though he was one of the strongest and certainly the most experienced American player. Following the match, Lt. Joseph W. Conrad won the British Amateur Championship. It marked the eighth consecutive occasion on which a member of the visiting United States Walker Cup Team had won.

The U.S. Walker Cup Team of 1955. Left to right: Joe Conrad, Billy Joe Patton (hidden from camera), Dale Morey, Bill Campbell (captain), Harvie Ward, Bruce Cudd, Don Cherry, Dick Yost.

The crowd around the 17th "Road Hole" during the Walker Cup matches of 1955.

1955 Walker Cup Team of Great Britain and Ireland. Left to right: Philip Scrutton, Cecil Ewing, David Blair, Ronald J. Whyte, Ian Caldwell, Ernest Millward, Robin Cater, Joe Carr, Gerald Micklem, John L. Morgan. Not shown: non-playing captain, Alec Hill.

1971

On the 50th anniversary of the first informal match between British and American amateurs, Great Britain and Ireland won the Walker Cup for the second time, defeating the United States, 13-11, at St. Andrews, Scotland. Formal competition between the United States and Great Britain and Ireland began in 1922, and the 1971 Match was the 23rd in the series. The British won last in 1938 at St. Andrews, and tied in 1965 at Baltimore. Great Britain and Ireland opened the 1971 Match by sweeping all four of the foursomes competitions the first morning. The United States then won six of the eight afternoon singles matches and halved

one other. After the first day the United States led, 6½-5½. The United States then won the two foursomes the morning of the second day, halved another, and with eight singles matches remaining, led 9-7. The tide swung to the British in the singles. Hugh B. Stuart, of Britain defeated Vinny Giles, 2 and 1. Warren Humphreys, of Britain, holed two monstrous birdie putts on the 15th and 16th, and then won the 17th when Steve Melnyk, his opponent made 6, to win his match, 2 and 1. Charles W. Green, of Britain, was the 16th to go 1 up over Allen Miller, but Miller won the 17th to pull even, and then Green won the 18th with a par 4, beating Miller 1 up. Roddy Carr, of Britain, was 2 up on Jim Simons with two to play. Simons won the 17th, but Carr holed a 30-foot birdie on the 18th to win, 2 up; Bill Hyndman, of the United States, was bunkered on the 16th and lost the hole and Dave Marsh won, 1 up. Jim Gabrielsen, of the United States, lost the 17th and the match to George Macgregor, 1 up. Only Lanny Wadkins and Tom Kite won their singles matches for the United States. Michael F. Bonallack was the playing Captain for Great Britain and Ireland, and John M. Winters, Jr., was non-playing Captain for the United States.

A view taken from the St. Andrews clubhouse of the Walker Cup teams of 1971 at the flag-raising ceremony.

Allen Miller, left, and John Farquhar of 1971 U.S. Walker Cup Team study a putt in the foursomes match. Courtesy Gerry Cranham.

John Farquhar, left, and Allen Miller study a mutual problem in the foursomes during the Walker Cup match of 1971. Courtesy Gerry Cranham.

Walker Cup matches of 1971. Playing the "loop." Courtesy Ian Joy, St. Andrews.

*1971 Walker Cup Team of Great Britain and Ireland.
Left to right: George MacGregor, John MacDonald,
Geoffrey Marks, Rodney Foster, Warren Humphreys,
Michael Bonallack, (captain), David Marsh, Charles
Green, Hugh Z. Stuart, Roddy Carr.*

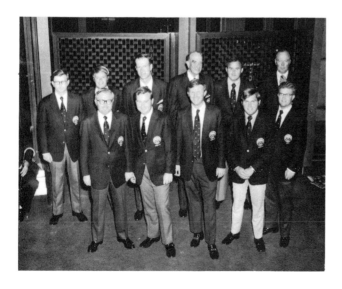

*1971 U.S. Walker Cup Team. Front row, left to right:
John Farquhar, Allen Miller, Marvin Giles, Lanny
Wadkins, Tom Kite. Back Row, left to right: James
Gabrielson, James Simons, William Campbell, John
Winters (non-playing captain), Steve Melnyk, William
Hyndman.* Courtesy Pan-American Airways.

9

Ladies' Golf

LADIES' GOLF AT ST. ANDREWS

According to Miss Enid Wilson, twice Ladies' Open Champion (1928 and 1930) as well as an excellent golf writer and historian, the Ladies' Golf Union of the British Isles had its formal beginning on April 19, 1893 when representatives of some fifteen golf clubs met at London to form an official Ladies' organization.

A Ladies' Golf Club had already been in existence at St. Andrews since 1868 and by 1886 there were five hundred members. There were regular tournaments for gold medals and by 1879 for a silver cross as a second prize.

The meeting of 1893 resulted in the beginning of the Ladies' Golf Union with representatives from all the clubs present making up the basis for the membership. The first official Ladies' Cham-

The ladies, in their "Sunday best," practice their putting in the 1880s.

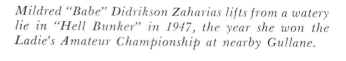
Mildred "Babe" Didrikson Zaharias lifts from a watery lie in "Hell Bunker" in 1947, the year she won the Ladie's Amateur Championship at nearby Gullane.

"Babe" Didrikson Zaharias seems unhappy with the results of her shot from the rough during a friendly game at St. Andrews in 1947.

LADIES' GOLF UNION.

THE SIXTEENTH

LADIES' GOLF CHAMPIONSHIP

WILL BE PLAYED AT

ST. ANDREWS, N.B.,

ON

Tuesday, Wednesday, Thursday, and Friday,
May 19th, 20th, 21st, and 22nd, 1908.

W. C. Henderson & Son, Printers, St. Andrews.

LADIES' GOLF UNION.

THE THIRTY-SECOND

Ladies'
Golf Championship

WILL BE PLAYED AT

St. Andrews, Fife,

ON

Monday, Tuesday, Wednesday, Thursday & Friday,
May 13th, 14th, 15th, 16th & 17th, 1929.

Miss Brigitte Varangot, Ladies' Amateur Champion of 1965. This tournament was only the third ladies' championship ever held at the Old Course. Miss Varangot also won the cup in 1963 and 1968.

when Miss Maude Titterton defeated Miss Dorothy Campbell at the 19th hole in the final round, the second in 1929 when Miss Joyce Wethered defeated Miss Glenna Collett of the United States, 3 and 1 and again in 1965 when Miss Brigitte Varangot of France defeated Mrs. Ian (Belle) Robertson by a score of 4 and 3.

Miss Cecil Leitch, Ladies' Champion of 1914, 1920, 1921 and 1926 has kindly supplied her reminiscences of the 1908 championship won by Maude Titterton. Miss Leitch herself was eliminated by Miss Titterton 1 up in the semi-final match. In her own words here is Miss Leitch's description of her own match with Miss Titterton and of the final match between Miss Titterton and Miss Campbell:

"It was a perfect morning when we set out, and my start was an auspicious one, for I was 4 up at the 7th. But at the 5th hole I found my brassie was broken and not being possessed of a duplicate, I began to fall back almost from that point.

Miss Titterton played a perfect tee-shot at the 11th or Eden hole, a one-shot hole of 148 yards, that finished 2 feet from the pin. The wind was

pionship was held that year over the Royal Lytham and St. Anne's links. The winner was Lady Margaret Scott who continued to win the championship for the next two years as well.

The Ladies' Championship has been held at St. Andrews only three times in more than one hundred years. Perhaps this might be viewed as a commentary on the state of welcome the ladies enjoy at St. Andrews but, on the other hand, it may be due to the fact that unlike the men's Open Championship which has a fixed "rota" or rotation among a certain few championship course sites such as Troon, Carnoustie, Birkdale and a few others, the Ladies have played their championships on many of the same courses as the men but also have added many other links to their schedule and have even occasionally played their championship in Ireland at Portmarnock near Dublin or Newcastle in County Down.

Three times a Ladies' Golf Champion has been crowned at St. Andrews. The first time was in 1908

Mrs. Ian (Belle) Robertson, runner-up to Brigitte Varangot for the Ladies' Amateur Championship of 1965.

170

Miss Dorothy Campbell, runner-up to Maude Titterton in 1908 for the Ladies' Amateur Championship. The match went nineteen holes before it was decided. Miss Campbell eventually won the championship in 1911.

dead against at this hole and she showed sound judgment in taking a wooden club.

For the first time she took the lead at the 12th; I secured a hard half at the 13th by holing an 18-yard putt after Miss Titterton had put her 3rd dead for a 4, I won the 14th, so we were all square with 4 to go. The next two holes Miss Titterton won in perfect 4's and she stood dormie 2. My backers looked very glum. They looked still glummer when I took 4 to reach the green of the famous road hole (456 yards) and was still some 12 yards from the hole.

Miss Titterton, however, was weak with her third, and 2 yards short with the like. To keep the match alive, I had to hole that long putt, and Miss Titterton had to miss her short one. Nothing seemed less probable. The first part was achieved, for I holed my putt, to the delight of a large section of the huge crowd, whose cheering caused a young horse in a jaunting car to bolt across the course. Whether Miss Titterton heard the crash as the car was smashed to matchwood I know not, but she missed the putt and on we went to the 18th, the home hole (360 yards) Incidentally when I holed that long putt on the 17th green, I was told that a spectator was heard to exclaim, "The child's inspired!"

On the 18th my drive was satisfactory, but Miss Titterton topped hers. The ball ricocheted along, hit the far bank of Swilcan Burn, rebounded thence on to the bridge, and finally came to rest on the fairway. Miss Titterton made no mistake about the next, and we both reached the green in 3 and were down in 5 without any further thrills. Miss Titterton thus winning 1 up and passing into the final. The other semi-final, between two dour fighters, required four extra holes before Miss Campbell could win, phenomenal putting marking the closing stages of this match.

The crowd that congregated for the final was worthy of St. Andrews, and so was the play that ensued. Miss Titterton led by a hole at the turn. At about this stage of the match a terrific hailstorm burst over the course but failed to damp the ardor of the spectators. At the 13th hole Miss Campbell was 3 down. To be 3 down with 5 to go is a terrible position, enough to daunt anyone. But Miss Campbell was one of those whom nothing daunts, and besides experience had taught her that a lead of that kind often has an enervating influence on the holder of it. So grimly and hopefully she stuck to her task, and actually won 3 of the next 4 holes, the two players standing on the 18th tee all square. A kind providence again watched over Miss Titterton's ball, for she topped her tee shot and this time jumped the burn. Had she not missed a short putt the match would have been over at the home green.

Away the players and spectators went again to the first tee. This hole, known as the Burn, is 365 yards, and short of the green is Swilcan Burn, a death trap for unwary second shots. Miss Campbell played short with her second, and Miss Titterton had to decide whether she would do the same or "go for it." It was a terribly anxious problem. On her decision might hang the issue of the championship. Her caddie put her brassie into her hand. Miss Titterton demurred but the caddie insisted.

"Well," said Miss Titterton, "I don't think I can do it, but if I do I'll give you five pounds." The caddie was justified. Miss Titterton carried the burn and won the championship and with it the admiration of all for a lion-hearted shot at the crisis of the match."

These articles first appeared in Cecil Leitch, *Golf*, and Enid Wilson, *Women's Golf.*

A rare photograph from the archives of the Ladies' Golf Union showing Miss Maude Titterton, on the left, Ladies' Champion of 1908. The other women, from left to right, are: Miss Cecil Leitch, Miss Mather, and Miss Dorothy Campbell. Miss Leitch went on to win the championship in 1914, 1920, 1921, and 1926, and was runner-up twice to Joyce Wethered, in 1922 and 1925. Miss Campbell was Ladies' Champion in 1911.

LADIES' CHAMPIONSHIP OF 1929

Miss Joyce Wethered, tall and thin, shy and unobtrusive, became a student of the game largely because of the enthusiasm of her brother, Roger Wethered. When he was Captain of Golf at Oxford, she met and played with his friends, was drawn into their arguments, and must have theorized on the perfection of style and the composition of the swing in a manner which no other woman had ever done before. Playing with the leading amateurs developed her game quickly and made her impervious to superior power. From a quiet house or a secluded part of an hotel, she would come to the first tee, smile charmingly at her opponent when they met at the commencement of their game, and then, almost as though in a trance, become a golfing machine. She never involved her personality, and those who played her had the impression that they, the crowd and the state of the

Glenna Collett, later Mrs. Edwin H. Vare, Jr., is pictured with the United States Women's Amateur Championship trophy, which she won no less than six times between 1922 and 1935. No one else has won so many. Glenna was runner-up to Joyce Wethered for the Ladies' Amateur Championship of the British Isles in 1929.

game had ceased to exist in her mind and that her entire faculties were being focused on swinging to perfection and holing the ball in the fewest number of strokes. The match concluded, Miss Wethered would vanish and be seen no more until the starter called her name for the next round. Her seeming remoteness from all the stress and strain that troubles ordinary people who go to championship meetings bewildered her opponents; her indifference to what they did became positively nightmarish to them, and made her task very much easier. This cloak of inhumanity was not created to frighten the enemy; it served to conceal an intense concentration, and to conserve its owner's physical strength. Miss Wethered was fragile in appearance, and there was nothing of the Amazon about her. Strength and stamina she must have had to withstand the physical and mental effort of a week's championship golf; but perhaps, knowing that her resources were not over-abundant, she

evolved the most economical method to suit her physique and, by shutting out everything of an extraneous nature, avoided the strain which others found so sapping and destructive, although this strain was not unknown to her in the later stages of her more memorable battles with Miss Cecil Leitch and Miss Glenna Collett. Joyce brought to her game power combined with perfection of style and a hitherto unknown degree of accuracy.

Miss Wethered annexed the English title for the third time in succession in 1922. As a matter of fact, she entered for the English each year between 1920 and 1924, and was never beaten. Furthermore, in 1924, she gobbled up the rest of her adversaries as a matter of course and so found herself holder of the British for the second time in three years.

So absorbed had we become in the affairs of our two great ones that we took little heed of what was happening on the other side of the ocean, and the progress of Miss Glenna Collett, who in 1924 swept the board in America and held every title of importance, apart from the National which she had held previously, meant little to us until she arrived here in the spring of 1925, to challenge Miss Wethered for the British, which was held at Troon. In no time, we had a very real respect for her, and the meeting between these two was an epic of the third round. In this match, Miss Wethered was greater than she had ever been before and although Miss Collett produced golf that would have eliminated anyone else with ease, she lost on the fifteenth, the score against her being level fours.

Miss Wethered decided then to retire from championship golf. She was then twenty-four, and having won the British title three times and the English title five, felt that she had earned a less active role. So she quit the stage; although, as it turned out, not for good.

Miss Collett brought to our notice that women's golf in the United States was making giant strides, and that any invasion party she might lead would constitute a menace to the British.

The lure of St. Andrews was too strong for Miss Wethered, who came out of her self-imposed retirement when the British was held there in 1929. It also attracted Miss Glenna Collett, and several other prominent Americans. Miss Wethered, with characteristic honesty, denied that her motives in entering were patriotic, that she wanted to keep the invaders away. The historic associations of the Old Course were more than she could resist. Only her intimate friends were aware of the quality of her golf, and the rest of the world had to wait patiently until her arrival in Scotland to see if any changes had taken place during the past four years.

About Miss Collett there were no uncertainties; we knew she was at her zenith and that she was easily the best and most powerful woman golfer on the other side of the Atlantic. She was fully acquainted with our courses and climate, and we were not a little afraid that she would achieve her ambition and carry off our cup. With Miss Wethered and Miss Collett in opposite halves of the draw, the concern of the entire golfing community was centered on the final to come. Had anyone upset the apple-cart and prevented the drama from taking place, they would never have been forgiven —especially in the light of what followed. The earlier rounds were training centers to build up form for the vital combat. Certainly nothing else was talked of at St. Andrews that week. The opinion prevailed that "she" would win; and yet, with all the implicit faith we had, there was a little gnawing worm of anxiety. Miss Wethered arrived at St. Andrews with no idea of the impending strain; but as the week wore on, she must have been fully aware of the hopes which she carried, and on the morning of the final the tension of this terrific meeting must have been very real to her.

The weather had wavered during the earlier part of the championship, and then relented, so that when the enormous crowd gathered to witness the piéce de resistance, the sun was shining from a cloudless sky. This lovely morning must have helped Miss Collett. In the previous rounds, the American had not quite produced the golf of which we knew she was capable. Now, with everything at stake, she rose to the occasion, and without a vestige of a mistake she reached the turn in 34. Such golf was almost unblievable, and Miss Wethered, who had played neither very well nor very ill, was five down. Up to the twelfth, Miss Collett was a woman inspired, beyond mortal reach. And then, with a putt to become six up, certainly no more difficult and not as long as some which she had holed with ease that morning, she missed. The spell was broken, and she became human once more. This was what Miss Wethered must have hoped and waited for, and slowly but surely she took command of the game and won back three of the six holes that remained before lunch.

A thoroughly scared and chastened crowd went to find nourishment and fortification for what the afternoon might have in store. The consensus of opinion was that Miss Wethered had passed the storm and would sail home with moderate comfort. The Elders of St. Andrews must also have been shaken by the best ball of the two distinguished ladies, which was 71. Nothing to equal this had been produced in a women's final before.

After lunch, Miss Collett's lead evaporated. The position at the twenty-seventh was Miss Wethered four up. She had taken 73 strokes for the homeward half of the first round and the outward half of the second one. All seemed secure, and then back came Miss Collett with two birdie threes, to make a fight and show that she still had shots left in her locker. Crisis loomed large on the thirty-third hole for Miss Wethered, who looked likely to lose it and be only one up with three to play; however, a six-yard putt rescued her, and provided the vitally-needed half. The match concluded at the Road hole. Miss Wethered had achieved her ambition of winning the British at St. Andrews, and the fulfillment of the wish had come to pass with superlative golf. Miss Collett never capitulated, never ceased from fighting, every inch of those thirty-five holes. What a glorious game it was!

Every generation swears that its sporting heroes and heroines are better than any before or since, and one spectator at least will always be happy in the belief that nothing could surpass the final of the British in 1929. Superb skill, artistry, sportsmanship and drama for an entire day! These qualities, and the classic setting in which they were framed, made this the finest moment in British women's golf.

This article first appeared in Enid Wilson, *Women's Golf: A History of Golf in Britain.*

Here is portion of Joyce Wethered's own description of the conclusion of the final match:
The fifteenth finally decided the result. I had sliced my drive and was unable to reach the green in two. A poor run up left me still six yards from the hole with Glenna lying practically dead in three. It looked very like being only one up, and in such a crisis, with still three holes to go, anything might have happened. But the most opportune putt I have ever made came to my rescue. I holed the six-yarder for a half and kept my lead of two, which I was able to hold on to till the seventeenth green. I did not feel in the least like holing the putt, and even when it was on its way I scarcely realized that it was going in. Generally there is an instinct about a putt which tells you what is probably going to happen. This time I had no such warning. I only remember feeling distinctly desperate and hitting the ball rather hard as the putt was uphill; and then the hole gobbled it up. Thank heavens there are still such happy surprises in the world!

The next hole we halved to make me dormy two. Then at the seventeenth, a very exacting hole in any circumstances, I was relieved of the responsibility of playing it really well, as Glenna took four to reach the plateau. All the same I shall not easily forget the anxiety of keeping the ball safely in play on nearing the dreaded green. It is the most trying of all experiences to keep cool just on the brink of winning; so easy to lose control and spoil it all. It was also impossible to ignore the pent-up excitement of the crowd which was ready to break out as soon as the last putt was struck. When the moment finally came it threatened very nearly to destroy us. Glenna and I were torn apart and became the centre of a squeezing, swaying, and almost hysterical mob, shouting and cheering themselves hoarse.

Thrilling as was the wild enthusiasm around us I was gratefully relieved to find struggling at my side two stalwart officers of the law. After what seemed an eternity we were able to force our way, yard by yard, through the crowd to the road by the side of the green, and from there gradually to the steps of the Hotel.

Quoted with permission from *Golfing Memories and Methods* by Joyce Wethered, Hutchinson and Co, London 1933.

PART III

A St. Andrews Miscellany

10

Why There Are Eighteen Holes on a Golf Course

Golf became an 18-hole game at St. Andrews, Scotland, a little less than 200 years ago, according to Robert Browning, Editor of the British magazine *Golfing*.

During the latter half of the eighteenth century, the rules, standards, and fashions of golf were set by the Honourable Company of Edinburgh Golfers, who played their golf over the Links of Leith. However, this leadership was gradually taken over by the members of the Royal and Ancient Golf Club, who played their golf over the links of St. Andrews. Until the middle of the eighteenth century, golf had been played over courses of no established length. Leith, for example, had only 5 holes. Blackheath, another ancient club, had 7, which was the most fashionable number; but other courses had as many as 25. Possibly 7 would have remained the traditional number for a round had it not been for the example of St. Andrews.

At the time, St. Andrews had 12 holes. The first 11 traveled straight out to the end of a small peninsula. After playing these the golfers returned to the clubhouse by playing the first 10 greens backward, plus a solitary green by the clubhouse. Thus, a "round" of golf at St. Andrews consisted of 22 holes. In 1764, however, the Royal and Ancient resolved that the first 4 holes should be converted into 2. Since this change automatically converted the same 4 holes into 2 on the way back, the "round" was reduced from 22 holes to 18. And since St. Andrews was the arbiter of all that was correct about golf, 18 holes soon came to be accepted as standard throughout Scotland and England and, eventually, the world. This is the accepted reason why a round consists of 18 holes.

This article first appeared in
Encyclopedia of Golf,
edited by Robert Scharff & the
editors of *Golf Magazine*

11

Early Golf

In Holland, in the 1600s there was a game called "Het Kolven." From contemporary literature and paintings it appears that the game was played in wide open spaces such as in roads or on frozen lakes or rivers, that a ball was struck from a tee and flew long distances in the air, that the game was played from hole to hole or from one stake or marker to another similar stake or marker. From literary sources we know, too, that the ball had to be played from the spot where it happened to come to rest on the ground or ice.

The clubs used were startlingly like the wooden shafted golfclubs of the late 1800s, were slender wooden instruments with leather grips and graceful heads or metal or wood which were attached to a supple shaft by "whipping" or wrapping with closely laid cord or line which effected a strong joining between the shaft of the club and its head. The ball then in use was small and light, probably stuffed with hair or a similar material and there is no question of doubt but that it flew long distances when struck fairly. In other words, in the 1600s the Dutch were playing a game close to the game of golf as we know it today. In the eighteenth century there was even a Dutch Amateur Championship which was contested for annually. The game in Holland later lost its popularity and fell into disuse.

The earliest reference to golf on St. Andrews links occurs in a parchment document dated January 25, 1552 in which the Archbishop, John Hamilton, acknowledges that while he has received permission from the authorities to raise rabbits in the "northern part of the common links adjacent to the water of Eden" the community continued to reserve the right among other things "to play at golf" not only where the rabbits were being raised but in other parts of the links as well.

Although this is the first written reference to golf at St. Andrews it is most likely that the game had been played for a hundred years or so prior to this time. As early as 1457 King James II was issuing decrees which sought to punish "anyone who wasted his time at the 'futball and the golf.'" In a schoolboy's diary, that of one James Melville in 1571 (Could he have been a forbear of the late Amateur Champion?) we find references to his "necessars for archerie and goff" and for his "glub and bals." James Graham, Marquis of Montrose, kept accounts of his expenses during his student days at St. Andrews subsequent to his entrance there in 1627. For example, he details such items as: "For two golf-balls, 24 shillings, for new clubs and dressing some clubs, and for balls 11 pounds and 8 shillings."

In the minute books of the Town Council of the City of St. Andrews on the 24th of September, 1776, the Council permitted one William Gib to use the links in the raising of rabbits but the links were "not to be spoiled where the golfing is used." The raising of the rabbits caused a great deal of consternation later on in the history of the links when it appeared that the little beasts would take over the golf course for their own personal use exclusively.

Later on, when a landowner named Dempster acquired the land there was a tenant on it, one Ritchie who pastured his sheep there, an unobjectionable situation we are sure because the sheep would help to keep the ground mowed properly. But Dempster, it appears, bought up Ritchie's lease and then leased the land at three times the former rental to a James Begbie for a "rabbit 'warren.'"

The rabbits, of course, acted like rabbits and pretty soon it was impossible for the custodians of the course to fill up the rabbit-holes as fast as the rabbits were making them. Later on, in the lawsuit which ensued George Robertson, "ball-maker and caddie" testified that in one day he and John Morris had counted 895 repairs and on another occasion 1197.

A number of residents of St. Andrews brought suit against Dempster claiming that "Since time immemorial the links have been used by the inhabitants for the exercise of golf which was claimed to be its "chief purpose" and since the conduct of the defendant in allowing the rabbits to damage the links was interfering with those rights of the citizens to play golf, Dempster should be enjoined from continuing his conduct or from "molesting the plaintiffs in exercising their rights," that he be ordered to remove and destroy the rabbits.

In the case of the Golfers of St. Andrews versus Charles Dempster, et. al. in 1813, the court with great unanimity gave judgment in favor of the "pursuers," that is, the Golfers of St. Andrews. The "pursuers" won the case but no one has been able ever since to convince the descendants of Mr. Dempster's original rabbits that they should not make their home on the Old Course. The local rules at the Old Course provide for a "free drop" from a rabbit burrow in which the golfer finds his ball. It is an amusing thought to consider the smiling rabbit descendant of one of Mr. Dempster's original family, as he peeks out of his rabbit-hole and watches a modern-day golfer drop his ball over his shoulder.

12

How the Royal and Ancient Got Its Name

The right to the designation "Royal" is bestowed by the favor of Sovereign or a member of the Royal House. In most cases the title is granted along with the bestowal of royal patronage in the Club. The Royal and Ancient was the first to receive the designation "Royal," King William the Fourth having bestowed the honor in 1834.

The silver and gold balls and other treasures of the Royal and Ancient Golf Club at St. Andrews. Andrew Wright holds the famous Open Belt.

13

Equipment

The rubber-cored ball was much more pleasant to hit and travelled better, but although the effect of its greater distance was profound, the change came gradually. (When the rubber ball was first on the market it was expensive and easily damaged. Many golfers could not afford the luxury of the more costly ball.) When the early difficulties in its manufacture were overcome and the rubber-cored ball became more serviceable the ball did completely replace the solid "guttie" ball. The revolution in golf balls was certainly not instantaneous and complete. It came over a matter of several years during which the leading golfers used both types of balls.

An interesting accessory of those early days was the india-rubber tee which was a strip of rubber moulded to hold the ball at one end and was attached at the opposite end to a "bob weight" which was meant to keep the whole contraption from flying away when the ball was driven from its rubber perch.

The London Times of August 15, 1898 had an interesting story about the finding of a well-preserved set of old golf clubs in a house at Hull, Scotland near Old Troon. The clubs had been boarded up in an old closet some time between the year 1700, when a serious fire burned the premises, and 1741, the date of an old Yorkshire newspaper found with the clubs. The article, after describing the circumstances under which they were re-discovered described them in this fashion:

Laurie Auchterlonie, Honorary Professional of the Royal and Ancient Golf Club, admires his handiwork on a new wooden putter, the "Auchterlonie" model. Note the brass sole. If this were a replica of an old putter he would have used ram's horn instead of brass.

183

"The clubs evidently form a set used by a golfer of the time. The set consists of six wooden clubs and two iron clubs. They must have been designed and made by the same person, and that person a golfer and experienced club-maker. The clubs are all noticeably heavier in the head and longer in the shaft, and in all respects bigger than modern clubs. (Author's Note: Remember 'modern clubs of 1898' is what is meant). The wooden clubs comprised drivers and spoons, there being nothing corresponding to the brassie and the putter. The heads are of unequal weight and the shafts of unequal length. The iron clubs appear to correspond to our cleeks and irons of today, but are much heavier and clumsier. The iron might be described as being as much of a niblick as an iron for it is evidently adapted to playing in sand. It is a formidable looking implement and has more the appearance of a weapon than a golf club. Its weight is 28 ounces, as compared with 16½ ounces, the weight of the irons with which Fernie, the ex-champion, plays. The length of the club from the top of the shaft to the ground is 43½ inches, about 4 inches longer than Fernie's iron."

The head is a rough piece of blacksmith work with a socket 3½ inches in circumference into which the shaft is fixed in exactly the way it is fixed in the present day. The cleek, which might be called an iron, is of comparable dimensions and character.

The wooden clubs are built in the same general way as those of the present day but there is a marked variance in the size of the head and the length of the shaft. In every case they have a flatter lie. The longest has a shaft 6 inches longer than the driver Fernie uses and there is a difference of eight inches (46 to 54) between Fernie's club and the old one measured from the top of each shaft all along the sole to the "nose." The head is abnormally large according to modern ideas. There is at least twice as much wood as in the average club of the present day. The weight difference is 4 ounces, most of it represented by the weight of lead in the head.

Three of the clubs have no added grip and it is not certain that they ever had. The grips, on the clubs that have them, consist of coarse woolen selvedge wound around the shafts. The shafts themselves and the heads are of a wood not unlike hickory.

When the Twentieth century opened and the "guttie" (gutta percha) was the ball everyone used, a whippy shaft was preferred to one that was on the stiff side. But then the golfers found that too much "whippiness" led to monstrous errors, especially slices from left to right and demand began to develop for a firmer type of shaft. The straight-grained hickory shaft filled the bill, it was found, and soon good hickory shafts became more and more difficult to find. Many of the clubs of those early days acted differently. It was the ideal of every golfer to obtain clubs that matched each other as closely as possible, in flexibility and "feel." Even the great "Bobby" Jones, who certainly had the ability to obtain the best in golf equipment because of his reputation and standing the the golf world, never did assemble what he felt was a truly balanced, matched set of hickory-shafted clubs. Jones himself said, in his book *Golf Is My Game*, "Prior to that time (November, 1930) there were no satisfactory iron clubs made in this country. The American irons were too long from heel to toe and had a "tinny" appearance and feel. Striking the ball off center produced a most unpleasant shock in the hands of the player. A satisfactory iron could be had only by using a British-made hand-forged head." All of Jones' clubs in the twenties were hickory-shafted with hand-fashioned forged heads. Most of them bore the famous "pipe" trademark of Tom Stewart of St. Andrews. Each time Jones would go to St. Andrews he would visit Stewart's shop and work with the club-maker as he "finished" a particular club to Jones' taste. The set of Jones' clubs which he used in winning his "Grand Slam" consisted of eleven irons and five woods, quite a heavy load for the caddie of that day, much in contrast to the set of the "ordinary" golfer who got by with two or three wooden clubs and an iron set which usually consisted of a mid-iron, mashie, mashie-niblick, niblick and putter or a total of eight clubs in all.

14

The Rules of Golf

On May 14, 1754 twenty-two "Noblemen and Gentlemen" who were admirers of the ancient and "healthfull" exercise of "the Golf," met together in St. Andrews, Scotland to consider the drafting of certain "Articles and Laws" relating to "playing the Golf." These twenty-two men, the original members of what we now call the Royal and Ancient Golf Club, were at that time known as "The Society of St. Andrews Golfers."

In the 1740s there had been established at Leith, Scotland, "The Honourable Company of Gentlemen Golfers," golf's first organized society. After "playing at the golf" in those days, these men were accustomed to meet at "Luckie" Clephan's tavern at Leith. One of the moving spirits behind the Society in Leith was Duncan Forbes, an eminent statesman, the Lord President of the Court in Session, who has been described as "a patriot without ostentation or pretense, a true Scotsman with no prejudices, an accomplished and erudite scholar." Forbes was such an avid golfer that in spite of his heavy official duties he would be seen knocking a golf ball along the seashore even on those days in the winter when snow made the Leith links unplayable.

For several years, the Honourable Company met at Clephan's without any formal organization, it seems. Then, stimulated to action by a gift to them by the Edinburgh Town Council of a silver golf club to be played for annually according to "the proper regulations" (drawn up at the desire of the

Magistrates by the "Gentlemen Golfers"), the Honourable Company decided that it had better get down to legal business and decide upon what the "proper regulations" would be.

It was clear that the Town Council considered the group as a true "body politic" (perhaps "golfing body politic" would be preferable), for the Minutes of the Town Council of March 7, 1744 document the recognition of the Society's existence and the beginning of their written records. The records have been kept since that time and constitute the oldest continuous records of any golf club in the world.

The first minutes of the Club prescribed the Rules of Golf to be observed on the links, as well as the regulations for the competition for the new trophy, the Silver Club. One of the conditions the winner had to observe, interestingly, was that he should append to the Silver Club a gold or silver coin or ball. This unique style of trophy is still contested for and at this writing there are three Silver clubs in the possession of the Honourable Company festooned with brilliantly polished silver golf balls, two of them completely filled with the silver orbs and the third nearly filled.

However, the Honourable Company of Edinburgh Golfers fell upon hard times. The Leith links were wet and drainage was an increasing problem. More and more members were finding golf at nearby Musselburgh more comfortable and were using those facilities. There were encroachments on the links from cattle and even military activities during the Napoleonic Wars. In 1831 there occurred a financial crisis which ended in the forced sale of their "Golf House" and all of its valuable historical contents. Fortunately, the club trophies were not sold, but the furniture and fixtures were. And so it was not until November 11, 1835, four years later, that the Honourable Company of Edinburgh Golfers would again come to life with a deposit of £ 260 18 s. 8 d. in the Royal Bank of Scotland.

In the meantime, the Society of St. Andrews Golfers had formed their own association in 1754, eleven years after the first rules and regulations of golf has been laid down by the Honourable Company. The St. Andrews group adopted the 1744 rules and regulations practically word for word when they decided to set down their official rules. There was only one small difference between the two sets of rules, and that difference seems to have been called for because of a basic variation in the conditions of the links themselves.

At St. Andrews a ball lying in water had to be picked out and dropped under penalty of one stroke while at Leith, the player was allowed to tee his ball up under the same circumstances. This is certainly understandable to us at this great distance in time, because if the Leith links had to be abandoned, as they were a few years later, because of the marshiness of the land, it would seem obvious that a ball at Leith links would be constantly in water or on soggy turf and the golfer therefore repeatedly subject to penalty upon penalty.

Here are the thirteen articles of the original Rules of Golf:

1. You must tee your ball within one club's length of the hole.

2. Your tee must be on the ground.

3. You are not to change the ball you strike off the tee.

4. You are not to remove stones, bones or any "break club" for the sake of playing your ball, except upon the Fair Green, and that only within a club's length of your ball.

5. If your ball come upon "watter" or any "wattery' filth, you are at liberty to take out your ball and, bringing it behind the hazard and teeing it, you may play it with any club and allow your adversary a stroke for so getting your ball.

6. If your balls be found anywhere touching one another, you are to lift the first ball till you play the last.

7. At holing, you are to play your ball honestly for the hole, and not play upon your adversary's ball not lying in your way to the hole.

8. If you should lose your ball, by its being taken up, or any other way, you are to go back to the spot where you last struck and drop another ball and allow your adversary a stroke for the misfortune.

9. No man, at holing his ball, is to be allowed to mark his way to the hole with his club or anything else.

10. If a ball be stopped by any person, horse, dog or anything else, the ball so stopp'd must be play'd where it lyes.

11. If you draw your club in order to strike and proceed so far in the strokes as to be bringing down your club, if then your club shall break in any way, it is to be accounted a stroke.

12. He whose ball lyes farthest from the hole is obliged to play first.

13. Neither trench, ditch or dyke made for the preservation of the links, nor the Scholar's holes or the Soldier's lines, shall be accounted a hazard. But ball is to be taken out and tee'd and play'd with an iron club.

NOTE: The references to "Scholar's Holes and Soldier's lines" were what would be called "local rules" today. The drilling of the local militia and cavalry undoubtedly caused strange holes and tracks on the course. The Scholar's holes were probably considered more "unfair" than the normal hazard and thus subject to this special exception.

By the year 1775 there were only five differences in the original code, and those were primarily differences of degree. The teeing ground was gradually moved farther and farther away from the hole. The greens were certainly suffering from the scrapes of the driving strokes of the players and it was thought better to give them a separate teeing ground. The first rule concerning proximity of the balls came into effect: a ball within six inches of another could be lifted without penalty. The problem of the "stymie" would continue to bother the rule-makers and the golfers of the world for nearly two hundred years, when it would finally be abolished in 1951.

Not until 1885, when the Royal and Ancient was approached and asked to act in the matter, was it thought useful for all golfers in general to play under the same set of rules. The Royal and Ancient was asked to form an Association under one set of rules. From 1885 until 1888 the momentous problem was studied, and at last uniform "Rules of Golf" were issued to the golfers of the world with an official status that carried the weight of authority. Finally, in 1897, the Royal and Ancient Club was given the sole control of the

Rules of Golf Committee. Until then other golf clubs had been represented on the Committee. In 1919, the Royal and Ancient took over the responsibility for the administration of the Open and Amateur Championships, a task which it has carried out in handsome fashion ever since. Truly, the Royal and Ancient Golf Club may be said to be a most benign and effective Parliament and Supreme Court of the Rules of Golf. For nearly two hundred years, the Rules of Golf have stood the test of time in glorious fashion.

15

Bobby Jones and St. Andrews

The United States Golf Association named Watts Gunn and me on the international team of eight members to play at St. Andrews, Scotland, for the Walker Cup, an event played every two years, alternately in this country and Great Britain. We also were to play as individuals in the British Amateur championship at Muirfield, Scotland, and four of us—Watts, Roland McKenzie, George Von Elm and I—were to stay over and play in the British Open championship at St. Anne's-On-The-Sea, England. When I started in the British Amateur I had already booked my passage home. I had decided not to play in the British Open, which was only a couple of weeks before our own open championship at the Scioto Country Club, Columbus.

I went fairly well in the opening rounds of the British Amateur. Anyway, I got to the top of my game by the fifth round and shot my head off against Robert Harris, 1925 British Amateur champion. I won nine of the twelve holes the match lasted, defeating him 8 - 6. And the next day, a youngster named Andrew Jamieson, about my age, gave me a tidy lacing, 4 - 3, in fifteen holes on which he was never above par, and was twice below it. I wasn't shooting par golf, but I wasn't so bad, at that. He just beat me.

I felt pretty blue when Jamieson stopped me. And more than ever, I wanted to go home. But

Bobby Jones with Ben Sayers in 1921. Caddie Martin, famous one-armed caddie, is at left.

here's the working of fate. If I'd been fortunate enough to go on through and win the British Amateur, I'd certainly have sailed for home a week later.

Then I got to thinking that if I went home now it would look as if I were sulking over failing to

An interesting shot of lady spectators in the 1920s straining for a view of Bobby Jones.

pretty regular, and they total as low a score as had ever been made in the British open championship to that time. I scraped my scores at St. Anne's if I ever scraped them; I used all the golf I knew and right up to the last few holes it looked as if it weren't enough.

I was two strokes down to Al Watrous with five holes to play. Watrous had done a 69 to my 73 in the third round and was leading the pack by two strokes. At the seventeenth Al and I were level. His drive was straight and in the fairway. Mine was at the left on an imposing acreage of sand, with dunes between it and the green. I had a medium iron left for a green I could not see from where I stood. The shot came off. My ball was inside Al's. He took three putts. I had a stroke in hand. I picked up another on Al at the finishing hole where his ball rolled into a bunker from the tee, and mine barely skirted it—plain luck. The two strokes were the margin.

This article first appeared in Robert T. Jones, Jr. and O. B. Keeler, *Down the Fairway*

win the British Amateur championship and I didn't want to think so. So I thought I'd stay on for the British Open, and try my best to show them a little good golf. No amateur had won it since 1897, when Harold Hilton's name went on the beautiful old trophy.

Jess Sweetser went on through several tough matches to the finals with A. F. Simpson and won handily and we all headed for St. Andrews, the home of golf, where the international team matches were to be played the following Wednesday and Thursday.

We won the big cup again, by a single point, and I feel it was George Von Elm's grim battle with Major Hezlett, resulting in a halved match, that gave us the margin. Watts Gunn performed nobly, getting a lot of revenge on the Hon. W. G. Brownlow, a most engaging youngster who had put Watts out of the recent championship. Watts beat him 9 - 8 in the singles matches at St. Andrews, and Watts and I beat Cyril Tolley and Andrew Jamieson in the foursomes. I met Tolley in the singles division and had the first really satisfactory round I had yet played in Britain, which, with Tolley's wildness in the opening holes, put me 9 up in the first round and closed the match 12 - 11 in the early afternoon. I was a stroke under par for the match and that is something to be happy about on the Old Course at St. Andrews, to my way of thinking the greatest golf course in the world.

I won the British Open championship, to quote Mr. Darwin again, "without ever being quite on my game." Or maybe that *is* my game, and the scores below 70 are merely flashes. Anyway, my cards were 72 + 72 + 73 + 74 = 291. They look

Robert T. "Bobby" Jones with his second Open Championship trophy, 1927. He had won the previous year for the first time at Royal Lytham and St. Anne's.

BOBBY JONES WINS AT
ST. ANDREWS

I wish Bobby Jones' admirers in his own country could have witnessed the scene at St. Andrews when he rapped the putt of three inches into the hole that made him, by six strokes, again British Open Champion. They would have realized that there is one respect in which Britain declines to be beaten by America, namely, in enthusiasm for Bobby.

It really was an astonishing, almost a terrifying scene. There were, at a conservative estimate, twelve thousand people round the last green. As soon as that last putt was holed, the crowd flung away stewards as if they were straws and, caring nothing for anyone else who was going to putt on that green, stormed the slope. In a twinkling of an eye the champion had disappeared. "One moment stood he as the angels stand" and then "the next he was not." He was just swallowed up. Either he or somebody else seemed bound to be squashed to death, but after what appeared an age, but was, I suppose, only a few seconds, he reappeared, borne aloft on willing shoulders and in turn himself bearing aloft his precious putter.

His cap soon vanished, but after the crowd had surged this way and that with their load for several minutes, he and his putter were safely on dry land again—not, however, before a rescuing party had set out from the Royal and Ancient clubhouse to save him.

There was another great scene when Bobby was handed the cup, but this time he was safe inside the clubhouse railings where he made his very modest and charming little speech of thanks and announced that he was going to leave the cup in the care of the Royal and Ancient Club, of which he is a member.

These scenes of unexampled enthusiasm were, of course, evidence of a very great personal popularity, but I think they were also evidence of something else: a general conviction that Bobby was so superior that it would have been a shame and an outrage if anyone else had dared to win. For a visitor to be able to force that conviction upon the whole of an intensely patriotic Scottish crowd is an astonishing thing, altogether outside the power of any other golfer in the world.

I am not going to tell again at length the story which has already long since been flashed across the Atlantic. It differed from the story of most of Bobby's triumphs in that he made his own pace and led from start to finish. As a rule he has come

Bobby Jones returns in 1927 after winning at St. Andrews.

190

up from behind. This time he got in front right away with his 68, and then had to stay there. To those of us who were looking on, there never seemed any real doubt that he would stay there, but to Bobby himself, I fancy that this making of his own pace was a very exhausting business and that he would have felt the strain less if he had only begun to come away from his field toward the end of the third round.

There were really only two moments when he looked like he was in the least pressed. One was on the second day. Bobby had reached the turn in 37, when we heard that Ben Hodson had added a 70 to his first round of 72. That meant that Bobby had to come home in 37 for a 74, which would make him tie with Hodson. Thirty-seven home at St. Andrews against even a slight wind is very good golf, and he was not playing convincingly. However, he took himself by the scruff of the neck, came home grandly in 35, and kept a lead of two.

The other doubtful moment was at the beginning of the last round. Fred Robson had gotten within four strokes of him and Bobby had started quite badly with five holes in 23. There was just a doubt, but a hole or two afterwards Bobby had begun to do his four 3s in a row, and that was that, once and for all. All through the tournament Bobby's driving was magnificent—long and straight. If one thing more than another won him the championship it was his wooden club play. The two long holes at St. Andrews, the fifth and the fourteenth, are both well over five hundred yards long, and, apart from their length, the nature of the ground makes them particularly hard to reach in two. The ordinary rank and file were working reasonably hard to play them in 5s apiece. Bobby himself could not quite reach the fourteenth in two, but his total for those two holes played four times each was just 33 shots. In the last round they gave him his great chance of gaining a clear stroke from lesser men and he certainly took it.

His pitching, on the other hand, was hardly up to his proper standard. Of course, he made many beautiful pitches, but he also made some downright weak ones; he was always inclined to be short with them, and once, on the last day, he fluffed one into a bunker in front of his nose.

But if he occasionally pitched weakly, he nearly always saved himself by his putting. Now and again, being mortal, he missed a putt, but he holed a great many and his approach putting was a model of free, clean hitting.

It was a long putt holed—ten yards at least—at the second hole in the first round which set him off on his 68. That hole had looked like a disaster, for it ought to be a 4, and it seemed almost certain to become a 6. He had drawn his tee shot slightly and had been trapped; he had failed to get out with his first effort, and, finally, when he reached the green in four, he was a good long way from the hole. And then down went that priceless putt for a 5, which was worth more than any orthodox, featureless 4s. He never again came so near to doing a 6 as at that hole, and, in fact, he went around the old course four times without a 6, a thing that has never been done before.

It is no derogation of Bobby's wonderful score of 285 to say that the conditions were ideal for scoring. The plain fact of the matter is that the weather came very near to making a fool of the classic course. Not only was there practically not a breath of wind, day after day, but the ground was unnaturally slow and grassy after much heavy rain. Those who know the course will realize that it was not its normal and interesting self in these circumstances. It was dull golf, with all the subtlety gone out of the shots, and none of that variety which an ever-shifting wind usually introduces. A big drive and then a high pitching shot, with some sort of spade mashie played right up to the pin in the sure and certain hope that it would not run over—that was the story of hole afer hole.

There were just two or three holes which gave the great player his chance against the merely good player; otherwise he could only assert his superiority by a slightly greater steadiness in the playing of obvious shots. Whatever had been the conditions—if it had snowed ink—it is my firm conviction that Bobby would have won; but a stiff wind and a faster ground would have made it more interesting to watch him do it. As it was, he did marvelously, but the battlefield was hardly worthy of the victorious hero.

This article first appeared in O. B. Keelor *Atlanta Journal*.

BOBBY JONES ON PLAYING AT ST. ANDREWS

Of all the courses I've played tournaments on if I had to be sentenced to play only one course the rest of my life, I would pick St. Andrews in Scotland because it changes so much, and there's nothing about it that's obvious. The way we build a course in this country, the fellow who designs it tells you how you must play it. He gives you a fairway and a green and some bunkers around it, and he tells you you've got to drive here. If you don't you're in the woods or some other place. At St.

Bobby Jones and Francis Ouimet at the start of a practice round in 1930.

Andrews, you can drive almost anywhere, but if you haven't picked the right spot according to the weather conditions and the conditions of the ground, you're at a disadvantage.

I didn't like St. Andrews at all when I first played it. (This was the time when Jones, then a nineteen-year-old "picked up" on the eleventh hole of a bad third round, the only time he ever withdrew from a tournament.) But pretty soon I studied the course and by the time I played there in '27 and again in '30, I felt that I knew it.

The difficult conditions at St. Andrews occur when the wind is blowing and the ground is firm and hard. It's easier if they've had a lot of rain— you see, they have no way of watering the greens over there—and if the course is soft. When the greens are fast and they don't hold, you've got to

maneuver around hazards rather than play over them. When you make a pitch shot, you've got to maneuver around so you're pitching into the wind. Then you can control the shot."

This article first appeared in *The Saturday Evening Post*, April 5, 1958, "A Visit with Bobby Jones" by Harry Paxton and Fred Russell.

BOBBY JONES IS MADE A FREEMAN AT ST. ANDREWS

The first World Amateur Golf Team Championship was, most fittingly, played at St. Andrews, Scotland. In the interest of international goodwill each nation of the world would send representative amateur golfers to the inaugural tournament, which was to be held in October, 1958.

Crowds following Bobby Jones and George Voight in the semifinals of the 1930 Amateur Championship.
Courtesy U.S.G.A.

Bobby Jones accepts the Freedom casket from Provost Robert Leonard.

193

Even before Robert T. Jones, Jr. was named Captain of the American team, he had decided that he would make his own personal pilgrimage to old St. Andrews to view once more the scenes of his early defeats and later victories, to revisit the charming Scottish people he loved so well. Bobby Jones at this time of his life was becoming increasingly more immobilized by the spinal disease with which he was afflicted for many years. Jones was well aware of his increasing physical disability and said, "I simply felt this might be my last opportunity to revisit the city and golf course that I love so well, and that I should by no means let this opportunity pass."

Jones was designated Captain of the team. Shortly before he was to leave the States he received a cablegram from the town clerk of St. Andrews, inquiring whether Jones would be willing to accept "The Freedom of the City" while there in St. Andrews on his visit. Jones did not know precisely what was meant by the "Freedom of the City" but, of course, realized that it was without question an honor to the recipient, probably somewhat similar to the American custom of presenting a distinguished visitor with the "keys of the city." As we shall see, the freedom of St. Andrews meant much more than that, but needless to say, Jones graciously accepted the offer. Then he began to worry about what he would say in an acceptance speech. Jones did not fancy himself as a speech-maker; he felt as embarrassed and nervous as most ordinary mortals in spite of his legal training. Soon afterward he received a copy of the presentation speech William Leonard, the Provost of St. Andrews, was planning to deliver at the ceremony.

After Jones had arrived at St. Andrews for the start of the tournament, the Town Clerk of St. Andrews called him to discuss the preparations for the ceremony which would take place on Thursday evening, October 9, 1958, at the Younger Graduation Hall of St. Andrews University. This was a beautiful auditorium which seated 1700 persons and possessed a large stage overlooking a lower floor and a balcony.

Jones was asked for a copy of the remarks he intended to make and he had to admit to the clerk that he had not yet been able to put anything on paper, though he promised that he would attempt to do so as soon as he could gather his thoughts. Now he began to get a bit panicky at his inability to "write his speech" and had the fear that he might find himself at the podium on that fateful Thursday night and be completely tongue-tied, unable to open his mouth. In his past acceptance speeches he had noted that he repeatedly spoke the same words and phrases except for the obvious changes in names, places and dates. Still, Jones knew that he had always been able to produce the proper words once he was thrust into the situation. He reassured the clerk, who was a little dubious now about the success of the evening, that his speech would come to mind later on, he was certain.

There was a rehearsal of the ceremony. The Town Clerk called Jones to invite him to meet with Provost Leonard and himself on the afternoon before the evening affair. It was then that Jones came to realize what an honor was being bestowed upon him, that only the most important six or eight personages of literary and political history in the last two hundred years had been similarly honored. Among those there was only one American who had ever been given the Freedom of St. Andrews, Dr. Benjamin Franklin himself, and that event had occurred almost two hundred years before to the very day. Jones was even more awed by thought of joining such illustrious company. Still the words of his speech would not come to mind. He decided that he would stuff his pockets with notes "in case of dire emergency" if the words didn't come.

The ceremony took place in the evening. Jones was driven in his golf cart up the steps and right through the entrance doors of the auditorium, down the center aisle. The cart was stopped and Bobby was helped up to the stage, aided by his hickory-shafted cane and by some of the participants in the event who watched to see that he did not fall. He was accompanied by his wife, Mary, his son, Bob III, and his youngest daughter, Mary Ellen. Unfortunately his elder daughter had to remain in the States to care for her children.

The Provost was dressed in handsome fashion, wearing a crimson robe with an ermine collar. A tremendous loop of gold chain with dazzling medals and jewels hung about his neck, symbolic of the importance of his office. All the members of the town council were there. In the audience were all the members of the World Cup teams, along with their various delegates and non-playing Captains. The house was absolutely full. It was reported that had the tickets been available the crowd would have been three times as large. Hundreds of people who were unable to get seats remained outside the auditorium doors hoping to catch a glimpse of their distinguished and beloved new "citizen" of St. Andrews.

The gathering started in solemn fashion with a prayer offered by the Reverend W.W. Rankin, and then the Town Clerk, wearing the white wig of his office, rose to read the proclamation of the Mayor and Town Council. Then Provost Robert Leonard proceeded to the rostrum before the hushed audience and spoke the sentiments of the people of St. Andrews, told of the high regard they had for their "Bobby" and why it was most fitting that he be given this signal honor. We cannot imagine what was going through the mind of Bobby Jones as he sat there, practically immobilized in his chair in the center of that stage, surrounded by his beloved family and "at home" once more in St. Andrews, the scene of his most cherished golf victories.

I think that the reader will agree that the comments of Mr. Leonard and the reply of Jones himself in the context of the entire scene, the packed auditorium, the thousands of friends of Jones, constitute one of the most memorable, heart-warming stories in the history of golf. Here are the actual words of Provost Robert Leonard:

Ladies and gentlemen, we are met here today to confer the Freedom of the City and the Royal Borough of St. Andrews on Mr. Robert Tyre Jones, Jr., of Atlanta, Georgia.

"Among its many other claims to renown, St. Andrews has for long been recognized as the metropolis of the golfing world—and the presence of golfers from all parts of the globe at this time to take part in a great new international competition for the Eisenhower Trophy is further confirmation of this fact. Mr. Jones is recognized as the most distinguished golfer of this age—one might well say of all time. Thus it is appropriate that just such a place and just such a personality should be linked together at just such a time as this.

"But the conferring of the freedom of a city, although it may have a certain formal symbolism of this kind, can never be a merely formal matter—and it can rarely have been less so than on this occasion. As representatives of the community of St. Andrews, we wish to honor Mr. Jones because we feel drawn to him by ties of affection and personal regard of a particularly cordial nature, and because we know that he himself has declared his own enduring affection for this place and for its people.

"Like many cordial and enduring partnerships, it was not, I think, a case of love at first sight. Probably few St. Andreans paid much attention to the visit of a relatively unknown young American golfer for the British Open Championship of 1921, and I believe that for his part, the first impression that Mr. Jones formed of the Old Course was something less than favorable, and

there—with any other person and any other place —the matter might well have rested. But back he came in 1927 to master the intricacies of golf at St. Andrews as they had never been mastered before, even by our own giants of the Nineteenth Century, and to win his way, not only to the Open Championship, but to the hearts of St. Andrews's people from that day to this.

"Even now, more than thirty years later, it is possible to recapture the thrill of that occasion in Mr. Bernard Darwin's incomparable prose.

"As he says—and remember that he is writing of the days before crowd control, when great multitudes surged over the Old Course in pursuit of their favorites—'Many vivid pictures remain in my mind's eye from this day, but there is one in particular. Bobby lay just short of the home green in the hollow called The Valley of Sin. He ran his long putt up dead, and the crowd stormed up the slope and waited breathless for a moment at the crest. He popped his ball in, and the next instant there was to be seen no green and no Bobby—nothing but a black and seething mass from which there ultimately emerged the victor bourne on enthusiastic shoulders and holding his famous putter, Calamity Jane, over his head in a frantic effort to preserve it."'

"Three years later, in 1930, when he won both the Open and the Amateur Championships of Britain and America alike—a feat never accomplished before or since—it was here that Mr. Jones attained what he himself probably regarded as the most perilous and desirable among these four contests for an American—the British Amateur Championship—a win that was acclaimed in St. Andrews almost as the triumph of a favorite son.

"Nothing could ever surpass the achievement of that memorable year—the climax of seven years scarcely less memorable, in every one of which he had won a major award. Let me detail them: the American Open in 1923 and the Amateur in 1924 and 1925; the American and the British Opens in 1926; the American Amateur and the British Open in 1927; the American Amateur again in 1928; and the Open again in 1929; finally all four in 1930. And so at the height of his attainments and still at the height of his powers, Mr. Jones retired from major competitive events—to reign forever after in our hearts, as Mr. Darwin suggests, as the champion of champions to the end of his days.

"And so we feel that when we welcome back Mr. Jones to St. Andrews, we welcome an old and dearly loved friend—as we welcomed him on his last visit in 1936 when he played around the Old Course attended, one might well imagine, by practically the entire population of the town.

"We welcome him for his own sake; we welcome him also as an ambassador in the cause of international understanding and good will which the competition of this week is designed to promote. We welcome him moreover not only as a distinguished golfer but as a man of outstanding character, courage, and accomplishment well worthy to adorn the Roll of our Honorary Burgesses. And that an American should once again be entered in that roll may well be thought timely, for it is just one year short of two hundred years ago, in October 1759, that our predecessors welcomed Dr. Benjamin Franklin of Philadelphia and accorded him the privileges of a Burgess and Guild Brother of the city of St. Andrews.

"What these privileges now are in any tangible sense, even the Town Clerk hesitates to suggest—though Mr. Jones may be interested to know that any that are ever mentioned relate specifically to the links—to cart shells, to take divots, and to dry one's washing upon the first and last fairways of the Old Course.

"These are homely terms—and perhaps in an American as well as British sense—but they may help us to convey to our new Honorary Burgess just what we mean by this Freedom Ceremony—that he is free to feel at home in St. Andrews as truly as in his own first home of Atlanta. One of our own number, officially now, as he has been so long unofficially."

This article first appeared in Robert T. Jones, Jr., *Golf is My Game*.

When his speech was ended, Provost Leonard placed the beautifully hand-lettered scroll of the citation which had been read earlier by the Town Clerk into a magnificent silver casket which was itself embellished with the seal of the City of St. Andrews. He presented the casket to Jones. Jones took the casket, placed it on the table in front of him (the rostrum was been installed in the center of the table) and then proceeded to sign the Burgess's roll, an act which signified his acceptance of the rights and duties of a Freeman of St. Andrews.

Bobby Jones, in his book *Golf is My Game*, tells of his emotions and sentiments as he received the silver casket from the Provost and began to collect his thoughts for his acceptance speech. In Jones's own words:

"Within the few seconds it took me to make my way to the lectern along the table so thoughtfully provided, I found out how a man's life, or

a great part of it, can flash through his mind in an instant. I knew in that instant that I had no need for the notes in my pocket. I knew that I would have no difficulty finding things to say to the people of St. Andrews. I was happy that the members of the international teams and the delegates were there; but after all, they were to me merely sympathetic witnesses. This reunion was mine with the people of St. Andrews, and it was to them that I intended to speak.

"I began by thanking the Provost for the kindly manner in which he had treated my early mistakes, and then I asked my audience to remember that at the time of my first appearance on the Old Course, I had reached the ripe, mature age of nineteen years. One thing I had learned about the Old Course was that she was not likely to be kind to young, inexperienced golfers.

"I told them of how I had started in that Open Championship of 1921 with two fair rounds, a total of something like 151. When someone among the players tittered, I hastened to state that that was for two rounds, not one. Since very few of the players in the tournament had been able to break eighty in either one of the first two rounds, it was not difficult for them to agree that this was not too bad.

"But then, I told them, the wind was really blowing on the morning of the third round. I had battled it as best I could to the turn in forty-six, had started home with a six at ten, and had put my tee shot into the Hill Bunker at the eleventh. Here, I wanted to correct a bit of their history recited in a guidebook I had read. I had not played two shots in the bunker and then knocked my ball over the green into the Eden River. My ball had come out of the bunker only in my pocket, and it was my score card that found its way into the river.

"I spoke of how the Old Course had come to have a real personality for me. Even in the beginning, I think I was never angry at the course, only puzzled and a bit bewildered. I think it was not long before I began to see her as a wise old lady, whimsically tolerant of my impatience, but all the while ready to reveal to me the secrets of her complex being, if I would only take the trouble to study and to learn. I did not try to develop this area of my thought, because it seemed too fanciful. But I did say that I thought the Old Lady had been satisfied with the early chastisement she had given me, and pointed out that she never again permitted me to lose a match or a contest. The more I studied the Old

Course, the more I loved it, and the more I loved it, the more I studied it—so that I came to feel that it was for me the most favorable meeting ground possible for an important contest. I felt that my knowledge of the course enabled me to play it with patience and restraint until she might exact her inevitable toll from my adversary, who might treat her with less respect and understanding.

"But," I said, "my thoughts are not of championships and trophies as I stand here tonight. You people possess a sensitivity which causes you to be able to extend cordiality and express friendliness in the most ingenious way."

"I was thinking, of course, of the scene at the final green when I won the Open Championship in 1927, the scene mentioned by the Provost. I was thinking of the murmur of warmth and approval that went through the crowd when I asked if I might leave the Open Championship trophy for the year of my possession with the Royal and Ancient Golf Club, of which I had the honor to be a member. I remembered, too, how after I had won the Amateur Championship of 1930, these people had made a lane through which I might pass from the side door of the Royal and Ancient Club to my hotel across the street, and how they called to me with 'Good by, Bobby,' 'Come again,' 'Well done,' etc.

"On the eighth tee I was paid the most sincere compliment I can ever remember. It was one of those things one does not talk about. I have never mentioned it before, and did not mention it at the Freedom Ceremony. But since this may be my last utterance on the subject of golf, I must put it down here.

"The eighth hole of St. Andrews is a short hole and the pin this day was tucked in behind a small mound to the right of the usual pathway leading to the front of the green. Having the honor, I had played a soft shot with a number four iron, which had faded neatly around the mound and finished some eight or nine feet from the hole. As I stepped back for Willie to play his shot and to slip my club back in my bag, my caddie, a pleasant-looking young man of about twenty years of age, said to me under his breath, 'My, but you're a wonder, sir.' I could only smile and pat him on the shoulder. I do not know his name nor where he is, but I hope he will now understand what pleasure he gave me.

"Four at the tenth was normal, but the eleventh put an end to my dreams. The hole that day was cut where I had never seen it before—on a flat area at the very back of the green and

directly behind Strath Bunker. The ground was firm and the wind following and slightly off the right. Never in a tournament would I have played directly for the flag. But this was quite evidently an unusual day, and I must say that at this point I was beginning to think that I could do no wrong. The five-iron shot directly on the flag was a bit too strong, and finished in a small pot bunker in the bank of the Eden directly behind the hole.

"The ball was lying cleanly. The bunker was shallow, and it was the kind of shot which held no terrors for me. But I tried to flick it up by the hole, left it still in the bunker, flicked again up four feet from the hole, and missed the putt. That five broke the charm. I three-putted two or three greens from there in, and finally holed a ten-foot putt for a three at the last hole to finish in seventy-two.

"I am happy to say that no one seemed to care about the forty coming home, and the thirty-two out was good enough for me. I spent thirty or forty minutes in the vestibule of the R & A Club House signing autographs for the crowd, mostly women and children. It had been one of the great days of my life.

"I talked some of this day, not, I am thankful to say, at the length I have here. And you may be sure I did not mention the caddie on the eighth tee. But then I wanted to tell the people of St. Andrews of something else they had done for me in their peculiarly entrancing way.

"A short while after the British Amateur Championship of 1930, without any warning or preliminary, I received at my home in Atlanta a package containing a wood box some eighteen inches high and of a cross section six inches on a side. Upon opening it I found the most perfect, gem-like miniature of the British Amateur trophy. It was a perfect reproduction in every respect, down to the last detail of lettering, and displaying the names of all winners of the championship up to date. The one thing not reproduced from the original was the following inscription engraved upon one of the plates on the base, 'To Robert Tyre Jones, Jr., a golfer matchless in skill and chivalrous in spirit, from some fellow members of the Royal and Ancient Golf Club.' Was there ever a more adroit flattery, and could there be anything more inspiring to try to deserve? I described the cup and told of my immense pride in it—that up to now it had been my most highly prized possession. After a slight pause I had to admit that I could not trust myself to repeat the inscription. 'And now,' I said, 'you have done this for me,' indicating the handsome silver casket containing the citation.

"Then it occurred to me to speak of my interpretation of the words 'friend' and 'friendship,' which are among the most important in our language, and yet are so often loosely used. Friends are a man's priceless treasures, and a life rich in friendship is full indeed.

" 'When I say, with due regard for the meaning of the word, that I am your friend, I have pledged to you the ultimate in loyalty and devotion. In some respects friendship may even transcend love, for in true friendship there is no place for jealousy. When, without more, I say that you are my friends, it is possible that I may be imposing upon you a greater burden than you are willing to assume. But when you have made me aware on many occasions that you have a kindly feeling toward me, and when you have honored me by every means at your command, then when I call you my friend, I am at once affirming my high regard and affection for you and declaring my complete faith in you and trust in the sincerity of your expressions. And so, my fellow citizens of St. Andrews, it is with this appreciation of the full sense of the word that I salute you as my friends.'

"Then, thinking of the World Cup competition and its purpose, I went on to say, "It seems to me, too, that it is entirely in keeping with the extreme good taste I have come to expect of this city that you should have chosen to sound this keynote of friendship at this particular moment during this first World Amateur Team Competition for the Eisenhower Trophy. For the fostering of friendship and understanding on an international scale is also the keynote of this event. We shall all be trying our very best to win in the golf competition because our high respect for our fellow competitors and for the game of golf demands that we do so. But all of us have come here with the hope that attachments will be formed here and reports will emanate from here which will provide an impetus toward a growing friendship among nations of the world. I am not so naïve as to expect that a golf tournament may accomplish miracles, but I do hope that we may sow some seeds here which may germinate later on into influences toward peace in the world.'

"Turning then to the Provost, I said, 'Bob, I am afraid I have talked too long, but I think I may best express my emotions if you will permit me to paraphrase your own closing remarks by saying to the people of St. Andrews that I consider they have now officially given me the right to feel as much at home in St. Andrews as I have for so long presumed to do on my own. I am grateful indeed for this honor.'

"Then we all stood and sang 'God Save the Queen.' One of my fellow Burgesses, a lovely lady, Mrs. McNaughton, presented a corsage of roses to my wife; my son assisted me down the stairs, and the Provost and I rode out of the hall in my electric buggy, which had been backed down in front of the stage, and in front, too, of the flag of the State of Georgia which my hosts had somehow acquired.

"I am not the least bit ashamed to admit that I had been deeply moved by the ceremony—as much by the awareness of the depth and sincerity of my affection for these people as by their expressions to me."

In his book, Jones made the claim, "But I did not weep or cry as I later read in some reports coming to my own country. I had to stop several times in my speaking in order to avoid a show of excessive emotion, and I did have to avoid saying a few things I had not the composure to utter."

Then, as he himself admitted, with a lump in his throat, Jones turned away from the podium and moved slowly on his cane to his seat. Everyone responded with a standing ovation, the Council, and the Provost standing at their places, applauding his speech and, more than the speech, the great man that was Robert Tyre Jones, Jr.

Now Jones made a move to leave the stage. As honored guest it was up to him to end the ceremony. The golf cart had been driving up the center aisle of the auditorium earlier and now had been reversed so that Jones could once more enter it and be driven out of the assemblage.

Jones looked at the thirty-foot distance between himself and the electric cart, the steps down from the platform. Every eye was on him, now a hushed silence had taken the place of the tremendous cheers. Jones stood up and with a great act of will, took a deep breath and without his cane or any other support made his way unassisted across the stage and down the steps to the cart. His son watched carefully from directly behind him. On this glorious occasion he would walk again as he once walked on the broad green fairways of the Old Course, and he *did* walk!

The cart moved slowly down the aisle. Everyone spontaneously broke out softly with the old Scottish song, "Will ye No' Come Back Again?" with its sad and touching lyrics:

Will Ye No' Come back again? Will Ye No' Come back again? Better lo'ed ye canna be, will ye no' come back again?

I have had the privilege of talking to several persons who were there in Younger Auditorium that night to witness this most unusual event. Each one has said that in his opinion it was a highlight of his life, that it was a great honor to be there, a never-to-be-forgotten experience. Bobby Jones claims that he did not cry. If he didn't cry the witnesses said that his voice choked up several times and that he had difficulty continuing to talk. As for the audience, there is no doubt whatsoever but that there wasn't one viewer who was able to fight back the tears that came unwillingly to his eyes that night.

Jones and everyone else truly knew that he would "no" come back again. The end of the life of an immortal golfer was happening before the very eyes of those seventeen hundred people. They knew it, Bobby Jones knew it.

THE MEMORIAL SERVICE FOR BOBBY JONES

Roger Wethered, a former Captain of the Royal and Ancient Golf Club, was invited to deliver the major address and tribute to Bobby Jones at the memorial service held in honor of the distinguished golfer. There could not have been a more admirable choice for this distinct honor. Wethered, a true gentleman golfer, as was Bobby Jones, had first played against Jones in 1922 in the Walker Cup matches of that year, which were held on the National Golf Links of America on Long Island, New York.

It does not really matter that Jones was the winner in that match and in later matches with Roger. As Roger himself says, "We met again at Sandwich and at St. Andrews with more or less the same adverse results from my point of view." The fact

The commemorative ceremony after the death of Bobby Jones.

199

remains that these two golfing "greats" became fast friends and remained so until Jones died after a long and painful illness.

The text of Roger Wethered's memorial address has been preserved, fortunately. Through the courtesy of Mr. Wethered himself, it is a pleasure now to allow the golfers of the world to share in his heartfelt sentiments of that sad day in May, 1972. Here are Roger's own words:

The days when Bobby Jones and I met were great golfing days, whatever the present generation of golfers may think of them, and I count myself unbelievably fortunate in having played with Bobby at the height of his majestic powers and to have remained, I like to think, his life-long friend.

Thinking back on those days, I wonder how many there are in this church who can recall that sturdy figure of the Twenties, that glorious swing that was the poetry of motion propelling the ball huge distances down the fairways in a seemingly effortless and simple manner, and who also can recall that truly beautiful touch on the greens?

I first saw Bobby Jones play in the United States Amateur Championship of 1920 at the age of eighteen. Even then, although he had not broken through to win, he was regarded as the most brilliant amateur in the United States. His swing had the same easy grace we all came to know, with, at the same time, perhaps an extra bit of dash and the impetuosity of youth. The only flaw that could be detected was the occasional missing of a short putt and the reaction of a temperament that was never satisfied with anything except the perfect shot.

The following year he came to England for the first time and played in the first International Match between Great Britain and the United States. The impact he made on the spectators at Hoylake, who had their own heroes in John Ball and Harold Hilton, was instantaneous. But it was not surprising to us who had seen him play the previous year on Long Island.

However, it is not on Bobby's achievements on the links, that we wish to dwell on on this occasion. What were those qualities, for instance, that made him so great a man and endeared him not only to his friends but even to strangers who only watched him play?

Undoubtedly his artistry and the simplicity of method with which he played, the modesty and quietness of his demeanor, were immediately attractive. Those who met him were also struck by his straight, direct look and, as someone remarked, his presence alone gave you a wonderfully good "feel." The gravity that hung about him was, I am sure, largely acquired as a result of the struggle he had had with himself during the first seven years of his career when, potentially America's finest golfer, he never won a tournament of the highest class. These years were probably the most significant in the forming of his character. As we know, he fought his way through those early disappointments and emerged complete master of himself and supreme golfer of his, or possibly any other, age. No doubt through this same period he acquired the strength of purpose to enable him to endure the long, drawn-out illness that caused his death, with the fortitude and patience that won the admiration of the world.

In those early days of which I have been speaking, days when intellectual attainments were less regarded than they are to-day, I do not think we realized the exceptional mental caliber that lay beneath Bobby's quiet, reserved manner. He was always a serious person, but a sense of humor also lurked beneath the surface and in his Southern voice.

The game of golf is said to contain many of the stresses that man has to contend with in life. To play as Bobby Jones did and to have remained, as an amateur, preeminent among the world's best golfers of his time must have required exceptional dedication and toughness of disposition. Yet, despite this, he never lost any of the values that make up the complete man: humanity, humour, consideration and courtesy to all about him. To have won through at golf after those years when nothing would quite come right was an epic victory in itself, but the second victory—the one in which he was reduced from walking with a cane and finally to a wheel chair —was a victory of the spirit that will also live as long as his name is remembered.

The words of Mr. Valiant-for-Truth, when he was departing this world, are so appropriate to the character of Bobby Jones, his life and his leaving of it, that I cannot end my address without quoting them to his memory and to those who come after him:

My sword I give to him that shall succeed me in my pilgrimage, and my courage and skill to him who can get it. My marks and scars I carry with me, to be a witness for me that I have fought his battles who now will be my Rewarder. So he passed over, and all the trumpets sounded for him on the other side.

(John Bunyan)

Bibliography

Blake, George, and Murray, W. H. *Scotland's Splendour*. Glasgow, Scotland: Collins Publishing Company, 1960.

Campbell, Sir Guy; Darwin, Bernard; Longhurst, Henry; and Wilson, Enid. *A History of Golf in Britain*. London: Cassell and Company, Ltd. 1952.

Cotton, Henry. *My Golfing Album*. London: Country Life, Ltd., 1959.

Cotton, Henry. *This Game of Golf*. London: Country Life, Ltd., 1948.

Cromie, Robert, ed. *Par for the Course*. New York: MacMillan & Co., 1964.

Darwin, Bernard. *The Golf Courses of the British Isles*. New York: D. Appleton and Company, 1941.

Everard, H.S.C. *A History of the Royal and Ancient Golf Club; St. Andrews from 1754-1900*. Edinburgh, Scotland: William Blackwood and Sons, 1907.

Hagen, Walter, and Heck, Margaret Seaton. *The Walter Hagen Story*. New York: Simon and Schuster, 1956.

Hutchinson, Horace G. *The Book of Golf and Golfers*. London: Longmans, Green and Co., 1899.

Jones, Robert Tyre (Bobby), Jr. *Golf is My Game*. Garden City, New York: Doubleday and Co., 1960.

Jones, Robert T., Jr., and Keeler, O. B. *Down the Fairway: The Golf Life and Play of Robert T. Jones, Jr*. New York: Minton, Balch and Company, 1927.

Keeler, O. B. *The Unofficial King of Scotland*. Atlanta, Georgia: *The Atlanta Journal*, July 10, 1927.

Leitch, Cecil. *Golf*. London: Thornton Butterworth, 1922.

Lema, Tony, and Brown, Gwilym S. *Golfer's Gold*. Boston: Little, Brown and Company, 1964.

Low, John L. *F. G. Tait: A Record*. London: J. Nisbet and Co., Ltd., 1900.

Park, William, Jr. *The Game of Golf*. London: Longmans, Green & Co., 1896.

Paxton, Harry, and Russell, Fred. *The Saturday Evening Post*. Philadelphia: Curtis Publishing Co., April 5, 1958.

Pottinger, George. *Muirfield and the Honourable Company*. Edinburgh, Scotland: Scottish Academic Press, 1972.

Rice, Grantland. *The Tumult and the Shouting: My Life In Sport*. South Brunswick and New York: A. S. Barnes and Company, Inc., 1954.

Robertson, James K. *St. Andrews, Home of Golf*. St. Andrews, Scotland: J. and G. Innis, Ltd., 1967.

Salmond, J. B. *The Story of the R. &A*. New York: MacMillan & Co., Ltd., 1956.

Smith, Horton, and Taylor, Dawson. *The Secret of Holing Putts*. South Brunswick and New York: A. S. Barnes and Company, Inc., 1961.

Stenhouse, Lawrence. *Scotland's Heritage*. Glasgow, Scotland: Collins Publishing, 1970.

Taylor, Dawson. *The Masters: Profile of a Tournament*. South Brunswick and New York: A. S. Barnes and Company, Inc., 1973.

Taylor, J. H. *Taylor on Golf*. London: Hutchinson and Company, 1902.

Travers, Jerome D. *Traver's Golf Book*. New York: MacMillan & Co., 1913.

Travis, Walter J. *Practical Golf*. New York and London: Harper and Brothers, 1902.

Vardon, Harry. *The Complete Golfer*. New York: McClure Phillips and Co., 1905.

Vardon, Harry. *The Gist of Golf*. New York: George H. Doran Company, 1922.

Wethered, Joyce. *Golfing Memorie sand Methods*. London: Hutchinson and Co., 1933.

Wind, Herbert Warren. *The Complete Golfer*. New York: Simon and Schuster, 1954.

Whitlatch, Marshall. *Golf for Beginners and Others*. New York: MacMillan & Co., 1921.

Index

206